Rights

Central Problems of Philosophy
Series Editor: John Shand

This series of books presents concise, clear, and rigorous analyses of the core problems that preoccupy philosophers across all approaches to the discipline. Each book encapsulates the essential arguments and debates, providing an authoritative guide to the subject while also introducing original perspectives. This series of books by an international team of authors aims to cover those fundamental topics that, taken together, constitute the full breadth of philosophy.

Published titles

Action
Rowland Stout

Causation and Explanation
Stathis Psillos

Death
Geoffrey Scarre

Free Will
Graham McFee

Knowledge
Michael Welbourne

Meaning
David E. Cooper

Mind and Body
Robert Kirk

Modality
Joseph Melia

Ontology
Dale Jacquette

Paradox
Doris Olin

Perception
Barry Maund

Realism and Anti-Realism
Stuart Brock & Edwin Mares

Relativism
Paul O'Grady

Rights
Duncan Ivison

Scepticism
Neil Gascoigne

Truth
Pascal Engel

Universals
J. P. Moreland

Forthcoming titles

God
Jay Wood

The Self
Stephen Burwood

Value
Derek Matravers

Rights

Duncan Ivison

McGill-Queen's University Press
Montreal & Kingston • Ithaca

ISBN 978-0-7735-3328-8 (bound)
ISBN 978-0-7735-3329-5 (paper)

Legal deposit first quarter 2008
Bibliothèque nationale du Québec

Published simultaneously outside North America
by Acumen Publishing Limited

McGill-Queen's University Press acknowledges the financial support of
the Government of Canada through the Book Publishing Development
Program (BPIDP) for its activities.

Library and Archives Canada Cataloguing in Publication

Ivison, Duncan, 1965-
   Rights / Duncan Ivison.

(Central problems of philosophy)
Includes bibliographical references and index.
ISBN 978-0-7735-3328-8 (bound).--ISBN 978-0-7735-3329-5 (pbk.)

   1. Civil rights--Philosophy. 2. Human rights--Philosophy. 3.
Natural law--Philosophy. 4. Political science--Philosophy. I. Title. II.
Series.

B105.L3I84 2008   323'.01   C2007-906830-8

Designed and typeset by Kate Williams, Swansea.
Printed and bound by Biddles, King's Lynn.

Contents

Acknowledgements

Someone once said of a book by V. S. Naipaul that it was philosophical but smelled of the earth. I can think of no better description of the ideal I had in mind when I sat down to write this book (although Naipaul is a master and I am not). My aim is to provide a fresh perspective on some familiar debates about rights and to open up some new questions about their past and their future.

In the course of writing this book I have received an enormous amount of help and encouragement that I want to acknowledge. First and foremost, I am especially grateful to Moira Gatens and Paul Patton, with whom I collaborated on a joint research project (generously funded by the Australian Research Council) out of which this book emerged. There are parts of the book where I am almost wholly indebted to their respective work, and I have tried to acknowledge that appropriately in the text. But my general debt to them is substantial and I acknowledge it here with gratitude.

My thanks to David Armitage, Annabel Brett, Andrew Fitzmaurice, Susan Mendus, Sankar Muthu and Phillip Pettit for many helpful conversations and for their expert advice. I am particularly indebted to Phillip Pettit, James Tully and Quentin Skinner for their generous support over the past few years.

I would also like to thank Stephen Macedo and Josh Ober for the opportunity to spend a year at the wonderful Centre for Human Values at Princeton, where the first draft of the book was written. I am grateful to the staff at the centre for being so helpful and supportive during my time there. Thanks also to my fellow Rockefeller Fellows for much stimulating conversation, including Anthony

Appiah, Chris Eisgruber, John Kelsey, Michael Kochin, Arlene Sax-onhouse, Bill Scheuerman, Jerry Schneewind, Tracy Strong, Stephen Wall and Roslyn Weiss.

At the University of Toronto I was privileged to join the remark-able political theory group and I am especially grateful to Ronnie Beiner, Joe Carens, Simone Chambers, Ran Hirschl, Grace Skogs-tad, Melissa Williams and Robert Vipond, Chair of the Department of Political Science, for being such understanding and supportive colleagues. At the University of Sydney, my thanks to Stephen Garton, Dean of the Faculty of Arts, Richard Waterhouse, Head of the School of Philosophical and Historical Inquiry, and my col-leagues in the Department of Philosophy, especially Moira Gatens and Paul Redding, for their encouragement and support during the last phase of writing.

I am grateful to Steven Gerrard for his patience and for being such an efficient and helpful editor. My thanks also to Kate Wil-liams and Coral Hauenstein for their help with the final prepara-tion of the manuscript. The anonymous readers commissioned by Acumen provided extremely helpful advice and criticism, almost all of which I have tried to incorporate into the final draft. Need-less to say the errors and problems that remain are entirely my responsibility.

Portions of Chapter 8 draw on material that first appeared in my "Emergent Cosmopolitanism", in *Between Cosmopolitanism Ideals and State Sovereignty*, Ronald Tinnevelt and Gert Verschrae-gen (eds), 120–34 (Basingstoke: Palgrave, 2006). I am grateful to the publishers for the use of some of that material here.

Finally, to Di, Hamish and Isobel I owe most of all. I cannot help but feel that in putting up with me over the past few years and yet continuing to provide me with their love and support, I am the ben-eficiary of something to which I have no rightful claim whatsoever. But I am so glad to have it.

Introduction

The aim of this book is to explore different arguments about rights in the context of various rich languages of moral and political philosophy. Locating rights in the midst of moral and political *argument* is crucial. Rights are often appealed to as part of a vision of the individual as radically disengaged from thick ethical theories that bind her to particular social roles or hierarchies. The idea of rights as providing a boundary around the individual, or at least around certain crucial aspects of her freedom, has been an influential image in the history of political thought. The image is true and powerful, but the conceptions of freedom and obligation that shape it are themselves the product of a particular set of moral claims. Boundaries abound in our talk about rights. But boundaries are also often ambiguous: they include as they exclude; they rule in as much as they rule out; and they stake out relationships as much as they separate.

Lawyers and moral philosophers frequently argue over the ultimate parentage of the concept of rights. But in this book, I shall be trying a different tack. I shall be focusing instead on the unavoidable *political* character of rights: the way arguments about rights are characterized by disagreement and conflict and by *movement* between the moral and the legal, and the abstract and the practical. It is a mistake to think that rights are either primarily a moral or legal concept. They are both. It is also a mistake to think rights are, by definition, "anti-powers" (to borrow a phrase from Pettit 1996), or fundamentally radical (or conservative). As we shall see, they have been deployed on the "radical" side of various forms of political critique, as well as by absolutists and "conservatives". They can be used to help create the conditions for the emergence of new kinds of political movements, as in many respects the language of human rights has proved (see Chapter 8). But they can also serve as conduits for new forms of power and regulation.

Nowheresville

One way to begin to think about the nature of rights is to imagine a world without them. Joel Feinberg, an American legal philosopher, referred to such a place as "Nowheresville" (Feinberg 1980). The inhabitants of this world lacked the capacity to claim anything on their own behalf of anyone or any institution. For Feinberg, *claiming* is central to what it means to have a right in the first place, and to lack that capacity is to lack the means to self-respect. There may well be duties in such a world – deriving from principles or rules associated with customs or social norms – and people might have the capacity to complain about their or others' failure to discharge them. But they lack the special capacity, without rights, to complain about the harm to *them*; they lack the capacity to be the self-originating source of a moral claim.

Sadly, the idea of Nowheresville is not only a thought experiment. The prison camp of Guantanamo Bay, to which "illegal combatants" in the US-led "War on Terror" have been sent – as well as those subject to state-sponsored schemes of "special rendition" – make Feinberg's imaginary world all too real. Claiming might not be as central to rights as Feinberg thinks, but the idea of a world completely devoid of rights seems to be one in which something crucial is missing. Part of our uneasiness, and even outrage, about the use of special rendition, or the existence of Guantanamo Bay, is surely connected to the fact that we see people in those situations as living precisely in a kind of legal and moral Nowheresville: held indefinitely; not told of the charges against them; lacking any effective form of legal recourse; and often subject to physical and psychological abuse. They are cut off from a world in which rights matter (see Steyn 2004).

Another way to think about a world without rights is to think of cultures and societies in more distant times that seemed to lack the very concept of a right. This raises some complex philosophical questions. We often speak of rights in universal terms: that all human beings, just because they are human, have rights. But if it turns out, as a matter of historical or anthropological fact, that some cultures did not (or do not) recognize those rights, then what does that show? It is certainly true that the practice and language of rights I shall be exploring below emerged out of a specific (yet complex) historical context. And we certainly will not find all of the various conceptual and normative tools of those languages in every tradition. Alasdair MacIntyre claims that if human rights, for example, really are universal then it would be a little odd that there is "no expression in any ancient or medieval language correctly translated by our expression 'a right' until near the close of the middle ages" (1984: 67).

This is an old theme. Benjamin Constant, in his famous 1817 lecture on the "Liberty of the Ancients Compared with that of the Moderns" (written in the aftermath of the French Revolution), argued that Greek city states failed to protect the individual sufficiently because they lacked, among other things, an adequate conception of rights. Repeating a charge made by his compatriot the Marquis de Condorcet, he claimed that the ancients "had no notion of individual rights. Men were ... merely machines, whose gears and cog-wheels were regulated by law" (Constant 1988: 312). The liberty of the ancients involved "the complete subjection of individual to the authority of the community ... No importance was given to individual independence, neither in relation to opinions, nor to labour, nor, above all, to religion" (*ibid.*: 311). The liberty of the moderns, on the other hand, involved:

> the right of everyone to express their opinions, choose a profession and practise it, to dispose of their property, and even to abuse it ... to associate with other individuals, either to discuss their interests, or to profess the religion which they and their associates prefer. (*Ibid.*: 310–11)

Now, Constant would ultimately call for the *combination* of these two freedoms, but the contrast he drew is clear enough. Later, Marx and Engels, in *The Holy Family* (1845), describe how the Jacobin leader Saint-Just, on the day of his execution:

> saw hanging in the hall of the Conciergerie the great tables of the Rights of Man, and with pride and self-esteem declared,

"After all, it was I who did that". But those tables proclaimed
the *rights* of a *man* who could no more be the man of ancient
society, than his national-economic and industrial relationships
could be those of antiquity.

(quoted and discussed in Williams 1995b: 153)

Of course, the literal absence of the word "right", or of some
close analogue, does not necessarily imply the lack of a related idea
or *concept*. In fact, some scholars have argued that the Greeks *did*
have a concept of rights close enough to what we understand by them
today. Josiah Ober (2000), for example, has argued that Athenian
democratic ideology of the fifth and fourth centuries BCE did distribute something like positive rights of participation, as well as negative
liberties of protection, to both citizens and non-citizens of the wider
Greek polis. Their understanding of these "rights" was very different from modern liberalism to be sure, but they are present to some
extent, in some recognizable form (cf. Oswald 2004).

A stronger claim would be that rights exist wherever there is a
morally valid argument for them. If all human beings have rights
in virtue of valid morally justificatory reasons, then it does not
matter whether or not the ancient Greeks had the phrase "human
rights" or "political rights" in their lexicon. Nor do we need to
search for some linguistic or historical analogue. Individuals in
ancient Greece, in so far as they were human beings, were entitled
to human rights, whether or not Greek philosophers formulated
the appropriate arguments (Gewirth 1996). This argument really
could only work at the most abstract level of analysis, if at all, since
it is clear that many of the rights that most people associate with
liberal societies presuppose specific institutions, material conditions
and ways of life that have developed over time (e.g. freedom of the
press, of information, the right to privacy, to education, etc.). These
rights are justified not only according to beliefs about the nature of
human agency and morality, but also by beliefs about the nature of
society and its economic and social structure, among other things.
Arguments about rights have to be anchored in *some* way to human
practices and ways of life within which they must gain their meaning and resonance. We shall return to this point in Chapter 1.

In the end, all societies distribute the benefits and burdens of
their ways of life along different lines. They all have rules and

norms that specify how certain actions can be performed by some but not others, or that regulate the relations between men and women, the weak and the powerful, adults and children, human and non-human beings. Whenever, precisely, the particular conceptions of rights with which we are most familiar today emerged, the basic concept is surely linked to reflection on and contestation of these kinds of norms and relations. In fact, as we shall see, rights – even in their most individualistic and modern form – are deeply connected to and shaped by social norms.

The importance of rights

The emergence of rights, and especially individual rights, is thus often heralded as a crucial turning point in man's moral and social development. We shift from a time in which the individual is conceived mainly as embedded within a wider whole, and whose purposes and actions are ascribed in terms of the purposes of that larger body, to something radically different: society now exists as a means of furthering the intentions and purposes of individuals, and not vice versa. Whereas Aristotle defines man as a *zoon politikon* – a political animal – who can only fulfil his true purpose as a member of the polis (Aristotle, *Politics*, 1.1), the United States Declaration of Independence (1776) declares that governments are instituted in order to secure those "unalienable rights" of men to "life, liberty and the pursuit of happiness" endowed by their "Creator". Needless to say, rights have featured prominently in some of the most inspiring social and political movements of our time, including movements for social and racial equality, religious freedom and the protection of minorities.

On the other hand, rights are also linked to some of the most intractable problems we face today. They are frequently associated with the rampant individualism and consumerism of liberal democratic societies, the growth of political alienation, the overly litigious nature of public life (at least in North America), the degradation of the environment and the entrenchment of economic inequality. Many of these criticisms have been part of a wider critique of liberal political thought, but many liberals too have been concerned about the consequences of too much "rights-talk". An overemphasis on rights can telescope and harden people's positions in politics, where often what is desperately required is a greater willingness for accommodation and flexibility. And it can encourage political solipsism; the focus is on the claimant and his needs and desires, and only to a lesser extent on the corresponding civic obligations and responsibilities they have in relations to the needs of others (see O'Neill 1996; Glendon 1991; Sandel 1996). As we shall see, some of these criticisms are essentially internal critiques. They accept the importance and value of rights, but seek to reform certain aspects of the practice. Others go much deeper. For these critics, rights manifest beliefs about the nature of persons or about society as a whole that must be overcome, not celebrated. Rights, it seems, are invested with equal amounts of hope and cynicism.

The aim of this book is to introduce different philosophical approaches to rights, and especially the political character of rights. As you will see, I take this to be a historical and theoretical task. One reason why is because it is helpful to get a sense of the way arguments about rights have emerged over time according to different circumstances and contexts. A historical survey of rights theories helps us to see the complexity and diversity of arguments about rights. This can help protect us against an overly reductive or simplistic approach that some critics and even defenders of rights often take. More importantly, it sheds light on the way conceptual change can occur in light of practical – and especially political – circumstances. Why is this important? It is almost impossible to see how any formal theory of rights – that is, an exhaustive conceptual elaboration of the nature of rights – could ever hope to settle disagreements about their fundamental value or the function they play in our society. These disagreements are normative through and through. Moreover, our beliefs about rights are shaped not only by moral arguments, but also by the historical, cultural and political contexts in which those arguments and beliefs are formed.

As I mentioned above, my aim is to take the political character of rights seriously. What does this mean? Political philosophy is importantly distinct from moral philosophy in at least this sense: although disagreement is endemic to both, in politics the persistence of disagreement – itself shaped by the passions and interests of the individuals and groups involved, along with the particular historical situation in which they live – must be reconciled with the need for the exercise of power.[1] Power is required, first of all, to create an order in which human cooperation becomes possible. But the exercise of power also creates demands for legitimization. A paradigm of injustice is a refusal to countenance the needs or interests of those over whom you exercise power. As Bernard Williams has put it, "'Might is not, in itself, right' is the first necessary truth, one of few, about the nature of right" (2005a: 23). But the move from this paradigm of injustice to the morality of a specific form of liberal rights does not dissolve the persistence of disagreement. There are many different ways of filling out that basic idea of injustice, none of which necessarily fit seamlessly together.

The distinctiveness of rights

What distinguishes rights from other kinds of claims – such as claims about moral validity *per se* – is twofold: first, in denying someone a right you have wronged them in a very specific sense; and secondly, rights aspire towards institutional embodiment and enforceability. This is another important dimension of the political character of rights. We want rights to be enforceable moral claims, and that is only possible in some kind of political community. If I have a right to something, then I have an entitlement, and that entitlement imposes obligations on others. But to realize my entitlement, the claim has to be enforceable in some way. Even a negative right requires not only that others forbear from acting, for example, but that the state acts so as to ensure such forbearance (see Shue 1996; Holmes & Sunstein 1999). But on what *grounds* are rights enforceable? What is the object of the right? To what extent do rights oblige? And enforceable by whom exactly, and in what circumstances? Are rights worth talking about even if they are not immediately enforceable?

We shall be discussing these questions in more detail below. At this point, however, let me introduce some basic distinctions and trajectories for the discussions to come.

Consider first the difference between *objective* and *subjective* senses of the term "right". There is, in fact, a complicated historical story about the separation of these two senses, about which, not surprisingly, historians disagree (see e.g. Tuck 1981; Brett 1997; Tierney 1997). But the basic idea is this: it is one thing to say that "it is right that Smith won the prize", or that "it is right to help the poor", and another thing to say "I have a right to enter the competition", or "I have a right to food". The use of right in the first instance is *objective* in the sense that the judgement is made not from the perspective of the individual agent making the claim, but from some more general perspective or viewpoint. I might think it is right to help the poor because it says so in the Bible, or because of some wider moral theory about what I ought to do, whether or not I assign any significance to any particular agent involved. In the second instance, the right is *subjective* in the sense that a particular person is seen as possessing or claiming a right. It starts from the perspective of the agent, and it refers to that agent in a particular way. It is this subjective sense of right, arguably, that is so distinctive about the *modern* discourse of rights, however much it might be the case that its origins can be traced back to medieval philosophy.

Now consider, briefly, two genealogies about the emergence of rights. The first is from Annette Baier. She summarizes the general conditions of the form of human justice in which rights come to play an important role in this way: the presence of moderate scarcity, limited generosity, vulnerability to the resentment of one's fellows and a limited willingness on the part of individuals to beg. "What we regard as ours by right", she suggests, "is what we are unwilling to beg for" (1995: 225–6). I would add another condition: an acute sense, drawn from historical experience, of the kind of *threats* that, in the absence of the kind of interests to which rights refer, are almost unavoidable. Rights emerge in response to specific threats, and they offer ways of dealing with them (see Scanlon 2003: 114–17).

The second genealogy is from Nietzsche. For him, instead of addressing inequality, justice only emerges when equality is actu-ally manifest: "justice originates between parties of approximately equal power" (1996: 92; see also 1989a: II.2). Recall Nietzsche's conception of the "will to power", where power consists, funda-mentally, in the expenditure of force or energy with which a given body is endowed (1989b: §36; 1989a: II.12). It offers itself as a psychological explanation of various kinds of human behaviour, which manifest through drives to self-preservation, self-overcoming and even self-destruction (e.g. Nietzsche 1989b: §13).[2] It applies also to explanations of justice and right. Partners act justly towards each other, suggests Nietzsche, only when they realize the parity of each other's strength, and continual aggression will only result in mutual attrition. So rights are not ascribed on the basis of some prior, abstract moral equality, but according to degrees of power, both actual power and the sense or *feeling* of power:

> Where rights prevail, a certain condition and degree of power is being maintained, a diminution and increment warded off. The rights of others constitute a concession on the part of our sense of power to the sense of power of those others. If our power appears to be deeply shaken and broken, our rights cease to exist; conversely, if we have grown very much more powerful, the rights of others, as we have previously conceded them, cease to exist for us. (Nietzsche 1982: II, 112)[3]

Hence the just man – the man who wants to be fair – is in constant need of the "subtle tact of a balance; he must be able to assess degrees of powers and rights, which, given the transitory nature of human things, will never stay in equilibrium for very long" (*ibid.*: 67).

So Baier and Nietzsche provide two very different stories. In one, rights emerge as a manifestation of an increasing sense of individual worth and dignity, part of the rejection of socially and culturally embedded hierarchy, and a check on the exercise of arbitrary power. In the other, rights are instead the *product* of relations of power (broadly construed). They represent a kind of mutual non-aggression pact, or a form of mutual recognition, subject to variation according to the changing perceptions, beliefs, capacities and actions of those who claim them against each other.

In many ways, these two genealogies underlie the discussion of the rest of this book. And I want to argue that understanding the political character of our theories of rights, in particular, requires seeing the ways in which both of these genealogies are getting at something fundamentally true about the nature of rights. We need to understand the differences between them as well, and I shall spend considerable time laying out these differences. But the basic thought is this: rights have been a vital part of the emergence of more liberal and humane forms of politics, but they are also, and always have been, implicated in various relations of power. They have been used to promote new capacities and freedoms, but have also brought with them new forms of power that act on those very capacities and freedoms. Our best understanding of the practice of liberal rights should seek to capture both of these aspects.

Using the language of rights is meant to signal that something important is at stake; one of the main reasons for invoking rights in the first place is to draw special attention to the object of the claim, whether or not it is already present in the extant legal, social and political culture. And yet this way of talking and acting is itself the product of particular historical processes, emerging out of specific historical periods and contexts, and thus with particular social and political pre-conditions. So as much as we use rights to criticize our legal, political and social practices and institutions, and to promote or protect those interests we deem to be the most vital or urgent, rights are themselves a social practice with a history. They simultaneously presuppose and reinforce various kinds of social and political arrangements and modes of interaction, and yet help bring new ways of acting and new institutional forms into being. In a very broad sense then, rights are not only, as Rex Martin has put it, "*established* ways of acting or *established* ways of ... being treated" (1993: 41, emphasis added), but also a means for *establishing* various ways of acting or being treated. To mark some interest or claim in terms of a right is not merely to *describe* a particular jural relation, but also to perform it: to help bring it into being, to make a normative claim on its behalf. Thus, rights need to be analysed in terms not only of their logical structure, but also their normative and historical structures. Philosophers are often keen to keep these elements apart, so the conceptual (what rights are) is distinct from the justificatory (what they ought to be). But they are hard to keep apart for long. Even those who seek conceptual purity are usually motivated by deep moral and political concerns; their criticisms often take the form of the language of rights becoming "degraded" or "debased" by overextension and misuse.

The dynamic character of rights

It is especially important, if we are concerned to capture the political character of rights, that we appreciate the fundamentally dynamic character of rights. Thus, when we say "*D* has a right to *X*", there are at least four aspects to this claim:[4]

- *Who* or *what* is the subject of the entitlement? (Individuals? Groups? Animals? Corporations?)

- What is the *substance* of the entitlement, or to what actions, states or objects does it refer? (To liberty? To free expression? To compensation? To self-determination?)
- What is the *basis* of the entitlement, or on what grounds does the claimant have the right(s) they say they do? (For moral reasons? Legal reasons? Political reasons?)
- What is the *purpose* of the entitlement? (To secure individual agency? Corporate agency? To promote well-being?)

To this basic quadratic structure we can add another layer of complexity (we shall turn to more concrete examples in the chapters below). The American legal theorist Wesley Hohfeld (1978) offered what has become a standard way of analysing the logical space of rights.[5] He tried to map the many different ways in which rights were used to cover an array of legal relationships, and to clarify exactly what kinds of jural relationships were at stake in each one. Hohfeld identified four key aspects to the family of legal relationships associated with rights:

- claim-rights;
- privileges (or permissions, or liberties);
- powers; and
- immunities.

Each then has a distinctive correlate: for claim-rights, it is duties; for privileges or permissions it is no-right (or no duty not to); for powers it is liabilities; and for immunities, it is disabilities. For Hohfeld, rights, in the strictest sense, are those claim-rights that are directly correlated to a duty. That is to say, if *D* has a *right* with respect to *H* to perform *X*, then *H* has a *duty* not to interfere with *D* in *X*-ing. The other relations work differently. If *D* has a *privilege* or *permission* to *X* with respect to *H*, then that means *H* has *no right* against *D* not to *X*. If *D* has a legal *power* with respect to *H*, then that means that some legal right or duty of *H*'s will be created, extinguished or altered by *D*'s exercise of that power, if he chooses to. Finally, since an immunity correlates with a disability, if D enjoys an *immunity* with respect to *H*, then *H* is *disabled* from changing or affecting *D*'s legal relations in some relevant way.

Hohfeld's analysis can be extended to moral and political contexts in interesting ways, although it becomes more controversial as it moves away from the more settled domain of legal analysis (see Edmundson 2004: 96–102). The most important result I want to point to here, however, is how the analysis shows that rights usually involve a bundle of Hohfeldian elements. If I have a right to free speech, for example, on Hohfeld's analysis I actually possess a bundle of things: a claim-right against specific others who have correlative duty not to interfere with my speech, but also an immunity – that the legislature (and others) are disabled from altering my legal rights to speech in various ways. Property rights too, on this analysis, are a bundle of relations. Owning my portable media player means that I have a claim-right against interference from others in my possession of it, but also permissions (or liberties) to use it in various ways. I have the power to sell it, give it away or lend it out on various terms. And I have immunities against others trying to alter the content of any of these relations. Even if we want to say that the core of the rights that matter most in politics are claim-rights, then that core is surrounded by a periphery made up of a range of different things, including permissions, powers and immunities.[6] The elements present at any given moment in time will vary given the nature of the right at stake, as well as the context. The rights I acquire in contracting with others may generate a periphery of relations that are very different from those associated with my right not to be harmed or killed.

As we explore different historical and contemporary arguments about the nature of rights, it is useful to keep the basic quadratic structure outlined above and Hohfeld's analysis in mind. One interesting result of doing so is to notice how the basic structure of rights is fundamentally dynamic. Rights have to be "housed" in a system or structure of beliefs in order to be justified. But these beliefs (and accompanying attitudes and habits) can come apart in various ways. Beliefs about who or what the subject of rights is, for example, can alter the sense of what counts as the substance or basis of rights, as well as what constitutes its core and periphery. Change along one axis creates knock-on effects along others. Beliefs about the subject of rights and their purpose, for example, are often bundled up with other beliefs to do with specific identities, practices and institutions. Moral disagreement and cultural change can cause disjunctions between those claiming rights and their effective recognition by the powers that be. We shall discuss a fascinating example of this kind of conceptual and historical change in Chapter 8, where we examine how attempts by indigenous peoples to claim rights to international recognition, as well as to land and self-government, raise fundamental questions about the nature of human rights.

Finally, the other general point I want to make about the fundamentally dynamic character of rights is the need to keep in mind how we see ourselves as both "authors" and simultaneously "addressees" of the law. That is to say, the laws and rules of a society are legitimate only if we are, in some sense – and it is a controversial point as to what extent we can be – self-governing. That means we have moral and legal claims to those rights that enable us to exercise self-government, for example, to political participation and collective action. But we are also, simultaneously, subjects of those very laws and rules, and that means we have another set of moral and legal claims to those rights that protect our non-public freedom. Jürgen Habermas (1996) has argued that this means there is, in fact, an internal relation (a "co-originality") between the rule of law and democracy, and thus between our "public" and "private" autonomy. We shall examine this particular claim in more detail in Chapters 4 and 8. But whether or not it is true, the perspective is valuable and useful to keep in mind. We are both the "artificers" and "matter" of the commonwealth, as Thomas Hobbes (*Leviathan*, "Introduction") put it. And that means that some of our most important political concepts, including that of rights, will be the object of constant collective construction and reconstruction, as well as frequent disagreement.

The history and future of rights

As will become clear, I expend considerable effort discussing the history of rights theories, and I shall say more about why in Chapter 1. But one thing I want to emphasize here is that the most influential theories of rights we have today, at least in the Anglo-American and European traditions of political philosophy, emerged from particular historical circumstances. In addition to the great scientific and philosophical developments of the early-modern era that helped shape moral and political thought, there were important political and historical circumstances. These circumstances included terrible civil and international wars, often fuelled by religious and ethnic zealotry and conflict, as well as the expansion of Europe into the "New World" and the geopolitics of competing imperial ambitions. And they included the emergence of the modern state and its distinctive conception of sovereignty, along with new forms of collective identities, especially in relation to the emergence of the nation-state.

We live in very different times, and yet the legacy of the nation-state and the civil, political and social rights that grew up around it is still a very powerful and important discourse in modern politics. Much has been written about globalization, and we shall explore some of its consequences below in our discussion of human rights. But what I want to mention here is that if our theories of rights have been deeply influenced over the past 250 years by the politics of the modern state as it emerged in Europe, the United Kingdom and the United States, then the next 250 years will present new challenges and hence new ways of understanding rights. Most states in the future will look more like Canada or Indonesia than the United Kingdom, Germany or the United States have in recent times.

What do I mean? Canada, for example, faces distinctive challenges to do with its history as a multinational and multiethnic state and the "deep diversity" that continues to characterize its politics.[7] As a condition of their continuing membership in the society, different founding groups have required recognition of their rights to language protection, education and, in some cases (e.g. indigenous peoples), to land and self-government. Migrants have sought protection from anti-discrimination provisions and the capacity to preserve some of their cultural practices. And we can see all of this reflected in Canada's constitutional structure, and in its distinctive rights culture more generally. The Canadian Charter of Rights and Freedoms, for example, which might look at first like a rather crass imposition from down south, is actually situated within a constitutional framework that recognizes a range of specific minority rights and distinctive constitutional norms. It contains protection for minority language rights and (limited) recognition of Aboriginal treaty rights. It contains a "notwithstanding clause" (Sec. 33), for example, which allows parliament, or a provincial legislature, to enable legislation that overrides sections of the Charter, albeit under strict conditions.[8] In 1998, the Supreme Court (Supreme Court of Canada 1998) issued a "Reference" that laid out constitutional norms and rules that would apply in the case of a potential secession by Quebec: an interesting example of a country literally setting the ground rules for its own deconstruction! Central to the court's argument was an appeal to the notion of ongoing democratic deliberation over the forms of mutual recognition acceptable to each of the parties involved, and the way to proceed in the face of ongoing disagreement.

All of this adds up to a rights culture deeply informed by the dilemmas and complexities faced by multinational societies. The same kind of complexity and hybridity, albeit in very different contexts and with very different challenges, is currently faced by emerging liberal democracies in other parts of the world, including in Africa, South Asia and South-East Asia, as well as even more dramatically and grimly in the Middle East. We shall discuss some of the challenges these contexts raise in Chapter 8.

The plan of the book

I have organized the book in such a way that I hope it can be read profitably by many different kinds of readers. The ideal, of course, is that you sit down and read it from front to back, taking in the full sweep of the argument. But I have also tried to structure the chapters so that they can be read on their own, or in different combinations, for those looking for a discussion of a particular set of arguments or debates. Each chapter can be read independently of the others, or as subsets, although they are all linked by a set of interweaving threads, the basis of which I try to lay out in Chapter 1. But I hope the book will also be of interest to those who are already well versed in some of these debates, but looking to refresh their views and find a new perspective on some familiar problems.

In Chapter 1 I try to provide the reader with some basic distinctions and methodological assumptions that will help them negotiate the various arguments about rights that are the subject of Chapters 2–8. But I also provide an account of my overall approach to rights, which I call a "naturalistic approach". The rest of the book does not depend on you accepting this view, and if you are not interested you can skip or skim that section, but it sets up the way I go about discussing the problems I present. My hope is that it will provide you with a distinctive way of engaging with the material discussed in the chapters that follow.

Chapters 2–6, then, go on to discuss five frameworks for justifying rights: natural law, property, dignity, mutual recognition and consequentialism. I explore the different ways these basic frameworks shape particular theories of rights, drawing on leading philosophers from the history of political thought and contemporary political theory to do so, including Grotius, Hobbes, Locke, Kant, Hegel, Bentham, Green, Rawls, Nozick, Foucault and Taylor (among others). Chapter 6 also uses some of the current debates over the threat of transnational terrorism to reflect on the nature of rights, especially those civil and political rights at the heart of liberal democracy.

In Chapters 7 and 8 the focus changes somewhat, as I turn to the idea of rights as "conduits" for relations of power more explicitly, and examine the challenge of justifying human rights today. In Chapter 7 I look at two distinctly critical approaches to rights, especially liberal rights: the Marxist critique of rights as a function of "bourgeois ideology"; and Michel Foucault's critique of social contract theory and "juridical" political thought in general. In Chapter 8 I turn to the question of what, exactly, we should want from a theory of human rights, and what role it should play in global politics. How can human rights be justified and enforced given deep disagreement about the foundations of rights, and the deep diversity of the global public sphere? Are we asking too much of human rights, or too little? What does the future hold for human rights?

1 A naturalistic approach

> A right, after all, is neither a gun, nor a one-man show. It is a
> relationship and a social practice, and in both of those essential
> aspects it is seemingly an expression of connectedness.
>
> (Michelman 1986: 91)

Introduction

Before we begin to engage with the various substantive theories of
rights on offer, I want to lay out my approach to these questions a
bit more explicitly. Although the book is intended as an introduction, among other things, its structure and organization reflect my
own substantive views about the subject. How could it not? There
are three ways in which I am going to approach the question of
rights and I want to introduce them here: first, we should think of
rights as representing a *complex social practice*; secondly, we shall
aim for what I shall call a *naturalistic* approach to rights in general;
and finally, among the different ways of characterizing rights, we
shall focus on rights as *statuses*, *instruments* and *conduits*. Let me
say some more about each of these now.

Rights as a social practice

Philosophers often want to keep two ways of approaching a concept or value separate, and for good reason. On the one hand, there
is the project of philosophical justification, and on the other, the
project of description or history. It is one thing to justify something,

and quite another to describe it or show how it works, or how it was used by such and such a culture or person. There have been complicated attempts to link these two modes of doing philosophy, most famously by Hegel, but the tension remains central to much philosophical work. We find it in the discussion of rights, too. Some philosophers set out to provide a formal theory of rights that sets out stringent conceptual and logical criteria for determining what counts as a right. Others posit some crucial property of or valid claim about persons, the presence of which warrants the ascription of rights. The idea is to provide a clear and rigorous standard against which to discipline our ordinary usage, as opposed to explaining how the concept arose. Rights, according to one version of this approach, are things that we *discover* – like laws of nature, or the structure of a chemical compound – as opposed to constructing ourselves.

Other philosophers start with the function of rights: what are people (or institutions, or corporations) *doing* when they appeal to rights? What role do rights play in our moral arguments or in our political practices? Looking at the function of rights can be more or less historically sensitive. Some see rights as having a single function across time and space – for example, to secure certain kinds of protected choices, or to promote a certain conception of well-being – or as having several such functions at once. Other theorists refer to a specific cultural or national "language" or framework of rights in order to explain the way it picks out specific interests or conceptions of well-being in a particular society (see e.g. Primus 1999). Here the claim is that the language of rights is itself derivative of, or at least highly dependent on, other more fundamental shared moral understandings, which themselves might be historically contingent in various ways. We can still talk about discovering rights as opposed to constructing them, but the discovery is now a distinctly historical and political one.

In what follows, I shall assume that rights are best understood as a *social practice*. What does this mean? First of all, rights are the kinds of things that are dependent on a social language of some kind, as opposed to standing independent of it, like atoms or molecules. At a minimum, a practice is any coherent (and complex) form of socially established cooperative human activity. Of course, the degree of coherence (and cooperativeness) will vary between

different practices, and some philosophers offer more specific defi-
nitions, such that planting turnips is not a practice but farming is,
or that chess is a practice but tic-tac-toe (noughts and crosses) is
not (MacIntyre 1984: 187). I shall leave aside these debates here.
Let us just assume that the social practice of claiming and recognizing rights is coherent enough to count as a practice in the broad
sense. This means that rights will only make sense given a particular
social context, one in which making a rights claim, for example, is
recognized as a legitimate move in a game, so to speak, that others
can understand and recognize. Charles Taylor (1985f: 32–4) uses
the example of voting to demonstrate what is involved in a social
practice: putting a cross beside someone's name on a slip of paper
and putting this into a box counts in the right context as voting
for that person (see Flathman 1976; Primus 1999: 28–34). In a
different context, without that particular social understanding and
without the particular social language of voting – involving the various distinctions and identifications between different social acts,
relations and structures – those acts would not amount to a vote.
Now sometimes practices are tightly rule-bound – think of chess
– but other times not. And in most cases, even with chess, we use
aspects of particular vocabularies in new and creative ways. This is
a particularly important point with regard to rights. Our practice
of rights is significantly open-ended or "underdetermined"; people
regularly refer to or claim something as a "right" that will often
stand outside normal usage, and yet still be at least comprehensi-
ble to others. As we shall see, this drives some philosophers crazy.
Rights "inflation" is seen as a problem that rigorous conceptual
analysis must eliminate.

So a practice-dependent approach to rights makes practices relevant not only to the application of a theory of rights, but also
to its justification. The content of that justification will depend,
in part, on the content and scope of the practices out of which it
emerges and to which it is meant to apply. A practice-independent
approach to rights, on the other hand, rejects the idea that any
practice-mediated relations people might have, or the culturally
distinct nature of particular practices, affects the justifying reasons
for a theory of rights. We shall explore both kinds of approaches to
rights in the chapters that follow, but what I am calling a "naturalistic" approach to rights clearly embraces something like the former.

Does this mean that a practice-dependent approach is incapable of criticizing extant institutions or practices? Does it mean that if a particular social and historical practice entails that a minority group is to be denied basic rights, there is nothing more than can be said? We shall explore this challenge in greater detail in Chapter 8, but the short answer is no. Social practices are complex and require interpretation and elaboration. There is more than one perspective involved in making sense of the nature of the practice in question. Moreover, as I suggested above, the very idea of rights is closely connected to the notion that "might makes right" is unacceptable as a way of justifying the exercise of power over individuals. If the exercise of power by governments or institutions affects the vital interests of individuals in significant ways, then their legitimacy is always potentially in question.

Thinking of rights in this way also means that rights are fundamentally *social* in character; they presuppose various kinds of interactions among people, and thus various social arrangements, including norms and institutions. As we shall see, many argue that the language of rights is intimately linked with political "atomism". Political atomism refers, basically, to the idea that we should seek to understand human social relations as reducible to relations between individuals. Society, according to this view, consists fundamentally of individuals seeking to fulfil their own particular ends (Taylor 1985e). Historically there are two examples of this shift. First, especially as the language of individual rights began to develop in the sixteenth and seventeenth centuries, we see a close relation between rights and property (*ius* and *dominium*). A tight link was often drawn between having a right and having the freedom (or sovereignty) to dispose of one's property, including one's person, in ways that were protected from interference (and especially state interference). Respect for rights was a condition for the legitimacy of state power, not the other way around. The second example is a sharp break from the Aristotelian view that one could not be a fully competent human agent outside the bounds of a particular kind of political society. Social contract theory and the use of the device of a "state of nature", operated with a very different conception of man's nature in relation to politics (or to the *polis* or city).

This picture of the moral individualism of rights is certainly true in important respects. But the language and practice of rights also introduced new ways of relating to others – new modes of sociability, in other words – as much as they mark the emergence of the moral importance of the separateness of persons. And so rights are also fundamentally *relational* in character (see Michelman 1986; Minnow 1990; Nedelsky 1993; Habermas 1996). Any account of rights will need to show how they operate as a *system*, or a *structure* of entitlements and responsibilities. In particular, they represent a particular distribution of freedom and authority. Rights entail, as we have already seen, various correlative and reciprocal duties, permissions, immunities, liberties and powers.[1] They establish patterns of relationships that impose benefits and burdens on people and institutions to varying degrees. Although rights can shield or protect individuals or groups from various kinds of interference (not limited to state interference), they also embed them in a complex web of social and political institutions and norms. To claim a right, for example, is by definition to affect the interests and actions of others, since you are seeking a particular form of recognition or acknowledgement of an urgent or important claim on your behalf. Moreover, rights can not only be claimed but waived; my not standing on my rights, for example, can signal a form of conditional trust in relation to others, or an assertion of autonomy on my part. More generally, the activities involved in the practice of rights – claiming, waiving, negotiating, accepting, recognizing, justifying, and so on – are all activities that go on *between* persons.

A system of rights therefore works not only to shield individuals from each other in various ways, but also to draw them together in others, often at the same time. They establish not only barriers but also lines of interaction. They can work to align individual behaviour with social and cultural norms, just as much as they can protect someone against them. For example, a legal right to sue for defamation or invasion of privacy can serve to align legal standards with a certain cultural or conception of civility, just as much as it empowers individuals to protect their autonomy.[2] The distribution of rights also depends on deeper and more systematic arguments about the interests or capacities they are said to protect and promote, and ultimately about the kind of society in which they are best realized or "housed". In short, rights presuppose a wider account of the social and political order in which they are to be situated. Rights presuppose community or, better yet, *communities*.

So the choice is not between a theory of rights that is relational and one that is not. Rather, it is between different kinds of social relations in which rights will play some part.

A naturalistic approach to rights

There are two ways of giving a "naturalistic" account of something. In contemporary analytic philosophy, naturalism tends to be closely aligned with the methodology of the natural sciences. To give a naturalistic account of X, then, is to give an explanation of it continuous with empirical enquiry in the sciences. But which sciences, exactly, and in what sense should our explanations be "continuous" with them? Sometimes this is intended in the sense that naturalistic explanations should replace traditional philosophical concepts and the practice of conceptual analysis and justification. More moderate versions suggest that we need to pay greater attention to empirical facts about the kinds of creatures we are and the world in which we live.

A second sense of naturalism is to give an account of X in terms that are continuous with the kind of creatures we are, subject not only to physical and biological laws but also as social and cultural agents. Here a naturalistic account of human behaviour is necessarily an account of human beings not only as part of nature, but also living under (and helping to create) culture. This means a naturalistic account of human behaviour needs to draw not only on the methodologies and approaches of the natural sciences, but also the human and social sciences, as well as the humanities. If it is an ethological truth that human beings live under culture, then we need also to make sense of the complex ideas and beliefs people form about those cultures. In particular, human beings live according to *norms*, and this provides a particular focus for the discussion below. So, what we are is a function, in part, of our biological or genetic make-up, in the loose sense of providing us with dispositions towards displaying certain properties or phenotypic traits in certain kinds of contexts. But what we are is also, crucially, a function of the way we are shaped and moulded by cultural and social factors and how these factors are in turn shaped by us. It is our nature, as Anthony Appiah (2005: 211) has put it, to shape our natures. A naturalistic ethics, and a naturalistic approach to moral and political philosophy, must account for these facts as well.

As applied to moral and political phenomena then, naturalism in this second sense is closely aligned with what I shall call a sense of *realism*, but not as this term is normally used by metaphysicians or in meta-ethics, nor by theorists of international relations. Rather, to give a naturalistic account of moral or political phenomena is to try to avoid both moralism and reductionism, an approach that analyses the capacities and intentions of human beings, as we think an "experienced, honest, subtle and unoptimistic interpreter might … [analyse] human behaviour elsewhere" (B. Williams 1995a: 68). For Williams, a naturalistic account of moral psychology, for example, avoids explanatory excess by pointing to the way various assumptions about the psychology underlying a particular (moralized) account of the will are themselves moral assumptions in need of explanation (*ibid*.: 65–76).[3] Nietzsche, according to Williams, offers just such a minimalist moral psychology; not for the sake of being reductionist, but rather in order to clarify at what point unwarranted idealizations about human capacities enter into our ways of explaining them.

If we turn to some recent political theory, we can find similar examples of this kind of approach. Carole Pateman (1987) and Charles Mills (1997), provide what I would call a naturalistic account of social contract theory. Against the grain of contemporary contractarian political thought, which seeks to distance itself from any kind of historical claim, Pateman and Mills reconnect contractarianism to the way it has been used in the history of political thought, especially as a means of describing and explaining the genesis of society and the moral psychology of its citizens (and especially its non-citizens) (e.g. Mills 1997: 5–6, 12–13). The point is to show how a supposedly ideal contract can end up as part of the rationalization of distinctly non-ideal aspects of the actual polity. For Pateman, that means exposing a hierarchical sexual contract underlying the apparently egalitarian ethos of social contract theory as it emerged in the early modern period. Mills, taking some inspiration from Pateman's work, focuses on the way various somatic norms shape assumptions about the capacities of the contracting agents and work to exclude non-whites from effective membership in the body politic.

What would it mean then to give a naturalistic account of rights? First, one could argue that rights are natural in the sense of being derivative of certain natural laws, as we shall see when we discuss these kinds of arguments in Chapter 2. Rights, for these theorists, are those moral qualities that form part of our rational and sociable nature, and that are prior to and independent of our belonging to any particular political community.

Secondly, one could argue that the language and practice of rights is conventional in certain crucial respects. Consider David Hume's account of the emergence of justice. In the original "frame of our minds", wrote Hume, "our strongest affection is confined to ourselves; our next is extended to our relations and acquaintances; and it is only the weakest which reaches to strangers and indifferent persons". It is this "partiality", he contends, that is an obstacle to the establishment of social arrangements that can overcome the "inconveniences" of human nature. The remedy, in part, is the emergence of conventions of justice and property, which are not "derived from nature, but from *artifice*; or more properly speaking, nature provides a remedy in the judgement of and understanding, for what is irregular and incommodious in the affections" (Hume 1978: 500). Artificial things have their causes in nature, but are ultimately the result of human action, and as such possess a certain function. (The sense of justice "arises artificially tho' *necessarily* from education, and human conventions" [*ibid*.: 483].) The rules of justice emerge then as a result of an individual's pursuit of a particular end, namely, the satisfaction of their "interested passions": that is, self-interest (*ibid*.: 429, 499–500). The unintended effect of the pursuit of these private interests, however, is the emergence of the institutions of justice and property, which, in the end, serve the public good. For Hume, there are certain constancies of human nature (a modified self-interest and confined benevolence) that, combined with a feature of the world (relative scarcity), lead to regularities in human behaviour, including the emergence of certain moral and political institutions.[4] But since these institutions ultimately rely on human beliefs and practices, they are subject to modification and change according to context. Thus, in the case of justice, who owns exactly what will vary from society to society, and even the kinds of things that might count as property will be variable (hence the importance of *de facto* possessions in his theory of justice) (see Haakonssen 1981: 38–44). For Hume, certain facts about human nature provide "test-principles" that necessarily refer to the existing value systems of the particular society in question.[5]

The naturalistic approach I am appealing to has certain structural affinities with Hume's, in that both seek to avoid an easy opposition between nature and convention, and between historicist and rationalist accounts of normativity. In particular, both seek to place the role of history (and the passions) at the centre of an account of normativity. But there are differences too. For Hume, the survival of a particular institution, and ultimately the moral beliefs that grow up around it, was sufficient evidence of it conforming to human nature, and thus of a kind of psychological necessity attached to those attitudes and beliefs. These laws of nature are not derived from statements about human nature, but caused by certain features of human nature ("confined generosity", etc.) placed in a world such as ours. And because men have an ability to balance long-term against short-term interests, they come to be bound by the rules they create, and hence they acquire a certain independent status (Haakonssen 1981: 37). But the contingency of the connection between our moral attitudes and the particular institutions and customs (or norms) of our society can be emphasized even more strongly than Hume does. The social and political institutions of Australia or Canada, for example, are not "natural" in the sense of conforming to (or being caused by) any deep facts about human nature, but rather in so far as they are the product of the collusion between "bare" nature – the basic, innate equipment all human beings have – and "second nature" – the particular interactions, relations of power and sociability characteristic of a particular community or society.[6]

The naturalistic approach appealed to here also has affinities with Martha Nussbaum (1992; 1995; 2000: esp. ch. 2) and Amartya Sen's "capabilities" approach to distributive justice. The capabilities approach draws on claims about there being basic and central capabilities required for any valuable form of human "functioning". The methodology combines a distinctive reading of Aristotle's discussion of human nature in the *Nicomachean Ethics*, John Rawls's theory of "reflective equilibrium" (in *A Theory of Justice*), and his grappling with the "fact of reasonable pluralism" in *Political Liberalism*. In short, for Nussbaum, the aim is to establish some basic, widely shareable and provisional judgements about human nature, and then build on these in wrestling with more specific ethical and political questions. In particular, Nussbaum argues that there are certain "central capabilities" of human beings – such as the capacity for practical reason and sociability (she goes on to provide a list of ten) – that almost everyone can acknowledge as essential to living a life that is recognizably human.[7] Human beings need some basic "innate equipment", or "basic capabilities", to achieve these central capabilities, but they also need material and institutional support to actually achieve them (e.g. education, adequate nutrition, etc.). The central capabilities are thus also "combined capabilities", since they combine "internal training" with "external" material, social and institutional support.

Once again, what is striking in this account is the presumption about the interaction between nature and culture, and the deep shaping of human behaviour and attitudes by the norms and institutions within which we act. Indeed, the whole notion of a "combined capability" offers an interesting way of thinking about the nature of rights in general (Nussbaum 2000; see also Ivison 2002: ch. 6). Human beings are complex assemblages of desire and affect as well as rational preferences and beliefs. Any genuinely political theory of rights has to make sense of both of these aspects of human agency.

Statuses, instruments and conduits

So take rights to be a (complex) social practice, not only an abstract set of metaphysical claims. And take a generally naturalistic approach to the analysis of rights, in the sense of paying attention to the dynamic structure of rights claims and their historical and practical character. What follows from doing so?

Rights, just like any other political value, have to be argued for and justified. They are not self-evident and they are not self-validating (despite what the drafters of the United States Declaration of Independence suggest). Two of the most common frameworks within which rights are justified are, broadly, *deontological* and *consequentialist*. We shall explore these different approaches in chapters to come, but it might help to introduce the basic differences here.

For the deontologist, rights are ascribed to individuals on the basis of their possessing certain capacities or attributes that warrant the special protection or recognition that rights purportedly provide. For the consequentialist, rights are ascribed on the basis that respecting them is a means of bringing about some desirable state of affairs, whether maximizing utility, promoting the interests of the worst off, or ensuring fairness and so on.

Some of the most powerful ways of representing the nature of rights in political philosophy has been to link them to the notion of an inviolable sphere or *boundary* within which the basic freedom of an individual is protected. This was encouraged, in part, by the close relation between the late medieval and early modern language of "*ius*" (right) and "*dominium*" (property). It was also encouraged by the development of the notion of rights as pre-political or "natural": as something that individuals possessed prior to entering political society and that structured subsequent political relations. (We shall be exploring these ideas in more detail in Chapter 2.) In more recent times, Ronald Dworkin has provided an influential metaphor of rights being akin to *trumps*, which has reinforced the idea of an inviolable boundary. A trump is a playing card that takes priority over any previous cards played. Thus, certain kinds of rights, according to Dworkin (1977), "trump" other kinds of political justifications that state a goal for the community as a whole. If an individual has a right to free speech, for example, then it is wrong for political officials to violate that right, even if doing so would make the community as a whole better off in some relevant way. Lying behind Dworkin's argument is a strong claim about the equal moral worth of each individual, and the way respect for individual rights helps to express and manifest that belief. (Note that it does not say anything about which rights should trump other *rights* when they conflict.) Robert Nozick (1974), who also linked rights to a strong sense of the inviolability of individuals, provided another way of thinking about rights in this way: rights as *side-constraints* on the pursuit of consequences, including even good consequences (such as the aim of maximizing the non-violation of rights).

Another way of justifying rights is broadly consequentialist or "instrumentalist". Here the basic idea is to locate a theory of rights in relation to the promotion of a set of desired consequences, or optimal distribution of interests.[8] Rule utilitarianism provides one such argument: respect rules that protect or promote individual rights in so far as doing so promotes utility overall. Utilitarianism is vulnerable to objections about whether or not it can capture the intuition about the inviolability of the individual discussed above, which drives many of the deontological arguments about rights. But as we shall see, utilitarianism is only one form of consequentialism and, moreover, the whole point of this approach is precisely to challenge the kind of intuitions deontologists appeal to.

Rights can also be justified as instruments for achieving goals other than the maximization of utility. Rawls, for example, a famous critic of utilitarianism, defined the optimal distribution of rights as that which would be chosen from the perspective of the original position. Rights are valuable to the extent that they promote justice understood as fairness. It so happens, though, that his first principle of justice is one that gives what he calls the "basic liberties" – essentially, basic rights to do with political liberty (voting, holding public office, freedom of speech, assembly, freedom from arbitrary arrest and the integrity of the person) – priority over other kinds of political justifications (Rawls 1999b: 52–4).

So rights can be understood to refer to the *status* of individuals, as an expression of the fundamental moral worth of individuals and their inherent dignity. And they can be understood as *instruments* or tools for promoting human well-being.

But we also need to see how rights can become embedded within various relations of power, as much as they are often deployed against them. And so we need to understand rights as not only statuses or instruments, but also as what I shall call *conduits*. The ascription of rights entails the distribution of a particular set of powers and capacities. We shall explore this in greater detail below when we turn to the critics of rights, especially those inspired by the work of Foucault. But one does not need to read Foucault to get a sense of how rights cannot, on their own, provide an automatic immunity against the exercise of power. The interaction and interpenetration of the social norms and the practice of rights, for example, means that the critical potential of rights claims will always be ambiguous to some extent. And the fact that rights are indeed so intimately linked to law and the juridical edifice of the state and its agencies means that the ascription and effectiveness of rights will be shaped by various historical and political forces at work in that society. Rights are one among a number of tools that individuals and groups can use to deflect or redirect various relations of powers that act on them. But they are *counter*-powers as opposed to inherently *anti*-powers; they never stand fully outside relations of power, even as they are deployed against them. Taking up the naturalistic approach helps shed light on the sense in which rights can be conduits of power just as much as they protect us from it.

Taking distinctions seriously

Finally, let us turn to the issue of how the general approach I am taking to rights might affect some of the standard ways of carving up modern philosophical discussions of rights. What I hope is that by the end of the book these distinctions will still be useful to you, but grasped in a new way. There are two, in particular, that I want to mention here and that we shall be returning to at different points as we proceed.

Moral and legal rights

First, although accepting that there is a distinction between moral and legal rights, the naturalistic approach adopted here seeks to recast it in various ways. Lawyers and moral philosophers have each claimed paternity over rights. Jeremy Bentham (1748–1832) famously observed: a "right is with me the child of law ... a natural right is a son that never had a father" (1987b: 334). Many contemporary critics of modern human rights have similar worries, concerned not so much to dispute the moral claims underlying moral rights as to cast doubt on the philosophical coherence and political sense of appealing to rights without any meaningful system of enforcement in place (e.g. Geuss 2001). However, others point to the fact that rights – especially human rights – often matter most precisely in the absence of any settled legal doctrine, or even any effective system of enforcement. They are manifesto claims, as Feinberg called them; aspirational claims meant to expose the moral shortcomings of our current legal and political arrangements, and intended to help motivate change.[9] So criticism of a state for their denial of basic political rights to minority groups, for example, is taken as evidence that there are rights that exist in some sense outside or apart from their legal enactment. This view accords with the language of discovery commonly employed when speaking about rights. For example, in relation to the recent history of "indigenous rights" lawyers and historians sometimes speak of the *acknowledgement* that Aboriginal people possess certain rights, or the *recognition* of those rights by the law.[10] In turn, this language of recognition and acknowledgement relies on an implicit distinction between legal rights and the underlying moral rights that find expression in legal form.

Many philosophers believe that rights exist if an acceptable moral argument for them can be provided. While they are happy with the idea that institutional rights evolve over time in response to changing beliefs and attitudes, they believe that if something is a moral right then it has always been so, even if people have failed to recognize it, or failed to extend it to others. To believe that moral rights are subject to historical change, according to this view, is to confuse rights with mere beliefs about rights, or to confuse the object of moral philosophy with that of historical sociology.

Consider, for example, Alan Gewirth's claim that the acceptability of a moral argument has nothing to do with the actual beliefs of individuals, and thus that there is a sense in which if a particular right exists (i.e. for which a morally valid justification can be given), then it must always have existed. Gewirth argues that the rights-bearing feature is the human capacity to act in pursuit of our chosen ends. This leads him to conclude that all human beings have a right to freedom and well-being since these are necessary conditions of such agency (Gewirth 1982: 6–7, 41–67). For Gewirth, the existence of human rights depends mainly on the existence of certain moral justificatory reasons. This means that even if human beings in the past did not claim human rights or even know whether they had them, they still had them. Human rights are discovered not invented.

These questions touch on very basic issues about the justification of morality, which we cannot hope to settle here. But at the limit, moral rights have to be anchored in some way to established human practices if they are to be knowable to creatures like us. The naturalistic approach sketched above departs sharply from Gewirth in a number of ways.[11]

First, as MacIntyre (1984: 65) and others have pointed out, and as the social practice approach to rights makes explicit, the very idea of claiming certain things as rights depends for its intelligibility on the existence of certain kinds of social institutions, norms and practices. Now, there is no *a priori* reason why we cannot say that particular ways of acting that are socially sanctioned might not amount to rights, whether or not the society in question employs the language of rights, and whether or not the sanctions employed correspond to the kinds of social institutions and practices with which we are familiar. But on my view, the practice of rights is a distinctive (albeit complex) practice that has its origins in a particular set of moral and practical discourses. That it has these particular origins does not necessarily affect its ultimate moral validity (as much as it will shape it in various ways), or its extension to very different circumstances or contexts. However, the naturalistic approach, given its emphasis on the dynamic interrelatedness between the moral, historical and institutional dimensions of rights, rejects the ahistorical approach expressed in Gewirth's argument. This ahistorical view is implausible as a concept of rights in general just because so many of the rights we take for granted are bound up with the material and ideological conditions of a particular kind of society. For example, freedom of the press, freedom of information, rights to privacy or to publicly provided health care, or the rights for equal access to education and employment are all rights that belong to people who live in a particular kind of society. They are justified not only by virtue of certain beliefs about desirable ways of being allowed to act and desirable ways of acting towards others, but also by virtue of certain beliefs about the economic and social workings of the society: for example, the belief that it is technologically and economically feasible to provide such entitlements without undue cost to the capacity to achieve other important goals. Although there might indeed be some general rights that come close to the kind of moral primitives appealed to by Gewirth, it's striking that this is very far removed from the list of rights familiar to most modern readers and embodied in the most famous human rights documents of the twentieth century, which are much more extensive and hard to reduce to a subset of basic (essentially negative) rights.

The naturalistic approach takes the interrelatedness between the moral, historical and political dimensions of rights seriously, and that means it is particularly concerned with the conditions of something becoming an effective moral right in a given society at a given time (or not, for that matter). For example, in so far as we now accept that indigenous people have a moral right to at least some of their traditional lands, it is implausible to suggest that this right always existed and that people were simply ignorant or unaware of it. In the Australian context, given what we know about the theories of property entitlement, racial hierarchy and the conditions of civilization that were common in the eighteenth and nineteenth centuries, and given what we know about the levels of ignorance with regard to Aboriginal culture, it seems a stretch to say that Aboriginal people actually had a moral right to their land at that time. There were dissenting moral views, of course, but the overwhelming weight of public and legal opinion was informed by versions of the natural law doctrine of "discovery", or the general attitudes embodied in law about the supposed inferiority of Aboriginal people denied them any justified entitlement to their lands or ways of life. By contrast, such prejudicial beliefs have become more difficult to sustain and justify in recent years. The commitment to equality has become stronger and more extensive. As a result, it makes more sense, I think, to say that new moral rights have come into existence, just as old ones have disappeared. Indigenous political movements have taken hold of both moral arguments and legal tools and tried to fashion new claims in light of changed historical and social circumstances.

The struggle to align legal and moral rights will become a particularly difficult issue when we turn to our discussion of human rights. For now, I think it is useful to think of the zone in between the moral and the legal as a crucial aspect of the political character of rights. The moral and legal aspects of rights are two sides of the same coin: two dimensions of a self-consciously political approach to rights.

"Interest" versus "choice" (or "will") theories of rights

Two of the most influential accounts of rights in analytic philosophy in recent years are the *interest* and *choice* (or will) theories of rights. On the choice account, as argued by H. L. A. Hart, the clearest (or strictest) sense of a right refers to an uncontested domain of *choice* for the individual. To be a rights-holder is to have control over the duty in question, in the sense of being able to demand or waive the performance of an action. So I have a claim-right against Y that Y φ just in case I have some measure of control (or "sovereignty", as Hart puts it later on in the article) over Y's duty (Hart 1984).[12] For Hart, furthermore, a right to liberty is fundamental to and presupposed by all other claims about individual rights. As Hart puts it, duties with correlative rights in this sense are a "normative property belonging to the right holder, and this figure becomes intelligible by reference to the special form of control over a correlative duty which a person with such a right is given by the law" (*ibid*.: 95). It follows that claim-rights cannot be attributed to things that cannot exercise the control and powers central to this account, such as babies or the very old, horses or a forest.

Now the advantage of this account is the direct link between my having a full measure of control over Y's duty, such that Y's duty is owed to me. A clear correlation is drawn between my right and Y's duty, which then can be customized according to the degree of control at issue (lesser or greater, etc.). As a descriptive theory of legal rights it has the advantage of matching closely the paradigms found in contract law and the criminal law, for example, as well as accounting for the asymmetry between the civil and criminal law (a point well made by Jones 1994; Sreenivasan 2005). It links the interests people have in claiming rights to a particular interest in autonomous choice. Recalling the quadratic structure of rights laid out in the Introduction, according to choice theory, the *subject* of rights is the free willing agent; the *substance* lies in the allocation of *powers* of control; the *basis* of rights lies in human freedom; and the *purpose* of rights is to demarcate "spheres of practical choice" (Steiner 1998: 238).

Once expanded to a story about moral rights, however, this conceptual fastidiousness quickly runs into trouble. First of all, it seems to limit rights to only those beings capable of autonomy, thus potentially ruling out as possible moral-rights-holders (except via proxy) the unborn, infants, the mentally disabled and animals. If moral rights are to act, in part, as constraints on the pursuit of goals, then babies or the mentally disabled (or animals for that matter) are here denied an important source of protection. Even if infants, for example, are owed duties of various kinds, if they are incapable of being a rights-holder themselves then the interests to which those duties refer might be vulnerable to the interests of *proper* rights-holders, or as mere inputs into a utilitarian decision procedure (see Edumundson 2004: 128). More generally, defenders of the rights of the unborn or of animals, for example, will not be impressed that their claims are ruled out of consideration by what seems to be conceptual fiat.

A second problem is inalienable rights. We might think that a rights-holder should be disabled from being free to waive certain rights and duties, for example, from enslaving himself.[13] This is usually justified as being in the interest of the rights-holder and as *strengthening* the claim-right, not weakening it. The idea is that I have a claim-right not to be enslaved, or not to be operated on without informed consent and so on (i.e. in these cases my capacity to assert my will is lessened, but at no cost to the force of the claim-right, which the choice theory must deny). For some, the inability to generalize from the paradigm cases of the choice theory to the cases of inalienability and incompetence reveal certain fatal flaws (see Sreenivasan 2005). Still, others have tried to refine choice theory to address the challenges (see Kramer *et al*. 1998). In so far as autonomy can be understood along a spectrum, as opposed to being all or nothing, there may be room for accommodating some of the concerns expressed by the counter-examples of babies and inalienability.

According to the interest theory, on the other hand, any necessary link between the capacity for choice and the pre-emptory force of a right is blurred, if not broken. In its simplest terms, the interest theory of rights just says: rights exist to promote or protect certain key interests of the rights-claimant.[14] To say I have a right to X is to say that someone else has a duty to perform some act (or omission) that is in my interests. But which interests exactly? Only those whose protection or promotion can be accepted as a reason sufficient for holding some other person (or persons) to be under a duty. However, to claim a right is not to have already justified the interest at stake, but merely to assert it; justification of the underlying claim has to be forthcoming. Thus Joseph Raz, a pre-eminent defender of the interest theory of rights, defines rights in this way: "To say of an individual or group that it has a right is to say that an aspect of their well-being is ground for holding another to be under a duty" (1986: 259).[15] Note that although the interest theory says that only those things capable of having interests are eligible for being rights-holders, this still entails a broad range of potential claimants (including babies, dogs and the mentally incompetent).[16] In fact, on its own, the interest theory does not identify the relevant interests or distinguish between those that really matter and those that do not. And so interest theory extends the notion of a claim-right to a much wider range of cases than does the choice theory. And it can readily acknowledge, depending on the arguments used, that some interests may be so profound as to warrant disabling individuals or groups from waiving them (since it makes no necessary claim between rights and autonomous choice, although autonomous choice may indeed be an important interest that should be protected). If I have a sufficiently strong interest in not being enslaved, or in not being operated on without my consent, then X's duties not to do any of these things is owed to me. The justification for doing so may depend on beliefs or arguments to do with things other than the exercise of autonomous choice, which might allow for a greater balancing of competing values, especially in conditions of deep disagreement about the good. However, as some critics assert, it might equally lead to incoherence about the nature of rights, since the language of interests is so general and promiscuous.

It is sometimes suggested by advocates of the choice theory that its descriptive austerity at least offers the possibility of a normatively minimalist account of the logical structure of rights, and that this will contribute to greater clarity about both legal and moral rights. But it turns out that the theory is difficult to sustain, even as a description of legal practice, let alone as a general account of moral rights. At best it represents a particular account of the force of rights in modern liberal societies, concerned above all to protect the formal structure of the law from becoming too heavily encroached on by promiscuous moralism and the short-term demands of policy (see e.g. Simmonds 1998: 213). To protect the integrity of rights, and particularly the connection between the value of choice and the pre-emptory force of rights, choice theory claims they should be interpreted as a set of especially important protected options, and not merely one set of interests to be balanced against others. But this now moves the choice theory some steps away from the conceptual austerity with which it began and more to the centre of contestable political debate, negating one of its supposed advantages over the interest theory.

The naturalistic account sketched above fully embraces the inevitability of disagreement over which interests matter most for our judgements about rights, and this raises some serious challenges for both it and the interest theory more generally. We should embrace an endogenous and historical approach to the emergence of the interests to which rights refer. And because the naturalistic approach conceives of individual choice and action as always enmeshed within various relations of interdependence and power, any claim about the necessary connection between autonomy and rights will have to be carefully qualified. So the interest theory is much closer to the general approach to rights I take in the book as a whole.

Having sketched the basic elements of the naturalistic approach to rights, and especially the focus on the political character of rights, let us turn to some of the most prominent arguments about rights in the history of political thought. We shall return to some of the points raised above as we work through these fascinating arguments, especially the distinctions between subjective and objective rights, moral and legal rights, and the choice and interest theories.

2 Natural law and natural rights

The Commonwealth of learning here is taking a complete holiday; we have all become politicians.
(John Locke to P. van Limborch, 7 August 1689)

Introduction

One of the most straightforward ways of thinking about rights is to say that people just have them: that it is a basic moral fact about persons. Just as our conception of a person includes things such as "has reason" or "is a conscious being", so it includes the idea that people have rights. The American philosopher Robert Nozick famously opened his critique of liberal egalitarianism, *Anarchy, State and Utopia*, with this claim: "Individuals have rights, and there are things no person or group may do to them (without violating their rights)" (1974: ix). Nozick was drawing on a rich tradition of thinking about the nature of rights. He did so in order to promote libertarian political ends, using the basic claim about the inviolability of individual rights – and especially property rights – to undermine the case for redistributive social justice and an expansive welfare state. But as we shall see, to assert that people have rights in virtue of their personhood, or their "humanity", that they have "natural rights", in other words, can lend itself to any number of different political ends. The Declaration of the Rights of Man and of the Citizen made by the French Assembly in 1789 proclaimed in its second article that "[the] aim of every political association is the preservation of the natural and inalienable rights of man", which it listed as liberty, property, security and resistance to oppression. A few years before that, in 1776, the United States Declaration of Independence announced that "all men are created equal ... endowed by their Creator with certain unalienable rights; that among these are life, liberty and the pursuit of happiness".

Here and in Chapter 3 we shall explore arguments about rights that begin from strong premises about human nature and about certain basic properties that men have (and here, often enough, they meant *men*). In particular, we shall explore how the idea of *subjective* rights emerged that, although increasingly distinguished from objective right, is nevertheless connected to wider moral theories and new visions of social and political order.

Another key theme for our discussion of natural rights is the way this tradition, complex as it is, contains different ways of conceiving of the ultimate purpose of rights that are often at odds with each other. The natural law tradition, in other words, has often disagreed with itself about what rights we have and why. One strand of the tradition emphasizes the basic connection between rights and protected choices; one has rights always over and against the city or one's fellows, including having the licence to attack or take pre-emptive action against them if your freedom is threatened seriously enough. Another strand of the tradition emphasizes the connection between rights and a prior conception of moral order, or of justice. Here rights are conceived as protected freedoms, but often for the purpose of fulfilling one's prior moral duties. The first strand is driven to its logical conclusion most dramatically by Thomas Hobbes, for whom the liberty protected by rights entailed war unless constrained by the state. The second strand can be found in a number of places. We shall pick up certain aspects of it in the work of Hugo Grotius below, and John Locke in Chapter 3.

Naturalism and rationalism

First, it might be helpful to pause and think more generally about what it means to call something a "natural" right or a natural law. Note first the basic difference between them: a natural right refers to a liberty of some kind, a natural law to a constraint. "Natural" refers to the *grounds* for a right or a law. A natural law is said to be a law that is true at all times for everyone, whoever they are and wherever they happen to be. A natural right is a right that all persons have *qua* persons, and independently of any special relationships or voluntary actions (see Hart 1984). The idea is that natural rights refer to certain moral relations that hold independently of the existence of any legal system, or perhaps any social or political system at all. Sometimes this is also used to restrict the class of basic rights that human beings have to a fairly narrow set, given that if they really do refer to basic capacities then the kinds of rights at issue will be relatively few and primarily "negative". But this does not follow automatically. It all depends on how the grounds are spelled out. A right not to be tortured seems to be a basic right in this sense, but so too might a right to subsistence or shelter. And most negative rights actually require extensive "positive" action on the part of others, especially the state, to be realized, for example, property rights.[1]

Recall the distinction between subjective and objective right. One route is to associate the natural with the objective; that is, we try to extract objective natural laws from nature. The appeal is thus to nature as providing a normative or critical standard against which to measure existing social and political practices. Even if we are born with different capacities and qualities, as well as into different civil and political orders, appealing to natural rights provides a regulative standard or benchmark against which to judge those relations. Grounding a moral standard in nature provides a vantage point independent of social, cultural and political differences. But how do we do this? Modern philosophers have generally been wary about what the English philosopher G. E. Moore called the "naturalistic fallacy": of identifying an ethical concept with a natural concept. Just because men are "naturally" physically stronger than women does not make that a good thing, or entail that they have certain natural rights that flow from their natural condition. Men and women are naturally inclined to do all sorts of things that we would not want to convert into moral claims on their part. Ancient and early modern philosophers were well aware of the need to distinguish between what is natural to men and what is naturally *justificatory*: the difference between describing the way men are and how they should be. But what is the basis of *that*? Just what, exactly, are the grounds on which we can base claims about the objective structure of ethics found in "nature", including human nature? What are our reasons for the visions and prescriptions of a social and political order based on natural rights? Moreover, exactly which rights do we have on these grounds and how do we know we have them? What is truly natural and what is customary? We are inevitably thrown back on to moral arguments and thus moral and political disagreement.

Aristotle (*Politics* 1254b26–32, 1255b3) spoke of nature in two ways: how a thing is born (*natura*) and how a thing grows (*phusis*). Human beings are by nature political animals (*Nicomachean Ethics* 1097b12; *Politics* 1253a2, 1243a7–8), which means that nature provides a standard (a *telos*) towards which human beings are ultimately oriented, and yet our nature is also partly *constituted* by politics. What nature "wants" it may fail to achieve, and here the work of politics matters.[2] This is an important and interesting distinction. Even in the sixteenth and seventeenth centuries, different readings of Aristotle could produce different accounts of the relation between rights and politics (see Brett 2002). Aristotle makes clear, especially in his *Nicomachean Ethics* (esp. ch. V), that the object of justice involves action towards or with regard to another, determined by the objective demands of equality as applied to the particular human relations at issue. Thomas Aquinas, adapting this idea in his synthesis of Christianity and Aristotelianism, defined right (*ius*) objectively as *the right thing* in a given situation. For Aquinas, men are naturally inclined to preserve themselves, as well as being naturally social and political animals (and religious). Thus, natural law was "the participation in the Eternal Law by rational creatures" (*Summa Theologica*, 1a IIae.91.2), something seemingly written into our cognitive software at birth. Through reason, men are able to participate in this "eternal law" and initiate action towards his natural good (*ibid.*: 1a IIae.90–97). But this freedom of action (*dominium*) is the capacity to understand and obey law, to realize the natural good to which he was naturally oriented. Here the good and the right are almost identical. Each individual does best by doing right, and that entails realizing the common good.

Now there are complicated historical issues about when this objective sense of right is superseded by more subjective ones, in which right is tied much more closely to the will and liberty of individuals (see esp. Tuck 1981; Brett 1997; Tierney 1997). Once natural rights are linked more closely to the wills of individuals, they become associated with voluntarist and ultimately contractu-alist forms of ethics and politics. This begins to happen with the great Protestant natural law theorists in the mid- to late-seventeenth century But even within the language of subjective rights, there is a distinction between those theorists who think it refers to some-thing like a property in or control over a thing, grounded in lib-erty, and those who think of right as a power of action under *law*, hence grounded in obligation and necessity (Brett 1997: 124). The argument between moral realists and voluntarists about rights goes back a long way.

If we conceive of the normativity of nature as existing over and above any man-made civil laws, then individuals are bound not only by these laws wherever they are, but can also appeal to them *against* the laws of their city or state. Natural law then consists of a substantive set of moral rules that ought to structure politics, and that no magistrate or king has the authority to violate. All individu-als thus have certain natural rights (*ius naturae*) in virtue of the applicability of natural law. It is this idea of natural law, along with a new emphasis on the accompanying natural rights, that informed the great sixteenth-century scholastic theories of natural law that played such a crucial role in the development of modern theories of rights.[3] The crucial innovation was the grafting of the idea of a right as a capacity for creative action onto the Thomist understanding of man as oriented by the good. Man had a right to self-preservation and self-defence, and yet also realizes his moral life in a political community (see Brett 2003: 102).

One extraordinary example of how this idea played out was the debate over the legitimacy of the Spanish conquest of the Americas after 1492. Spanish theologians, and especially the Thomist "School of Salamanca", took up this question in the language of natural law and natural rights (for background see Skinner 1978b: ch. V; Pagden 1982, 1995; Brett 1997). Francisco de Vitoria (*c.*1485–1546), one of the most influential Thomist theorists of this era, argued in his "On the American Indians" (1537/9) that the indigenous peoples of the Americas, given the existence of their civil societies and evidence of their common humanity, possessed natural rights that entailed that Spanish domination over them was unjust (Pagden & Lawrence 1991: 250). Since they are human they have *domin-ium*, and therefore their jurisdiction and properties are legitimate (*ibid*.: 247–51). Colonists and others had argued that the Indians' "ungodliness" and inhumane social practices justified their submission to colonial rule and the expropriation of their lands. Vitoria rejected both claims; if the latter was true, he argued, the King of France has a perfect right to invade Italy (*ibid*.: 225). So on what basis could the Spanish legitimately settle in their lands? Once again he turned to his Aristotelian training and appealed to the natural sociability of men, a universal claim, which entailed that all men have the right to "commerce" – to communicate with and move among their fellow men for peaceful means (*ius communicandi*). In fact, to reject such communication and fellowship is to violate natural law and potentially create the conditions for a just war, an argument that would be exploited by later theorists for justifying imperial expansion (*ibid*.: 274–86).[4] Here is an excellent example of the fundamental ambiguity of the language of natural rights during this period; in closing the door to one form of imperialism, Vitoria (perhaps unwittingly) opened the door to another.

Another important way that political philosophers conceived of nature, however, involved breaking with this Aristotelian framework and seeing it as marking the *absence* of politics. In other words, politics must somehow accommodate nature and work to either contain the damage it can do, or at least harness it towards civil ends. One crucial issue driving the break between nature and the city was the relation between religion and the politics. Catholic and Protestant resistance theories appealed increasingly to the right of an individual or group to practice their religion as one held against the *civitas*, at least when there was a conflict between the two.[5] The religiously fuelled civil wars in France, the Netherlands and England demonstrated just how devastating such conflict could become. This led to new ways of thinking about the relation between nature and politics, and new ways of thinking about the nature of rights. Thus, a political community is conceived not so much as an association created for the sake of perfecting man, but rather as an artificial device created for the sake of mutual advantage between "free" agents. Thomas Hobbes (1588–1679) and John Locke (1632–1704) famously argued that the state of nature was that condition in which men existed *before* civil society was established. Unlike Aristotle and his followers, the human sociability that led to the formation of the *polis* was not prior to the individual and independent of his will, but rather the creation of it (Pagden 2003: 180–81; Tuck 1981). Human beings had a basic degree of natural sociability to be sure, but not to the same extent that Aristotle suggested when he described man as by nature a *zoon politikon*. There was no necessary line of development between man's innate capacities and reason and the fulfilment of his true nature in the city. For Hobbes, the state of nature was a state of war. This meant we needed a powerful sovereign capable of holding individuals to their shaky grasp of the laws of nature (as "precepts of reason") through fear of the consequences of civil war. For Locke, the state of nature was a more peaceable condition, albeit "inconvenient", which entailed a very different conception of the state. In both cases, however, nature was something to be overcome, not realized.

Scepticism, contingency and the city

Natural law theory was one of the dominant European understandings of morality in the fifteenth and sixteenth centuries. It has Catholic and Protestant variants, although there are continuities between them. We shall be concentrating on Protestant natural law theory, for the most part. Natural law was taught in the major universities and often provided the basic moral framework within which major political questions of the day were framed and debated. Of course, one thing that haunts any account of natural law is *scepticism*: the thought that there really is no objective, binding moral law built into the structure of the world – or our minds – that we can intuit or discover through reflection. It is one thing to think that it is just plain hard to ascertain moral knowledge of this kind, or that we need the help of divine revelation, but it is another to doubt that such knowledge is even possible. Sceptics press hard on the latter worry. Indeed, any sensible person looking around Europe in the sixteenth and seventeenth centuries would have good reason to be worried. The consequences of deep religious and cultural disagreements were plain to see: ethnic cleansing, civil and international conflict and imperialism were rampant. Moreover, there were major changes occuring within philosophy and the natural sciences to do with how best to understand nature and the universe in general.

So one problem the natural lawyers faced was the sheer improbability that there were universal laws governing our moral conduct that we could discover through our reason. And this made for fertile ground for scepticism about the kind of answer Aristotle and his followers gave to the question of how one should live. Philosophical scepticism has deep roots in ancient thought (on ancient scepticism see Burnyeat 1984; see also Popkin 1979), but its most important modern restatement was in the widely read *Essays* of Michel de Montaigne (1533–92). The kind of scepticism he discusses, however, is not quite scepticism about knowledge *per se*, but rather how one can *live* without having access to secure knowledge of the highest good or natural law. In his essay "Apology for Raymond Sebond", Montaigne takes direct aim at natural law. There are no doctrines about right or wrong or about how to live that are universally accepted: "Let them show me just one law of that sort – I'd like to see it" (Montaigne 1965: 437). What are we to make of the radical difference in customs that we find around the world? Are many of our beliefs about morality not the product of circumstance and context as much as anything else? Does that not explain the variation in practices and beliefs as much as anything else, and does that not fundamentally undermine the claim of the natural lawyers to have discovered the true foundation of morality? Montaigne, in fact, is a fideist: the weakness of human reason only serves to exalt God and divine grace (see Schneewind 1998: 46). We cannot have natural knowledge of natural law, and thus most of what passes for morality is a human creation. We have to ask about how best to live without hope of supernatural aid, or even of the "many and the wise", as Aristotle recommended. Although there are some universal bads – torture and the burning of witches, among other things – there is no universal common good. We can only ask for ourselves, and try to discover our own pattern of life.

Another response, less to do with scepticism, but equally corrosive of key aspects of the classical worldview, was that of Niccolò Machiavelli (1469–1527). He is notorious for attacking the standard humanist account of a just city in *The Prince* (*c.*1513). A prince must possess *virtu* to maintain his state, but this has very little to do with the standard humanist or Christian story. For the classical humanist, the key princely virtues included possessing wisdom, justice, temperance, courage and especially honesty: the virtue of keeping faith with others (*fides*). According to the standard humanist line, the most effective way for a prince to secure his city was to act virtuously, defined in these ways. The good city was one in which the common good was placed above the calculation of self-interest, knowledge of which we gain either through our reason, or via a wise ruler who uses his wisdom and rhetorical skills to shape us accordingly. The city is a genuine *unity* only when it is character-ized by justice and concord.[6]

Machiavelli inverts this standard picture most dramatically in *The Prince*. For him, the *virtuoso* prince must be prepared to act cruelly in order to snuff out potential threats to his rule; he should prefer to be feared than to be loved; and, above all, be prepared to act unjustly, at least as defined by the classical and Christian accounts, when circumstances dictate – namely, whenever his city is under threat. Christianity sent all the wrong signals: too much emphasis on the afterlife instead of this one; too much meekness and passivity in the face of threats from enemies. Religion was important to the success of a city, but it had to be of the right kind: one that promoted the right kind of active virtues and attitudes. As Machiavelli puts it in Chapter 18 of *The Prince*, there are two ways of fighting – as a lion and as a fox – and the virtuous prince is skilled at both: "since a ruler … must know how to act like a beast, he should imitate both the fox and the lion, for the lion is liable to be trapped whereas the fox cannot ward off wolves" (Machiavelli 1988: 61). Cruel deeds, well committed, may indeed sometimes be expedient. That does not mean that anything goes. You do not want to end up like Agathocles: murdered in his bed as a result of his wanton cruelty. He was after *imperio*, not true *gloria* (*ibid*.: 33). The successful prince can achieve true glory, but only if he is will-ing to act decisively and free of conventional moral constraints, as circumstances require.

In Machiavelli's *Discourses* (*c*.1518/19) the emphasis is different. Here he is concerned above all with how *republics* achieve great-ness, as opposed to principalities, and Rome is his main exemplar. The greatest cities, by which he means the richest and most exten-sive, are those "at liberty": "we see by experience that city states have never been successful, either in expanding their territory or in accumulating wealth, except when they have been free (Machiavelli, *Discourses*, II.2). By "free" Machiavelli means (mainly) free from external domination and thus self-governing, which in turn requires having the right institutions (*ordini*) to help secure self-government

(*Discourses*, I.18). Once again he thinks that this means sometimes that extra-moral acts will be required to secure the republic, since sometimes they will be faced with extraordinary threats or circumstances, and *virtu* will have to be mixed with prudence. And here Machiavelli means that *the people* will have to possess *virtu*, not just their rulers.

But the people, taken as a whole and individually, are not inherently good. They are not moved naturally by love of the good, or by reason. In fact, most people are selfish and narrow-minded. But if the laws are properly constructed they can channel most people's interest in being left alone to pursue their own projects into supporting the public interest, and they can constrain the most ambitious from doing too much harm. The law can help balance the various interests at play in a republic by ensuring that each has some capacity to participate in the ruling of the city. A well-governed city is one in which the people are free and willing to act to preserve their freedom. Unlike in the classical ideal, however, the aim is not concord or harmony, but rather proper management of the inherent "tumults" of a city, allowing for robust contestation of the laws and policies (*disputendo*), but not to descend into actual fighting and civil war (*combattendo*) (for more discussion see Ivison 1997: ch. 3). Properly structured, a popular government can be more stable, prudent and capable of handling the unforseen events (*accidenti*) thrown up by fortune than a princely one (Machiavelli, *Discourses*, I.58). A well-ordered city is still one in which each part of the city has its proper place, just as in the classical ideal, but for very different reasons. It will also be expansive, since that is the best way of preventing domination from the outside, as well as offering opportunities for its citizens to achieve honour and glory. But expansion also increases the risks of defeat and of corruption (see Hornqvist 2001). Still, there is no other option. Fortune catches up on those who try to hide from it. We have only those institutions we construct ourselves, along with the leaders we choose to put up with, to rely on in facing "the times". There is no appeal to divine guidance, or to natural law.

The unsettling arguments of Montaigne and Machiavelli provide two sources of disquiet for the early modern civil philosopher faced with the social and political upheavals of his day. Philosophical scepticism threatened to undermine confidence in the moral structure of human society, and suggested there might not be a common good to which human beings naturally aspire. Machiavelli's rejection of Christian morality, along with his frank advice of the necessity of acting immorally in some circumstances, radically undermined the grounds of civil society. But these are not problems only for early modern philosophers. We still worry about scepticism and the special demands of the political placed on our leaders (and ourselves). Machiavelli seems to describe a world, and a form of politics, in which the moral considerations that underlie rights are set aside, or at least are likely to be frequently suspended. The desire to anchor rights, especially human rights, in the deep structure of either human nature or reason continues to motivate much moral and political argument. And the demands of politics – the permanence of disagreement and conflict and yet the need for the exercise of power nonetheless – continues to complicate our judgements as to which rights matter most and in what circumstances.

The Grotian problematic

One way to put the differences at issue here is like this: either natural rights are derivative of natural law, or natural law is derivative of natural rights. In other words, we can understand rights as providing a foundation for moral and political order, or as derived from a prior objective moral framework. The former might seem to entail moral subjectivism, the latter that rights are not foundational, but ultimately derivative of an objective moral theory in which duties are primary as opposed to rights. In fact, many historians of early modern political thought have recently challenged the view that the dominant natural law theories of rights in the seventeenth and eighteenth centuries are fundamentally individualist and subjectivist; some are, but they are the exception to the rule. As we shall see, this means that rights are conceived often in relation to a power or a liberty of an individual to act, but act in *a certain way*, in relation to a particular conception of moral and political order.

Two big issues emerge at this point. First, as we saw earlier, if rights are derivative of an objective account of natural law, and God is the source of natural law, then how do we know what these laws are? Revelation was a notoriously opaque source, as well as radically underdetermined; how could we really know what God's intentions were in relation to how we should act in all manner of different situations? Secondly, the world itself seemed to provide examples of a great diversity of moral practices and standards. How were these to be understood and judged? If reason was to play a greater role as the seat of natural law, then the danger was that God could be displaced from the story: the alternatives included positivism, or the appeal to some set of actually existing cross-cultural moral universals. These challenges were also connected to a deep debate about the basic metaphysical status of morality. On one side were those who saw morality as inherent in the structure of the world and accessible to human reason; on the other were those who saw morality as "superadded" to the world through acts of will, whether divine or human. This represents one important difference between Protestant and Catholic natural law theory. Scholastic natural law theory seemed to presuppose that we could know things about God's intentions for us and about the world he designed around us: that there was some moral continuity between ourselves and God. For many Protestant thinkers, this was impossible. There was a radical discontinuity between man and God, such that it was impossible to give a rational account of morality with reference to God. Only faith could bridge that gap. As scholars have pointed out, this led many Protestant thinkers to either end up relying on faith alone as a foundation for morality, or pushed them more and more – somewhat paradoxically – towards explicitly human and temporal foundations for not only morality but politics.

One of the leading figures in the history of the emergence of modern rights discourse is the Dutch philosopher Hugo Grotius (1583–1645). Grotius was deeply engaged in some of the leading political debates of his day in the Dutch Republic, and this shaped his most important work on rights. There are three contexts worth mentioning here. First was the problem of religious toleration: how could Catholics, Protestants, Jews and others live together peacefully? The second was colonialism: on what grounds could the Dutch, English, Spanish and Portuguese claim property or jurisdiction over the peoples they were encountering in the "new world"? And the third was philosophical: how could the challenge of scepticism be addressed? Recall that Grotius was writing in the midst of the ferocious wars and conflicts of the seventeenth century. He wanted to find a way of grounding natural law such that it holds *between* different states as much as *within* them. He accepted that there are customary laws that have emerged between nations over time through their interactions, derived from the will of particular peoples, which he calls the "laws of nations" (*ius gentium*). But these laws should be distinguished from natural law. He will argue that there is a form of justice applicable in peace and in war, as well as across boundaries, that is not merely customary. Nor does he think such a law is grounded merely on prudential reason – that it is in our interest to avoid conflict (although clearly it is) – but also on the basis of justice.

In 1604, Grotius began work on an essay intended to justify armed incursions into the East Indies, including attacks on Portuguese shipping. The Dutch had been fighting for their independence from Spanish domination since the late-sixteenth century, and a truce was in the process of being negotiated (for detail and background see Tuck 1993; Grotius 2004: xi–xxiv). Among the issues to be decided was Dutch access to the lucrative silk, spice and porcelain markets (among other things) of the East Indies, where, along with the Dutch, the Spanish, English and Portuguese were also keen to secure trade. Access to trade was seen to be crucial for Dutch security and prosperity. One of the questions Grotius was concerned with was whether force could be used against those who sought to restrict free commercial competition (i.e. the Portuguese). One part of this essay, published in 1609, became *The Free Sea*, which attacked Portuguese claims to exclusive rights of possession, control of navigation and trade. But it is the broader framework of his argument that is of interest here, and it is laid out in much greater detail in the longer essay from which it is taken, *De Jure Praedae*, or *Commentary on the Law of Prizes and Booty* (Grotius 1950), which was not actually published until the nineteenth century. Here Grotius defends the Dutch actions in the East Indies according to natural law.

For Grotius, natural laws were derived originally from divine will, but for the content of the laws we need to turn not to scripture but to the design of nature. God created man "free and under his *sui iuris* so that the actions of each individual and the use of his possessions were made subject not to another's will but to his own" (*De Jure Praedae*, I:18). The two primary laws of nature are self-defence and self-preservation, where self-preservation entails being able to acquire and retain things useful for life, the means of which God has provided to all through his creation (*ibid.*, II:10–11). This provides a distinctive account of property. The world is common, argues Grotius, in the sense that each of us has the right to use those things we need for our self-preservation, but not to continue to exclude others from the enjoyment of an object they need for theirs. Things we need for immediate consumption have to be private, and then by extension come to include other objects, both moveable and immoveable (e.g. fields but, crucially, not oceans – see below). Thus the primary motivation of human action is essentially the pursuit of one's own advantage, albeit rightfully understood. So God is the source of natural law, along with utility: the will of God juridicalizes the pursuit of utility (from Brett 2002: 39). Still, these first two laws are essentially permissive in form, and by the time we get to his great work *De Jure Belli ac Pacis*, or *On the Rights of War and Peace* (1625), they have been redescribed as *rights*: the right of "recurring to Force, in defence of one's own Life" (*De Jure Belli*, I.ii.3), and the right of "innocent Profit" (*ibid.*, II.ii.11).

These natural rights are in turn limited by two natural laws: "Let no one inflict injury upon his fellows" (the law of inoffensiveness), and "Let no one seize possession of that which has been taken into the possession of another" (the law of abstinence) (*De Jure Praedae*, I:21). (See the summary in Grotius 2005: "Preliminary Discourse", VIII.) The question of in what circumstances rights of nature take precedence of these laws of nature became deeply contested (see discussion in Tuck 1993: ch. 5; 2005: xxi–xxii; cf. Haakonssen 2002).

Note how this argument served Grotius's immediate political ambitions. First, freedom of navigation and trade could be construed as exemplary instances of the basic laws of nature (e.g. using common things without harming others) (Grotius 2004: 6). But also, it followed from his emphasis on the right to self-preservation that men had a right to property as well. Men were entitled to use whatever they required to preserve themselves. But it did not follow from this that they could continually exclude others from things they could not justifiably use, since the world was "common" in the sense that each could use what they needed in order to survive. Nor, obviously, could they take from others what they needed to preserve themselves, which would be a case of wanton injury and cause for justifiable war. This delivered two happy results, as far as the Dutch were concerned. First, the Portuguese could not claim to own the sea and therefore exclude the Dutch, since it was clearly not something that could be appropriated from nature and used in the way that land could be, subject to the limitations sketched above. The sea is too fluid and its products too abundant to be possessed and used in the requisite manner to qualify as property. Secondly, the Portuguese could claim no right of possession in virtue of first discovery – of having discovered the East Indies as unoccupied land and available for appropriation – since it was in the possession of the native inhabitants. Drawing on the arguments of Vitoria, whom we discussed earlier, Grotius argued that even if the natives were radically different from Europeans, whether culturally or politically, this provided no grounds for dispossession. The only possible claim for that was a right of conquest, but Grotius denied that the natives had provided any reason for thinking a war was justified in this case (*ibid.*: 15).

But it is the moral analysis of right that is also important for us here. Grotius explains the laws of nature in terms of rights. Everyone has the right to self-preservation, and we must understand our relations to others – for we are also sociable creatures – in terms of respecting each other's rights. But how are we to understand the nature of these rights? First of all, rights must be understood in relation to justice. In the "care of maintaining society", Grotius writes, "in a Manner conformable to the Light of human Understanding is the Fountain of Right properly so called" (2005: "Preliminary Discourse", VIII). He offers two further senses of the word "right", arising from this initial designation. The first, "which relates directly to the Person: In which sense right is a moral quality annexed to the Person, enabling him to have to or do something justly" (*De Jure Belli*, I.i.iv). The second is that it "signifies the same thing as law, when taken in its largest extent, as being a rule of moral actions, obliging us to that which is good and commendable". He goes on to summarize his view:

> Natural right is the rule and dictate of right reason, showing the moral deformity or moral necessity there is in any act, according to its suitableness or unsuitableness to a reasonable

nature, and consequently that such an act is either forbid or commanded by God, the author of nature. The actions upon which such a dictate is given, are in themselves either obligatory or unlawful, and must, consequently, be understood to be either commanded or forbid by God himself; and this makes the law of nature differ not only from Human Right but from a voluntary divine right; for that does not command or forbid such things as are in themselves, or by their own nature, obligatory and unlawful; but, by forbidding, it renders the one unlawful, and by commanding, the other obligatory.   (*Ibid.*, I.i.x)

Having defined natural right in this way (note in the passage above that he suggests we are obliged by what is good according to our moral judgement, as opposed to the fact that God commanded it), Grotius turns to the foundation of civil right. Consent is the origin of civil right, and thus the origin of civil society lies in "pacts" or agreements since, for Grotius, God created man "free and *sui iuris*". Why do we enter into civil society in the first place? We do so for the sake of utility and to protect ourselves. This means that *in extremis*, at least, these rights hold even after we have entered civil society, and we have accepted the demands of the public good. However, in just about every other respect Grotius argues that one can be legitimately subject to the demands of civil society: to the demands of general utility, as it were, as against private utility. The freedom to exercise one's right includes the freedom to alienate it:

It is lawful for any man to engage himself as a Slave to whom he pleases; as appears both by the Hebrew and Roman Laws. Why should it not therefore be as lawful for a people that are at their own Disposal, to deliver up themselves to any one or more Persons, and transfer the Right of governing them upon him or them, without reserving any Share of that Right to themselves? ... In vain do some alledge the Inconveniences which arise from hence, or may arise; for you can frame no Form of Government in your Mind, which will be without Inconveniences and Dangers ... But as there are several Ways of Living, some better than others, and every one may chuse what he pleases of all those Sorts; so a People may chuse what Form of Government they please ...   (*De Jure Belli*, I.iii.viii)

It might be surprising to discover that an argument justifying the existence of natural rights also ends up justifying political absolutism.[7]

Note two things here. As I argued in the Introduction, although rights are clearly linked to theories about *limiting* the power of the state, there is nothing inherently limiting about the concept of rights themselves, even subjective rights. Sometimes they were used to limit rulers' power, in other cases not. If rights form part of the complex of concepts central to liberalism, as they clearly do, we must not forget that liberalism is concerned not only with *limiting* state power but also *justifying* it. Liberalism is as much a *form* of government as it is critique of it. Secondly, the link between subjection to slavery and subjection to government is one that Hobbes, as well as critics of both Grotius and Hobbes (e.g. Jean-Jacques Rousseau), will exploit, as we shall see. It is connected to a general concern about what we might call rights fundamentalism. If individual rights constitute all there is to morality, or at least its most important aspects, then men and women not only have the "right to do wrong" (i.e. where wrong is defined in any way over and above the violation of the rights of others), they are free to alienate the very freedom and agency to which the concept of right refers. If I am the judge of what is in my interest or utility, then subjection might follow if I think it the best way to realize or promote it. Freedom appears limitless, and yet for the sake of our own freedom – *properly understood* – we should renounce it. More disturbingly, and this is a conclusion only Hobbes, typically, is ready to contemplate, if rights really are radically subjective, they risk being divorced from the direction of an objective law of nature. If that is true, then we are left with potentially irresolvable conflicts of rights, not merely due to human weakness but to the fact that our moral world is not, in fact, ultimately harmonious.

Right and justice

It is time to draw together some of the consequences of Grotius's argument. First, Grotius clearly connects rights *both* to the "moral quality of a person" and his subjective freedom, and to objective relations of justice stated by the law of nature. Part of what it means to be a moral agent is to have rights in one's person and to claims on the world. And just because we have individual rights we can alienate them, or retain them. But a right is also something that enables us to exercise our freedom *justly* or *lawfully*. And so Grotius also, importantly, links the proper exercise of and respect for individual rights to relations of justice. These rights do not exhaust morality. We have to recognize the rights of others that do not infringe our rights, but we are also capable of recognizing rights that might, strictly speaking, do so. These are what Grotius calls "imperfect rights". They are important, but not absolutely essential to social life and therefore less universal and less strictly enforceable. A perfect right, on the other hand, is perfectly enforceable. A rich man ought to give alms to a beggar, but he cannot be compelled to do so. The beggar has a right to receive charity, but it generates a duty that cannot be compelled in the same way as when someone is claiming their (justifiable) right to property. (However, the poor *do* have a "perfect" right to the property of the rich *in extremis*, for example during a famine. In these circumstances, something like a "community of goods" is reasserted: the idea that the world is held in common by all human beings in the negative sense that no one can exclude anyone from the basic means required for self-preservation.) The distinction between perfect and imperfect rights is an important one, and we shall return to it in our discussion of Kant in Chapter 4 and of human rights in Chapter 8.

Historians of political thought disagree about the ultimate relation between rights and political justice in Grotius. On the one hand, the emphasis on the subjective nature of rights and self-preservation has led Richard Tuck to argue that Grotius is offering a radically un-Aristotelian, "minimalist" conception of natural law. This argument is geared especially, argues Tuck, to addressing the philosophical problem of scepticism and the political challenge of finding peace in the midst of violent religious and ethnic conflict (Tuck 1987; 1999). On the other hand, some scholars have insisted that there is some continuity with various Aristotelian themes in Grotius's emphasis on the conformity of *ius* with right reason (see Brett 2002; Haakonssen 2002). Justice, in the strict sense, means abstaining from harming the rights of others. But what are these rights? They are what our right reason or capacity for moral judgement tell us they are: claims having to do with liberty, property and contract. But on this reading, subjective rights are not prior to and therefore constitutive of justice, but are derivative of a substantive claim about human nature. The contrast between these interpretations is thus between thinking that subjective rights are foundational for political morality, or thinking they are derivative from a more substantive conception of moral judgement ("right reason").

Grotius also ties the language of rights to a kind of pluralism, although we should be careful not to confuse it with modern value pluralism. First, in his earlier work and in the *Rights of War and Peace*, Grotius makes it clear that the religious principles to which all men are under a moral obligation to submit are fairly basic: that there is a God and that he has "care of human affairs". The moral point of religion, for Grotius, is to help elicit the right kind of conduct to enable men to live together in society. All other religious beliefs, especially to do with various specific doctrinal issues not essential to the functioning of moral and social life, ought not to be punished or enforced by the state (*De Jure Belli*, II.xx.47). Although he clearly thought Christianity was superior for promoting the right kind of moral conduct, at least as compared with Islam and Judaism, Grotius sought the broadest interpretation of its basic tenets compatible with promoting civic peace among deep disagreements over religion (for detailed discussion see Tuck 1993: 179–90). In the process he was also, of course, limiting the extent to which religion could be used as an extra-civic standard to which individuals could appeal against the state. Remember too that, although Grotius accepts the role of right reason inherent in our human nature, we are also born needy and seek utility, both of which give rise to civil right and civil society. This means that our motivation for obeying the laws of nature rests as much on utility or self-interest as it does on God. In a notorious passage from *The Rights of War and Peace*, he declared: "All we have now said would take place, though we should even grant, what with the greatest Wickedness cannot be granted, that there is no God, or that he takes no Care of human affairs" (2005: "Preliminary Discourse", XI). Thus, even a city founded on consent can be a proper "unity", as the classical theorists might put it, albeit for Grotius on the basis of very different reasons (*ibid.*, II.ix.III).

Finally, note the last sentence in the long passage cited above from *The Rights of War and Peace*: "there are several Ways of Living, some better than others, and every one may chuse what he pleases of all those Sorts; so a People may chuse what Form of Government they please". In the next sentence he goes on: "Neither is the Right, which the Sovereign has over his Subjects to be measured by this or that Form, of which divers Men have divers Opinions, but by the Extent of the Will of those who conferred it upon him" (*De Jure Belli*, I.iii.8). The immediate context of this passage is to explain why a people might, in fact, "deliver themselves up" into slavery. However, it has wider implications too. People can live good lives in different kinds of states, although their rights are best protected and realized in those where the frame of government rests on their utility and consent. So constituted, and dramatically reconfiguring the classical language with which we began this chapter, Grotius calls such a city a proper "unity" or body (*ibid.*, II.ix.III).[8]

Thomas Hobbes: politics against nature

The philosopher who was most prepared to state unambiguously that laws of nature were reducible to a set of precepts tied to our reason and a proper consideration of our self-interests was, of course, Hobbes. And it is really only Hobbes who accepts the fundamentally subjectivist and relativist conclusions that are often attributed to fundamentalism about individual rights. Like Grotius, Hobbes had a humanist background that shaped his subsequent political theory in its attempt to reconfigure the classical categories of citizenship, virtue and the city. And like Grotius he was concerned with the challenge presented by scepticism, both epistemological and psychological.[9] But unlike Grotius, there is no doubting his repudiation of much of the *content* of classical humanist political theory, if not its methods.[10] Against the Aristotelian view that right reason was written into human nature, Hobbes scoffed that those "commonly ... that call for right reason to decide any controversy, do mean their own" (Hobbes 1969a: 188–9). Against the Aristotelian view that our perception gives us access to the real properties of objects, or that colour, for example, inheres in the object perceived, Hobbes argued that they were attributed to them on the basis of the observer's perceptions. And he extended this claim to moral properties: "Whatsoever is the object of any mans Appetite or Desire; that is, which he for his part calleth Good; And the object of his Hate and Aversion, Evill; And of his Contempt,

Vile and Inconsiderable" (*Leviathan*, vi.7; see also Hobbes 1969a: 29).

What is the solution? Hobbes suggests that if there is any kind of "right reason" shared by all human beings it is the desire to avoid death: "It is therefore not absurd, nor reprehensible, nor counter to right reason, if one makes every effort to defend his body and limbs from death and to preserve them. And what is not contrary to right reason, all agree is done justly and of Right" (1998: 27). Men have no direct knowledge of the external world, or indeed other minds. Nor do they have access to the divine mind by way of reason, but only through experience. And yet the attempt to use the empirical facts of human nature or history to intuit or make sense of God's will has, Hobbes thinks, been one of the main sources of the kind of disagreement and disorder that has led to so much war and bloodshed. So we need to try to understand what kind of moral order we can have relying on the most minimal and least deniable claims possible. All of us should want to avoid death, and all of us should acknowledge that each of us possesses a right to defend themselves from wanton attack. But even here Hobbes felt the force of the sceptical challenge. In the state of nature, that is, in a condition without government, although everyone has a right of nature ("the liberty each hath, to use his own power, as he will himselfe, for the preservation of his own nature"), the result is chaos: a state of war (*Leviathan*, xiii.9). Just because each of us is judge of what is in our own best interest in terms of self-preservation, if we both desire some object which cannot be shared, or we judge each other to be a threat to our security, we come into conflict. There is no easily accessible "natural" or even inter-subjective agreement of what really threatens my security.

So disagreement and conflict attend the exercise of even the basic right to self-preservation. And this made Hobbes's reconfiguration of natural law theory so unacceptable to many of his contemporaries, stripped as it seemed to be of any real meaning, and bereft of an appeal to the ultimate moral orderliness of the world. For Hobbes, the only solution to moral confusion is political: we must construct an artificial person, through human agreement, that can fix and regulate those moral terms and conditions required for us to live in peace. Individuals have to be brought to see that it is in their longer-term interest to agree to bind themselves so that this can occur. Like

Grotius, Hobbes takes advantage of the idea that just in so far as agents have rights, they are free to relinquish them. But he goes one step further by suggesting that people *must* relinquish them (and in the right way), if they are to escape from the state of nature. Thus natural law is ultimately reducible to a basic precept of reason: *seek peace* (*Leviathan*, xiv.3–4).[11] And the only way to ensure that one can live peacefully is to relinquish your natural right to the sovereign in such a way that he is (they are) effectively empowered to make all judgements, and take all necessary actions, about what is most conducive to the preservation of civic peace (including to do with almost all religious matters). Our natural motives to preserve ourselves have to be transformed into a commitment to observe allegiance to the Leviathan. This occurs only if the promise of allegiance is mutual – if there is a coincidence of judgement (or what Hobbes called a "concourse of wills" [1969a: §12.7]) about what is needed to get out of the state of war.[12] To preserve the freedom that you should really care about entails giving up right, understood strictly as the liberty and power we have to preserve ourselves. The only right you retain is the natural right not to be killed, or at least to defend yourself against getting killed, since that is the primary reason for agreeing to establish a commonwealth in the first place.[13] But this falls far short of any generalized right to resistance: citizens can never be said to retain the right to exercise private judgement about when the security of the commonwealth is in jeopardy. Nor can they appeal outside the political morality constituted by the establishment of the commonwealth, including to religious authorities or scripture, to question its veracity.[14]

Samuel Pufendorf (1632–94) would try to combine the central insights of Grotius and Hobbes in his enormously influential *On the Law of Nature and Nations* (1672) and *On the Duty of Man and Citizen According to Natural Law* (1673), through his account of the "unsocial sociability" of man. Man is both naturally sociable and self-interested. But he can only realize his most important interests within a legal and civil structure that constrains everyone equally. Both civil society and property thus arose through "compact", whereby the individual agrees to surrender his rights to society in order to further his self-interest.[15] In what sense are you obliged by such a surrender of your rights? "An obligation is properly laid on the mind of a man by a superior", argues Pufendorf, "by one who has the strength to threaten some evil against those who resist him, and just reasons why he can demand that the liberty of our will be limited at his pleasure" (*On the Law of Nature and Nations*, I.vi.9). What are these just reasons? Some interpret them along neo-Aristotelian lines, others along lines that anticipate Kant's conception of self-legitimizing reason and the higher rational part of our nature from which it comes (see esp. Schneewind 1998: 125). Ian Hunter, on the other hand, claims that Pufendorf grounds obligation in the good of political security, not moral perfection or our higher rational nature: that is, "in the relations of dependency and protection linking a being in need of security to one who is in a position to provide it" (2001: 135–63, esp. 156; cf. Tully 1991: xxxii–iv; 2003: 493–5). He does this, Hunter claims, because it provides a way of grounding civil government (in security alone) that is as independent as possible from controversial moral-theological positions that were the source of the murderous political conflict that so engulfed early modern Europe during this time. But this was not the only way of making sense of the idea of civil society and the state as the product of human will. As we shall see in Chapter 3, an alternative approach is to argue that mutual subjection does not entail the alienation of our powers and rights to a sovereign, but rather only their *delegation* on condition that the sovereign acts for the public good.

Conclusion

The period 1500–1700 was one in which a vision of ancient citizenship was both revived in Renaissance humanism and attacked. It was a time when the language of virtue and civic perfectibility was revived, but also opposed by one that emphasized rights against the city and the preservation of property. For Aristotle and his followers, human sociability and the capacity for citizenship was in some sense independent of human will; it was part of our nature and *telos* as political animals. But for Grotius, Hobbes and Pufendorf, civil society was the creation of an act of *will*; the desire for preservation, mixed with varying degrees of sociability, led to the creation of society. Given different circumstances, it might not. This is one very important consequence of seventeenth-century voluntarism: that although moral values might ultimately be the product of God's will, because we have no direct access to the divine mind through our reason, and attempts to discern divine providence in nature are so elusive and/or divisive, we should look to certain natural facts about human beings and construct our social theories in light of them. As Knud Haakonssen has put it, this meant that, for Protestant natural law theory, a focus on the human will became the "key explanatory factor in understanding the value schemes that make up humanity's cultural world" (2004: 96). How then to provide social explanations of the interactions of agents of will, and how to explain the ties or obligations that arise between individual wills? Through the language and practice of *contract*. God might make the laws of nature genuine laws by commanding them, but that is about it. The rest is up to us.

One of the interesting consequences of this emphasis on the will, as opposed to the notion that the mind is hardwired with a substantive conception of right reason, is that it led to a focus on how the will is shaped by factors external to the natural cognitive powers of the mind (see Haakonssen 2004). This is true even of Hobbes, something often missed by readers focused on his authoritarianism. Although fear is clearly the "passion to be reckoned upon" to "forme the wills" of subjects (*Leviathan*, xiv.31), it cannot do all the work. A state cannot always effectively deter, through fear of punishment alone, those who are determined to cause "intestine disorders" (*ibid.*, xlvii, xxx). Hence the importance of the "well-government of opinions" (especially about where sovereignty lies), in which "consisteth the well governing of mens Actions in order to their Peace and concord" (*ibid.*, xviii.9). If men are not well-governed, Hobbes argues, then they remain all too ready to take up arms on the basis of their ill-considered beliefs: they live, as it were, "in the precincts of battle continually" (*Leviathan*, xviii.9). Good government necessarily involves a degree of (re)socialization and the internationalization of virtuous behaviour, reconfigured by Hobbes as those actions conducive to peace. The "liberty of subjects" is clearly a *lawful* liberty; it would be absurd to demand liberty if we mean by that exemption from the laws, since that would be to ask for the liberty of others "to master their lives" (*ibid.*, xxi.6). Only the commonwealth can provide us with the protection we need to prevent that from happening. The danger that it will be the *state* that ends up mastering our lives without greater opportunity for the exercise of our natural (and civil) rights is, for Hobbes, far less worrying than the destructive disorder that will accompany any attempt to constrain its authority. One of Hobbes's deepest and most poignant claims is that civil society is ultimately extremely vulnerable. Unconstrained by collectively established institutions, the exercise of our natural rights, taken to their limit, entails disaster. In fact, it is not even clear that we can ever fully leave behind the destructive potential of the state of nature; the danger of slipping back into that condition in whole or in part is ever present. In a world in which genocide, ethnic conflict and transnational terrorism continue to loom large, Hobbes's arguments remain frighteningly prescient.

3 Rights as property

Rights are not fruitfully conceived as possessions. Rights are
relationships, not things; they are institutionally defined rules
specifying what people can do in relation to one another.
Rights refer to doing more than having, to social relationships
that enable or constrain action.   (Young 1990: 25)

Introduction
One familiar way of making sense of rights is to think of them
as related to control over our property and ourselves. This intuition lies behind the attractiveness of the "choice" theory of rights
that we discussed in Chapter 1. In this chapter, I want to take a
closer look at this way of understanding rights, which also has
interesting connections with the natural law tradition, which we
have been discussing in Chapter 2. Central here is the notion of
self-ownership; I "own" myself in the sense that no one else has
the right to use my body, or control my choices, unless I consent.
What is striking about this idea is how it has been central to a range
of different political ideologies and traditions. Libertarians take
it very seriously, but so too do Marxists and egalitarian liberals.
A central theme of this chapter is the way conceptions of the self
inform and shape our conceptions of rights. The normative idea
of self-ownership points to a set of ways of thinking about what is
most distinctive or significant about human beings and why they
should have rights. But I also want to examine how an emphasis on
choice and self-ownership shapes our conception of the legitimacy

of political power. An emphasis on self-ownership is strongly correlated with an emphasis on consent as the basis of political obligation and legitimacy.

I want to explore these ideas through the political philosophy of John Locke. Locke provides us with a rich philosophical approach to rights in which the ideas of *property* and *self-ownership* are central. His influence on the drafters of the American Constitution is self-evident (see White 1978; Pangle 1988; Lacey & Haakonssen 1991). Our discourse of rights, and our public culture more generally, despite all the distance between our time and his, still bears the imprint of many of his arguments.

Another thing Locke does is link the language of rights to *consent* in a particularly dramatic way, through his account of political obligation and popular sovereignty. I want to draw out two important ideas here. First of all, it has proved to be a remarkably influential conception of political power. But as I argued in Chapter 1, we should resist a too easy assumption that rights are best grasped as always fundamentally opposed to social and political power. We saw in Chapter 2 how both Grotius and Hobbes, starting from premises that granted that everyone was naturally free and possessed certain natural rights, ended up justifying absolutist government. For Locke the story will be different, but equally illuminating. Consent grounds the exercise of political power, but the very capacities and powers required for the effective exercise of rights are themselves the object of "government", understood more broadly to include not just *the* government, but other forms of social power too. So consent and the ascription of rights can explain some aspects of the exercise of power, but not all. We need to keep this broader conception of government and social power in mind if we want to grasp what rights *do*, as much as understand what they *are*.

The other important thing we shall discuss is the link between the ascription of rights and a particular conception of human agency: the rational, autonomous, contracting self. Although Locke himself does not use the language of autonomy *per se*, others have extended his argument in this direction. Certainly the conjunction of the idea of self-ownership and the idea of rights as something people possess and own lends itself to such a conception of human agency. As we shall see, this offers not only a powerful conception of what it means to be treated as a free moral agent, but also a means of denying freedom to those who lack the requisite capacities for self-ownership.

Finally, Locke was also able to link the language of rights with some of the themes of its apparent ideological competitor: republicanism. Locke is not a civic humanist or a neo-Roman, but he does offer us an interesting example of the overlap between the language of rights and virtue. Part of this is due to the overlap between the language of duty and virtue. Virtuous behaviour was a duty, and a duty to act in a certain way described virtue (Haakonssen 1991). Rights feature here, but often in a subordinate role. This makes the familiar distinction between rights-based "liberalism" and republicanism in early modern political thought (and beyond) much less obvious than often assumed.[1] And it also points to some of the challenges of conjoining the language of rights, and especially individual rights, to a theory of citizenship that is more than simply an ascription of a legal status. We still struggle with the relation between rights and a rich theory of citizenship that emphasizes our duties to others as much as the entitlements we have. The language of rights is too often understood exclusively in terms of the advantages it confers on individuals claiming them. Rights confer advantages but they also impose duties, and no system of rights is complete without an account of how and why they do so.

Rights and equality

Like Grotius, Locke thinks of men as sociable and self-interested, and that the laws of nature are valid even in the state of nature (against Hobbes). And like Grotius and Hobbes, conflict and disagreement is endemic to human interaction, in part because men are fundamentally equal. God created all of us to live in a state of "perfect freedom" and equality, "wherein all Power and Jurisdiction is reciprocal, no one having more than another" (Locke, *Two Treatises*, II.4). This does not mean that all men are, in *every respect*, equal. What I shall call *basic equality* is consistent with a range of other inequalities. As Locke makes clear, "Birth may subject some, and Alliance or Benefits others, to pay an Observance to those to whom Nature, Grattitude or other Respects may have made it due". But these differences do not impugn, Locke thinks, basic equality: "that equal Right that every man hath, in his Natural Freedom, without being subjected to the Will or Authority of any other Man" (*ibid.*, II.54).

This raises the more general problem of the relation between rights and equality. Ascribing rights to individuals is a way of expressing the sense in which we believe people are fundamentally equal. But in what sense, exactly? Rights help us translate a belief about the basic equality of individuals into concrete legal and political form. They allow us to see each other, and relate to each other, across the many obvious differences between us, whether natural, historical, cultural or conventional. The structure and content of rights is also linked to particular conceptions of the agent. Or, to put it another way, systems of rights are usually designed with a particular conception of human agency in mind. So, putting these two points together, all human beings – or all citizens (and the difference between these two reference groups is crucial, as we shall see) – are equal in the sense of being bearers of certain basic rights. Individuals are *owed* certain rights and these rights in turn refer to certain basic capacities that all human beings (or citizens) share. This sometimes sounds like an empirical or descriptive claim: that an agent has the relevant capacity/attribute *A* and therefore should be treated equally. But why should a descriptive claim have any necessary moral consequences? And what kinds of attributes or capacities matter and why? Some of us might have them to greater or lesser extents. Does that mean we do not deserve to be treated equally? One way to express this idea is to say that rights express a sense of *respect for persons*. Everyone is entitled to equal respect, and ascribing rights is a way of expressing that respect; they protect or promote capacities that we ought to respect. But *why* are people owed equal respect? And what does respect actually entail in terms of what rights people have?

For many contemporary egalitarians the claim grounding the basic equality of persons, distinct from what it might mean to actually treat them as equals, often seems like an article of faith: human beings *just are* fundamentally equal in this sense. There is no proof that can be offered to someone who disbelieves it, someone who claims, for example, that women are intrinsically inferior to men, or that whites are intrinsically superior to blacks. Others are less sanguine. Brian Barry, for example, argues that there is a complex relation between assumptions about natural equality and fundamental equality. In the United States Declaration of Independence and the French Declaration of the Rights of Man and of the Citizen, for example, both God and nature are said to endow men with the attributes and capacities in respect of which they are to be treated equally. Today, we often appeal to more secular versions of the relation between natural and fundamental equality. All human beings share certain basic capacities and needs in virtue of which they are members of the respective class of creatures deserving of equal treatment (whatever that means in practice). Among the kinds of things we appeal to here are often the capacities for forming a point of view about the world and one's place in it, for pursuing projects, for making claims: for possessing the potential for moral agency, in other words. We also tend to associate these capacities with activities connected to certain kinds of human societies – ones in which people can express themselves freely, form beliefs about religious or metaphysical views, participate in political affairs (or not), or will their property in particular ways – in other words, in ways that the United States and French declarations (among others) attempted to describe very generally. It is not just sentience as such that commands respect, or the mere capacity to have interests, but a richer sense of what it means to be human. In ascribing rights we are not only issuing a negative injunction – do not mess with these capacities! – but we are also saying that these capacities are worthy of respect, that they are good, and that they ought to be not only protected, but fostered (Taylor 1985a: 194).

But of course some of us fail to meet these thresholds: irreversible brain damage or severe mental illness, for example, might mean someone fails to display the necessary attributes. On the one hand, even though the ascription of rights requires certain preconditions, and thus the patient with irreversible brain damage, or the infant with severe physical disabilities, might be said to fall short in some way, they are still "one of us" – part of our species – and we include them within our practice of rights ascription. We often do so even while denying other non-human animals with a similar (or even higher) level of capacity the same kinds of rights.[2] This raises the spectre of speciesism, which critics argue is akin to racism or sexism. But a short response to this charge is that the analogy is false. The racist denies that certain races are owed equal political rights, among other things, because they are fundamentally of less equal worth than his racial group. But the care or preference shown for one's own species as against others is not of the same order: we do not have to believe that human beings are the most important thing in the universe to think they are more valuable to *us* (Williams 2006: 139). Almost no one thinks that all non-human animals, for example, deserve the same set of social and political rights that human beings have, not even most animal liberationists. A better analogy is with the special obligations we feel towards our children. A belief in basic equality is compatible with the thought that I am justified in caring more for my children, over and above whatever basic duties of justice I owe to others (see e.g. Haksar 1979; Barry 1992; Williams 2006). Still, hard questions remain, especially about the ultimate nature of our relation to non-human animals and our responsibilities towards them.[3] And we might well want to expand our sense of species solidarity to include animals that do seem to share certain important capacities with us, as proponents of the Great Ape Project have claimed (quite convincingly, I think) (Cavalieri & Singer 1995).

Jeremy Waldron has argued recently that it is not clear that "we – now – can shape and defend an adequate conception of basic human equality apart from some religious foundation" (2002: 13). Why not? Because, Waldron thinks, we need a much more philosophically explicit account of the sense in which human beings are fundamentally equal. We cannot just take the claim for granted. And he is not sure a mainly secular account can do the job either, especially as developed by recent work in Anglo-American political theory under the influence of Rawls (see esp. *ibid*.: 13–15, 236–43).[4] For this reason he recommends taking Locke's theological grounding of equality very seriously. Waldron's argument begs some pretty big questions: why assume that we need foundations like these, and can they really provide the grounds for equality in modern, pluralist societies like ours? But for now, let us see how Locke goes about justifying the equality that informs his account of our natural and civil rights.

In *An Essay Concerning Human Understanding* (1690), Locke is an anti-essentialist about species. Thus it seems that what counts as a "man", and what is eligible for the attribution of equality, is mainly conventional. This suggests that the boundaries of humanity could be drawn very narrowly indeed (or widely, for that matter) (*Essay*, II.6.26, IV.7.16; see also Bracken 1984: 54–6; Ayers 1991: vol. II, 65–90; Waldron 2002: 62–82). Hobbes, not surprisingly, addresses this possibility directly. For him, (natural) personhood is linked closely to speech and language; to my ability to communicate my desires and wants to others, so that others see them as mine (that I own my words and actions, so to speak).[5] Thus personhood is deeply social. Obligation, as we saw, is tied very closely to these capacities. As a result, "Children, Fooles and Madmen" are excluded from the full ascription of personhood, since they are apparently incapable of communicating with others in the right way, of taking responsibility for their actions, even those undertaken by their guardians (see Hobbes, *Leviathan*, xvi.9–10).[6] Although a good working definition of man might very well be that he is "a rational animal", for Hobbes, it is ultimately up to the *state* to decide what falls under that category, especially given the stakes attached to such descriptions and the controversies that arise in light of them.[7]

For Locke, what we need – at least for moral purposes – is the complex idea of a "corporeal rational Creature; What the real Essence or other Qualities of that Creature are in this Case, is no way considered" (*Essay*, III.11.16). Equality is associated with the real resemblance of corporeal rationality between beings. Those beings that exhibit corporeal rationality are entitled to be seen and treated as equals, which for Locke means (essentially) not being subject to the non-consensual control of others. But this raises the question we encountered above; what is the threshold for these capacities?

There are four different categories of beings that Locke thinks fall outside the law, and therefore may lack any rights and duties at all, or be entitled to only some. Lunatics and "idiots" fall beneath the line, since they lack the capacity to reason, and thus are incapable (ever?) of grasping the law of nature and thus their rights and duties (Locke, *Two Treatises*, II.57, II.60). "Terrestrial irrational creatures" – non-human animals – have been given to man by God for their use, and lack the capacity for reason entirely and thus have no rights or duties. Lawful slaves, that is, individuals who have entered into a state of war and been captured, have quit the law of nature and thus forfeited their rights and can be treated as "noxious beasts of prey" (*ibid.*: II.16, II.85).[8] Finally, children are not fully under the law of nature until they reach maturity and the capacity for understanding, although they do possess some rights against their parents in general (*ibid.*, II.59–60).[9]

So the basic idea is that men are equal in the sense that each has reason "enough to lead them to the Knowledge of their Maker, and the sight of their own Duties" (Locke, *Essay*, "Introduction"). It does not follow, therefore, that not actually knowing God's law is grounds for falling below the line, since many of us do not and we will get there via different paths. The capacity for abstract thought is what seems to be crucial, at least for moral purposes (*Essay*, II.11.16). We are capable of relating to God's existence and thus to a law that is to govern us, and from that to a set of duties and rights that apply to our conduct, however difficult it might be to actually grasp them. So what grounds basic equality is our capacity to grasp how we are all the product of God's workmanship and capable, in principle at least, of being able to work out what this means for our social and political relations.[10]

In *A Letter Concerning Toleration*, Locke makes the connection between equality and rights explicit. He mounts a number of different arguments for toleration. Some are explicitly religious in character, based as they are on the nature of faith (that it has to be freely arrived at, etc.), and others more pragmatic. But he is also clear that toleration flows from the fact that people have equal rights: rightful claims over not only their property, but their person (we shall explore how Locke links these two ideas together later). "The Sum of all we drive at", he argues towards the end of the *Letter*, "is that, every Man may enjoy the same Rights as are granted to others" (1983: 53). How men actually worship should not affect the ascription of equal rights (the political consequences of certain theological principles, however, raises a different issue). This includes dissenters from the Church of England as much as orthodox Anglicans, Catholics and Jews: "neither Pagan, nor Mahometan, nor Jew ought to be excluded from the civil rights of the commonwealth because of his religion" (Locke 1983: 53–4).[11]

But there are problems, and this lands us back in the relation between natural and basic equality. First of all, by "men" does Locke mean *men*? In the *First Treatise* Locke seems to make clear that God gave the world not to Adam alone, but to "the Species of Man, for 'tis certain *Them* can by no means signifie Adam alone ... *They* then were to have Dominion" (*Two Treatises*, I.30). However, among early modern social contract theorists, although women are sometimes conceived of as naturally free, they usually end up subject to the apparently legitimate authority of their husbands. Perhaps this is not surprising, at a time when women in England, for example, literally disappeared under the legal personage of their husbands (see e.g. Blackstone, *Commentaries*, bk 1, ch. 15, §111). For Locke, political subjection was conventional and based on consent, but conjugal power (the power of husbands over their wives) was natural (*Two Treatises*, I.47–8, II.2, II.71, II.81–2; see also Pateman 1987, esp. ch. 3). As Mary Astell put it so vividly in 1700: "If all Men are born free, how is it that all Women are born slaves? as they must be if the being subjected to the inconstant, uncertain, unknown, arbitrary Will of Men, be the perfect Condition of Slavery" (1996: 18–19). Still, in many instances Locke was much less forthright about the natural subordination of women than many of his contemporaries. He was clear that a husband did not have the power of an absolute monarch over his wife; that marriage was a contract and not (in principle, at least) perpetual; that women could own property; and that the fifth commandment applied equally to fathers and mothers (*Two Treatises*, I.61, II.82, II.183). This is of little comfort to women, no doubt, but less draconian than many of the attitudes and practices of his contemporaries.

But we are still left with a difference in authority based on natural differences. Locke might well have believed a husband was not akin to an absolute monarch, and that women could own property and divorce (once they had raised the children and inheritance was taken care of), but this still left the husband with natural and civil rights over his wife. Pateman has argued that this means that Locke does not see women as part of the relevant class of agents entitled to *full* political equality and citizenship. Since the state of nature is a condition in which all "power and jurisdiction" is reciprocal, and women are naturally subject to the authority of their husbands, they do not count as free and equal individuals who establish civil society, and therefore can never be genuinely equal citizens (Pateman 1987: 52–3, 86–96).

Thus, even minimal or formal claims about the essence of human agency shape the *kinds* of rights we ascribe to people, along with who is eligible for them. I shall return to this point towards the end of the chapter.

Rights and freedom

For Locke, our having rights was not only a function of our being fundamentally equal, but also naturally free. However, unlike Hobbes, for him the state of nature is not a state of war. Like Hobbes, Locke thought that men in the state of nature had rights – hence natural rights – including a natural right to property (something Hobbes denied). But he also thought that although men were naturally free, this did not mean they were free to do anything they liked: liberty was not licence. It was not "a Liberty for every Man to do what he lists", but rather "to dispose, and order, as he lists, his Person, Actions, Possessions, and his whole Property, within the Allowances of those Laws under which he is; and therein not to be subject to the arbitrary Will of another". What is the nature of such law? In its "true notion", law is "not so much the Limitation as the direction of a free and intelligent Agent to his proper Interest, and prescribes no father than is for the generall Good of those under that Law" (Locke, *Two Treatises*, II.57). The "good" referred to here is not the eudaimonistic good of Aristotle's *Ethics* or *Politics*, or the idea that we naturally work for the good of others. Rather, Locke means the good of the security each of us has in acting how we want to (and ought to) in relation to our person and possessions. Like Hobbes and Grotius, there is no appeal to the idea of a substantive common good since, given his generally hedonistic psychology (we like what we take pleasure in, and dislike what pains us), the plurality of likes and dislikes makes this difficult to imagine (Locke, *Essay*, II.xxi.55).

So what natural rights do men have? At first glance, rights appear derivative from more fundamental duties. Man is the "workmanship of God", and his proper function is to act according to his reason, which is both the actual faculty of reason and the principles so discovered, which is natural law (*Two Treatises*, II.6). What is the fundamental law of nature? Recall that for Grotius and Hobbes it was basically "preserve yourself". For Locke, crucially, it is "preserve *mankind*". This means that men have positive duties to preserve themselves and others by providing aid to others, where it does not conflict with their own survival. They also have negative duties to abstain from harming others. And each has a natural right to the means to preserve themselves, that is, to property. Although God originally gave the world in common to all, natural law allows men to appropriate property, without the consent of others, by "mixing their labour" with it. But there are limits. You must leave "enough and as good" for others, and you cannot appropriate more than you can reasonably use (*ibid.*, II.25–7). In conditions where others need access to your property in order to survive, their inclusive right may trump your right to exclude them.[12] Finally, each has a natural right to compensation from injuries, and the right to punish transgressors of the law of nature; this is a logical corollary of man's natural freedom and his right to preserve himself in mankind (*ibid.*, II.7, II.87–9).

It is very important to see that for Locke, property refers not only to stuff – to land and moveable objects, for example – but to our (moral) rights in general. Thus he uses "property" in both a broad and narrow sense. Men join civil society for the "mutual preservation of their lives, liberties and estates, which I call by the general name, *property*" (*Two Treatises*, II.123). In the broad sense, then, property refers to basically whatever is one's own, to whatever belongs to or is part of oneself: "Though all the earth and inferior creatures be common to all men, yet every man has a property in his own person; this nobody has a right to but himself" (*ibid.*, II.26).

The idea of self-ownership that forms part of Locke's conception of property has been remarkably influential in modern political thought. It has been taken up by liberals and Marxists alike, as well as more broadly in the public culture (see discussion in Kymlicka 2002: 107–27, 180–82; Cohen 1998). It also marks a crucial way of thinking about rights in general: that rights are best understood *as* property – as things bound up with and possessed by individuals. This idea is central to many aspects of modern societies. We value bodily integrity and often conceive of freedom in terms of the right to determine what shall be done to and with our bodies. And yet just because we are self-owning, we are said to be capable of giving up control over our bodies in various ways. This opens up the possibility that self-ownership can lead to subjection: in exchanging our capacity to labour for wages, for example, we subject ourselves to a potentially exploitative relationship with the owner of the means of production. Or, in exchanging our capacity for self-government to the state for protection, we end up in a relation of subjection or domination. Even more seriously, as we shall see, to say someone *lacks* self-ownership – because they lack the requisite capacities for self-government, or indeed the right kind of body – is to say, potentially, that they are not eligible for the ascription of rights in the first place, or for equal political rights.

We shall return to the general issue of the relation between self-ownership and rights below, but before we do, how should we understand the basic structure of Lockean rights? I suggested above that for Locke, natural rights are ultimately derivative of our duties to God and, through him, to each other. This makes them seem rather conservative. However, Locke is also able to extract a radical theory of popular sovereignty from his theory of natural rights, albeit one combined with a conservative social thesis about the likelihood of revolution ever occurring. But first, what *kinds* of rights are Lockean rights?

For some, the emphasis on natural rights is taken to entail a claim about rights being foundational to natural law. In other words, that rights are primary, not duties. This is often connected to a broader claim about rights-based morality, or to what Charles Taylor (1985e) has called "atomism".[13] For Taylor, atomism represents a view about the nature of human agency and human society; society exists for no other reason than the promotion of individual ends. The basic view is one of moral individualism: individuals are the primary unit of moral concern and whatever social obligations we have are derivative of more fundamental principles to do with individual rights. Is Locke an atomist in this sense? It is hard to see that he is. The right to self-preservation is not a liberty to do anything one wills, but derives from natural law: the duty to preserve mankind. Whatever else we might call it, Locke's theory is surely a *limited* theory of rights (Tully 1980: 63; Sreenivasan 1995). But does that mean the converse is true: that all Lockean rights are derived from duties, and that duties are primary, not rights? Are the only rights we have those that are necessary for the fulfilment of our duties?

Recall our discussion in the Introduction about the conceptual landscape of rights. Hohfeld introduced four different kinds of jural relations that he argued captured the logical space of rights: claims, permissions (or liberties), powers and immunities. The most significant kind (but certainly not the only kind) of right we find in the *Two Treatises* is a *claim-right*.[14] A claim-right is a protected liberty; there exists a direct correlative duty on the part of someone else to allow the exercise of that right. For example, according to Locke, each of us has an equal right to preserve ourselves, and others are duty bound to enable us to exercise that right (*Two Treatises*, II.4–6). Parents have a duty to raise and care for their children, and they have the rights that enable them to do so (*ibid.*, II.58).

Of course God, ultimately, has rights over us too, and therefore *his* rights might be considered primary. But this does not have the same consequences for *us*, in this world, as those who claim that rights are primary often think. God is the obligator of the law of nature, but we are the beneficiaries. The benefits we receive are our rights, and we have duties to not interfere with the exercise of those rights. But Locke also thinks that it is a logical corollary of our having duties that we have the right to perform them. But we do not have rights *only* to do what our duties require, namely, to preserve mankind; all of our rights are not soley the means to perform our duties. Instead, our natural duties set a boundary around those rights or liberties we have to act other than in relation to our duties. In other words, although Locke clearly does think we have rights that are directly correlated to duties, we also have rights that create moral space for the pursuit of other kinds of activities.[15] We have rights not to be harmed or interfered with, even when not doing our duties. That does not mean we have a right to do wrong – we are always bound by the law of nature – but we have a right to do what is not always best (see Simmons 1992: 77–8).

Rights and the legitimacy of the state

Because men are by nature "free, equal and independent" and possess natural rights, any legitimate political order must be based on consent, and any political power government has based on the exercise of those rights "resign'd up into the Community" (Locke, *Two Treatises*, II.96, II.87). In fact, Locke defines legitimate political power as the *right* to make laws for the public good (*ibid.*, II.1). There are other forms of power – tyranny and "usurpation" are two possibilities – but these are examples of illegitimate as opposed to legitimate exercises of power. What they lack is the rational consent of those over whom power is exercised. (It follows, therefore, that for those who are unable to give their rational consent, because they lack – or at least *seem* to lack – the appropriate capacities to do so, other forms of power may be exercised over them.) Note, therefore, that our natural rights are antecedent to the establishment of political society and are supposed to condition the exercise of political power therein. Locke, famously, uses the language of *trust* in relation to consent: we entrust our natural powers to government to protect our property, broadly understood to include not only our possessions, but our lives and liberties too (*ibid.*, II.124, II.129, II.134). We consent with each other to create a political community, and simultaneously to be bound by its majority decisions (*ibid.*, II.96).

But what counts as a "sufficient Declaration" or sign of consent? Consent can be express or tacit. The former involves a "positive engagement" and express promise to be bound by membership in a community. The latter, more typical, is given by "having possessions or enjoyment of any part of the dominions of any government". And this can involve no more than "the very being of anyone within the territories of that government" (*ibid.*, II.119, II.122). Many have criticized Locke (and modern Lockeans) for holding a far too loose sense of what counts as consent. But Locke's problem is not necessarily that of the contemporary libertarian. His main concern is to distinguish between legitimate and illegitimate political societies; the former are those for whom the state's right to govern is derived from the consent of the people, as opposed to natural subjection or conquest.

Political power then, is to be exercised on the grounds of the people's delegation of their original natural powers and liberty to form an association and then a government in order to protect their "lives, liberties and estates". It is also grounded in a relation of trust. Any laws made and executed must be in accordance with natural law: "[The legislative power] in the utmost Bounds of it, is limited to the publick good of the Society. It is a power that hath no other end but preservation, and therefore can never have a right to destroy, enslave or designedly to impoverish the Subjects" (*ibid.*, II.135). If it does, then consent can be withdrawn and the government reconstituted. This is the upshot of Locke's radical theory of popular sovereignty: the power to judge whether my trust is violated reverts to the individual citizen. Trust plays a mediating role between our consent and the *actual* exercise of power. It is an attitude that falls somewhere between faith and suspicion: we have to allow governments to act in ways they judge to promote the public good, but never forget they might violate our rights in the process (adapted from Ignatieff 2000: 33). However, government also has the right to exercise power beyond the law, as part of its "prerogative" power – "the power of doing publick good without a rule" (Locke, *Two Treatises*, II.160) – and what Locke refers to generally as the "arts of government" (see Ivison 1997: chs 4–5).

In Chapter 1, I argued that rights not only provide a bulwark against political power, but also distribute and reinforce relations of power in various ways. Locke's argument provides a striking example of this. In his other philosophical writings, including his *Essay Concerning Human Understanding*, his memorandum on the reformation of the Poor Laws, his various responses to critics of his *Letter Concerning Toleration* and his colonial writings, Locke is clear that the exercise of political power often reaches beyond and into the apparent "zone of indifference" protected by our natural and civil rights. Religious beliefs and practices can be interfered with if they threaten public order. The poor can be coerced to work and placed in poor houses if they refuse to do so. Indigenous peoples can have their property taken from them if they fail to cultivate it in the appropriate way and block others from doing so.

In fact, in the *Essay*, Locke pointed out that more than just civil law shapes the behaviour of people. Divine law governs us as well as what he called the "law of opinion or reputation" (Locke, *Essay*, II.27.20). For Locke, morality involves conformity to one or other of these laws. We have already discussed the basis of civil law. But what are we to make of this third form of law? In the discussion in the *Essay*, Locke points out that much of what people think of as virtue or vice often arises from what is regarded as worthy of praise or condemnation in the particular community in which the actions take place. We may give up our natural powers to be regulated by the state, but men "still retain the power of Thinking well or ill, approving or disapproving of the actions of those whom they live amongst, and converse with" (*ibid.*). Of course, the law of reputation will only work on those who actually care about their reputation, but Locke thinks it is still a fairly powerful force in society. The attribution (and distribution) of praise or blame is an extremely effective form of "government" (in the broad sense of the term) in society: there is not "one of ten thousand, who is stiff and insensible enough, to bear up under the constant Dislike, and Condemnation of his own Club" (*ibid*., II.27.12).

As long as political power – construed formally in terms of civil law – is exercised legitimately, Locke seems to assume that the morality of the law of opinion will, in general, coincide with it. It too, in a sense, is a product of the will and interactions of individuals, albeit in a more decentralized and diffuse way. When power is usurped or abused, then there might well be discontinuity between civil law and the other two forms of law. Civil law might become arbitrary, and the other forms of law might need to be invoked against it. Divine law is ultimately, of course, the basic touchstone of moral rightness for Locke, but the law of reputation still plays a very important role in political society. Indeed it is an early elaboration of what was to become an influential account of the idea of civil society, or the "public sphere", as seen as standing apart from the state and as a source of critical reflection on it. But notice here too how it acts to shape people's behaviour – and very effectively, as Locke notes – but is not, strictly speaking, something to which people can consent (or at least only if the idea of tacit consent is stretched to the point of meaninglessness). So consent legitimizes the exercise of political power, but the very capacities required to exercise consent and political judgement are themselves the object of other forms of "government" which are not capable of being regulated by consent.

Locke makes clear that citizens require an extensive set of capacities and dispositions in order to be capable of exercising the political judgement required of them. Individuals must be capable of judging not only according to the law of nature, civil law and the law of reputation, but also with regard to the scope of executive power and the arts of government. On the one hand, the ascription of rights to individuals might be taken to signal that these capacities are *inherent*, either naturally or historically (or both). Locke, for example, like other theorists in England at this time, insisted that these natural rights were also historical rights: the rights of

Englishmen, guaranteed by their "ancient constitution" (see Pocock 1987). These rights preceded the Norman invasion and their imposition of feudal law through conquest, an event that was for Locke (as well as others) deeply problematic (*Two Treatises*, II.175–6).

On the other hand, the ascription of rights is dependent on whether someone *actually* does possess the requisite capacities implied in the particular account of rights. Think of what is implied by Locke's theory. The appropriate subject of rights is someone who has "property in their person"; someone who can reason properly and is thus capable (mentally, legally and morally) of consenting to political arrangements to which they are subject; and someone who can be trusted (i.e. is a responsible moral agent). To lack any or all of these capacities casts serious doubt as to whether or not you can be a proper member of civil society. Even more strongly, it may cast doubt as to whether or not rights can be properly ascribed to you. If some of our most important rights inhere in us because of our possession of certain natural powers and capacities, and I am said to lack some of those crucial natural powers, then it might follow that I am not eligible for rights-ascription. Worse, it might mean that I am considered less than fully human. In both cases, the justification for the exercise of legitimate political power drops away. Consent is not required because it cannot be offered, in the proper sense of the term. In fact, as we shall see below, this is the starting-point of a radical critique of the whole conception of rights conceived in relation to the notion of self-ownership. Feminist political philosophers as early as Mary Wollstonecraft have pointed out how these kinds of presumptions were used to justify treating women (and others, including non-Europeans and non-whites) as incapable of possessing equal rights.

Rights and self-ownership

So conceptions of the self play a crucial role in shaping our theories of rights. And there are important questions about *which* conceptions of self lie behind our most influential conceptions of rights, and moreover, which conception of the self (or family of conceptions) *ought* to inform our theories of rights. One important question our discussion in this chapter raises is this: if rights are fundamentally about human *agency* then what do we mean by agency? Are we referring to the natural powers and capacities of agents? Or are we referring to something else? Are the powers and capacities that are relevant to the ascription of rights the product of particular circumstances and relations of power? Or are they a claim about the universal capacities of all human agents, inferred from the natural structure of the self, independent of particular circumstances and power?

Self-ownership provides a powerful way of conceptualizing the self and the rights it ought to have. It often features in arguments that stress a connection between a rich conception of individual autonomy and the role that rights play in protecting and promoting autonomy. How should we understand the nature of this autonomy? Recall Locke's emphasis on a capacity for abstract thought, on the ability to take responsibility for one's choices, as well as his claim that we have property in our person. Or recall Hobbes's emphasis on being in control of one's speech and attitudes, such that others see that they are genuinely yours. Both arguments appeal to the notion of some form of reflective self-direction. Some philosophers think there is an important difference between an emphasis on human *agency* and an emphasis on *autonomy*. The former is supposed to be thinner than the latter, or to signal an account of human action that is less moralized than autonomy is often taken to be, especially as formulated by John Stuart Mill (in *On Liberty*), or more recently, by Joseph Raz (1986). To have agency is to be capable of pursuing, in some way, one's own projects, plans or values. It is distinct from the further claim that one has arrived at one's beliefs about those projects or values in a suitably autonomous fashion. For the sake of simplicity I will assume that talk of agency and autonomy, at least here, amount to roughly the same thing. But we shall revisit the whole idea of what is human agency in Chapter 8.

Locke's emphasis on consent as the best way of thinking about the legitimacy of political power is a natural corollary of this idea of self-ownership and autonomy. Recall also the claim by Nozick with which Chapter 2 began: "Individuals have rights and there are things no person or group may due to them (without violating their rights)". He goes on to say that society must respect these rights because they reflect "the underlying Kantian principle that individuals are ends and not merely means; they may not be sacrificed or used for the achieving of other ends without their consent" (1974: 30–31). We shall examine this Kantian idea in more detail in Chapter 4, but notice how it leads Nozick to a strong claim about rights.

According to Nozick, rights are "side-constraints": *boundaries* that it is almost always morally wrong to transgress, whatever the value of the project or goal in the name of which a violation may be justified. Equal freedom, for Nozick, entails self-ownership: that I am my own master, as opposed to being in the power of someone else. People should never be used as "means" towards some social goal, or have their rights violated for the sake of benefiting others.

The Lockean view thus gives us a very powerful conception of rights: that all rights are essentially property rights; that conceptually they are deeply linked to the idea of vesting in the right-holder control over a domain of choice. Locke is one of the most important intellectual forefathers of the modern "choice theory" of rights discussed in Chapter 1. In one of the most influential articles on natural rights in the modern era, H. L. A Hart summarized the basic idea in this way:

> Rights are typically conceived of as possessed or owned or belonging to individuals, and these expressions reflect the conception of moral rules as not only prescribing conduct but as forming a kind of moral property of individuals to which they are as individuals entitled.   (1984: 83)

One way of drawing out the logical conclusion of this way of thinking about rights is to say that rights must ultimately be "compossible", that is, coexistent without conflict. If rights really are protected choices – control vested in the individual over actions that are linked to capacities central to what it means to be a human being – then they really should not conflict, especially if the duties are correlative ones (i.e. each entailing a moral right). This was, you may recall, part of Hobbes's analysis of what was wrong with the state of nature; where correlative duties are "competitive", people have a right to invade the rights of others, and that entails war.

Hillel Steiner (1994) has offered a fascinating elaboration of this idea. For Steiner, duty-conflicts between correlative duties are highly undesirable. If moral rights are supposed to provide us with standards to evaluate our legal system, among other things, then they fail to do so if there are fundamental conflicts between them. So he asks: what characteristics must a set of rights possess if its entailed set of correlative duties are not to conflict? A right, for Steiner, is a vested liberty, that is, a liberty surrounded by what he calls an "impenetrable perimeter" (*ibid.*: 87). When someone has a right they occupy – literally – a certain spatiotemporal location and have exclusive use of certain material objects. These are the "physical elements", as he puts it, of the conduct required by the right (and the correlative duties). For two duties not to conflict, it is necessary that the respective sets of physical elements not intersect or overlap (*ibid.*: 74–101). Steiner lays out this argument with great subtlety and complexity, but the basic idea is this: for rights to be "vested" requires that others not be able to physically interfere with the means of my exercising those rights (and duties). To have a right to freedom of speech is to say that *at this time* and *in this place* you are free to speak. To have a right to freedom of religion is to be free to practise your religion at this time and in this place. If others can significantly alter or affect my control over the domain to which my right (and the correlative duties) refer, then I do not have the right. For example, if others have a claim-right to equal protection and equal benefit of the law, and that is extended to include pro-tection from certain kinds of speech (e.g. "hate" speech[16]), then on Steiner's reading, I do not have the right to freedom of speech (and vice versa).[17] So rights are conceived as "domains over which claim-holders have controlling powers" (Steiner 2006: 470). If our moral rights are not in principle compossible then they fail to provide the requisite moral standard for legal (and political) decision-making.

The clear contrast here is with the *interest* theory of rights. Recall that the interest theory says that persons have a right if and only if some aspect of their well-being is sufficiently important in itself to justify holding other persons under a duty to perform or not perform some action. This pretty much makes conflicts of duties (and rights) inevitable. We have a range of important interests to which rights claims might be attached, and there is clearly every possibility that many of the duties involved will conflict. As we shall see, our interest in security, and the duties they may generate, can conflict with our equally strong interests in freedom of speech or association and the duties they generate. Our interest in freedom of choice can conflict with our interest in an equal distribution of resources. And so on.

Incompossibility is a problem for theorists for whom rights form part of the foundation of a theory of justice. It is also a problem for those for whom rights are linked fundamentally to choice and control over a specific domain of non-interference. In the real world, of course, rights, including basic rights, do conflict and hard choices have to be made between realizing some rather than others. We criminalize hate speech, for example, or we wear some of the consequences of broadly unregulated speech as the price of freedom of expression. We restrict freedom of association in order to ensure public safety. Theorists such as Steiner and Nozick do not deny this, but they seek to clarify as precisely as possible what follows when we say that someone has a right to x. If rights cannot be distinguished clearly enough from other kinds of moral claims, then we lose sight of the distinctive role they are meant to play in our moral and political theory.

Rights republicanism

In Chapter 2 I pointed out that the emergence of natural law in the seventeenth century, and especially the emphasis on subjective rights, provided a sharp alternative to the language of civic humanism and republicanism. For Grotius, Hobbes and Locke, citizenship is conceived of in terms of rights, property and contract, as opposed to virtue and the realization of our true nature in the city. We undoubtedly do have two languages of politics here, but it is not clear that they are fundamentally incompatible. Locke helps us to see this.

In a series of influential books and essays, the intellectual historian J. G. A. Pocock (1980; 1985) has taken aim at what he calls the "myth of John Locke":[18] that everything in intellectual life after 1688 could be explained by Locke's presence in this context. Pocock has instead emphasized a complex "non-Lockean republic of letters",[19] and alternative set of political languages, that had their roots in ancient constitutionalism, classical republicanism and worries about corruption, politeness, civility and sociality. This has been part of a general "republican revival" in the history of especially American political thought, as well as in political theory more generally (see Skinner 1997; 2001a; Pettit 1997). In particular, Pocock's excavation of an alternative language of civic human-ism has emphasized the central role of civic virtue in securing the common good against tyranny, and hence the dangers of commer-cial society and the exclusive pursuit of "interest". Pocock's extraor-dinary thesis was that this "Machiavellian moment" in Northern European political thought (actually, one influenced by the redis-covery and interpretation of Aristotle's *Politics* as much as Machi-avelli) migrated to the New World and helped shape the ideological origins of the American revolution. What it also did was provide a much richer and more detailed landscape on which to re-place Locke's *Two Treatises*, and thus gain a more complex understanding of Lockean thought in general (Tully 1993c: 253–5).

It turns out that Locke's position in relation to the debate over the origins of liberalism and republicanism in early modern politi-cal thought is much more ambiguous than usually thought.[20] If the ancient forms of political economy and virtue were inappropriate to a time of rapidly changing domestic and geopolitical circum-stances, that does not mean the language of virtue was completely irrelevant. Steve Pincus has argued that defenders of the English Commonwealth in the 1650s folded discussions of virtue into those about interests, and mixed arguments for the common good with claims for material improvement. They combined a commitment to commerce and the politics of interest with a republican conception of liberty (*salus populi* not *majesta imperii*). It is this amalgamation, suggests Pincus, that constitutes the origins of liberal political phi-losophy: the desire to be "modern, commercial, and polite on the one hand and to defend the common good on the other" (1998: 735; see also Armitage 2000: 168–9). Locke becomes, on this read-ing, a kind of modern republican.[21]

Is this reading persuasive? I think it is, for two reasons. On the one hand, Locke's political theory of consent, limit and resistance – a scheme central to radical Whig and republican writers of the early 1680s and 1689 – entailed that "[the legislative power] in the utmost Bounds of it, is limited to the publick Good of the Soci-ety" (*Two Treatises*, II.135). The boundaries of the law of nature – that mankind ought to be preserved – are the "rule of virtue and vice" (see *Two Treatises*, II.7, II.16, II.134–5; also *Essay*, II.28.11).[22] Natural law commands what is in the best interests of mankind as a whole, and this leads to "'public happiness'" by helping secure the preservation and prosperity of society (Locke, *Essay*, I.2.6). Locke hovers between naturalistic and supernatural means of getting men to act rationally (for discussion see Dunn 1983: 192–9; Simmons 1992: ch. 1; Tully 1993b), but the emphasis on acting so as to fulfil one's moral duties and benefit society – and not only oneself – remains clear.

On the other hand, since most people most of the time have great difficulty in clearly discerning their obligations under natural law, and hence in promoting the public interest, a complex array of forms of government were required to keep partiality and corruption in check. This was a consequence of having to combine an essentially hedonistic psychology, as outlined in *the Essay Concerning Human Understanding*, with a non-egoistic moral theory (for a defence of which see Tully 1980: 103–4; Simmons 1992: 37–47). To do so meant that the virtue of which the classical republicans spoke belonged to a distant "Golden Age", which was impossible to maintain given the development of money, expanding populations, growing trade and the rise of "Ambition and Luxury", all of which radically reshaped human desires (Locke, *Two Treatises*, II.111). But this did not mean that men were no longer required to act in such a way that promoted the common good.[23] Instead, it meant providing a different account of the nature of virtue to suit the philosophical programme outlined in *An Essay Concerning Human Understanding*, and the new social, economic and political circumstances of late-seventeenth-century Europe.

So Locke does, in fact, offer a combination of natural law and republican arguments – a "constitution-enforcing" conception of rights – in which the people subject their rulers to the rule of law through the threat and practice of resistance (Tully 1993a: 259–61; Skinner 1997: 18–21, 55). According to this reading, rights can promote republican forms of civic liberty, however much they may be compatible with non-republican forms of government (Skinner 1997: 55 n.177). Liberty as non-interference may indeed remain an important good of such a society, and rights a means of realizing that good, but the range of what counts as a constraint on a citizen's liberty is expanded to include living in a state of *arbitrary* dependence on others. This is a crucial feature of what Quentin Skinner (1997) has called the "neo-Roman" conception of freedom (see also

Pettit 1997). Defenders of republican freedom then, *pace* Pocock, can perfectly well accommodate the language of rights, but they end up endorsing a particular account of the way we possess rights. We only truly enjoy a right, according to this tradition, when others – especially governments and monarchs – are prevented from being able to interfere arbitrarily with our exercise of them. The mere fact that the king, for example, had discretionary powers to arbitrarily suspend or invade the basic liberties of his subjects led English "Commonwealth" theorists in the seventeenth century to declare that anyone living in such a condition was living akin to a slave (see Skinner 2002; 2006: 258–60).[24] Of course, this conception of freedom also entails that forms of non-arbitrary "interferences" – for example, to do with enforcing the rule of law, or ensuring people have the capacities to make effective choices and decisions about their ends – are not, in themselves, violations of one's liberty (Skinner 1997: 84–5; see also Pettit 1997). And thus it is not a purely "negative" conception of freedom either, to borrow from Isaiah Berlin's (1969) classic discussion, which says that I am free only to the extent to which I am not interfered with.

This is not just a historical point. Rights are frequently accused of being narrowly individualistic and incompatible with any conception of the common good, apart from the protection of individual rights. The conceptual claim is that as an essentially negative locution – the idea of a right as a protection *against* the state, or as grounded outside the norms of the city – it is difficult, if not impossible, to marry it with a positive notion of citizenship (Brett 2003). This is also a key aspect of the communitarian critique of rights, which we shall examine in Chapter 5. But this critique presupposes that, first, rights are essentially negative and, secondly, that moral individualism is fundamentally incompatible with community. Both claims should be treated with care. Rights are often criticized as providing only the thinnest of bonds for a sense of political belonging. But this neglects the ways in which rights can help create and sustain community, as much as constrain it. If rights are fundamentally relational, then they do not only set boundaries, but also distribute powers and capacities in various ways, and thus structure particular kind of relationships between citizens (and noncitizens). Moreover, since rights always have to be interpreted and implemented in particular circumstances and in relation to existing social norms, it is actually hard to separate them from "community", even when we want to (this is a challenge for interpreting human rights, as we shall see).

Because rights discourse is associated with claims of equality, it provides a way into public debates for groups and individuals trying to claim or make real the status that rights presuppose (just as these presuppositions can work to exclude). Rights can operate as levers in this sense, helping to raise a set of political claims into the main register of political debate and discourse. They provide a language for democratic argument in so far as they signal the importance of the interests at stake, and the need for special kinds of justification with regard to those interests. Moreover, rights are an institutionally dependent concept; to realize the value of rights requires institutions. And the institutions of the modern state are vital in this regard (just as they are also always, at the same time, a threat to rights), and in turn require extensive public support and expenditure (Homes & Sunstein 1999). Also, in multi-ethnic and multicultural states such as Canada or South Africa, where appeal to a common ancestry, history or language is incapable of providing the bonds of national unity, the appeal to a commitment to equality, manifested in a particular constitutional structure or tradition of rights, is often invoked. Even if it is hard to draw a sharp distinction between civic and ethnic nationalism, it is clear that rights have become an important aspect of different forms of liberal democratic nationalism in recent times (see Kymlicka 1995; cf. Miller 1998).[25] A shared commitment to equal rights is hardly a sufficient condition for social unity in complex liberal democratic states, but it may well be a necessary one.

Against natural rights

Here and in Chapter 2 we have been exploring a range of arguments concerning natural law and natural rights. Both remain influential notions and natural rights have often been invoked in contemporary discussions of human rights. But they are also vulnerable to powerful criticism, and it is useful at this point to stand back and conclude our discussion by looking at some of these critiques.

One of the most direct and forceful critiques of natural rights was offered by Jeremy Bentham, scourge of both the United States Declaration of Independence and the French Declaration of the Rights of Man and of the Citizen. Bentham's critique is grounded ultimately in a consequentialist analysis of morality and the public good: "Nature has placed mankind under the governance of two sovereign masters, pain and pleasure" (1962: vol. 1, 1). The public interest was an aggregation of the interests of individuals, expressed in terms of their experience of pleasure and pain. The calculus of utility was thus the best and only reliable principle and test for both moral thinking and public policy, including concerning the nature of rights. A course of action was right, in the substantive sense of that term (recall our discussion in the Introduction), if it promoted utility.

For Bentham, law had to be understood in terms of the determinate commands of an identifiable sovereign, backed up by threats of sanction. Laws and processes of law-making were to be evaluated on the basis of their propensity to promote utility. Thus the jurist was charged with explaining what the existing law was, along with its effects on society. And he should seek to work out what utility demanded in the circumstances of that society and propose whatever rules, institutions and sanctions would help realize those demands. Bentham was an active social critic and supporter of democratic reform – he offered his services as a kind of political consultant on reform to governments around the world – but he did not think the doctrine of natural rights helped serve progressive change. In fact, he thought it did the opposite. So his objections to natural rights are both philosophical and practical.

In *Anarchical Fallacies*, Bentham took direct aim at the Declaration of the Rights of Man and of the Citizen. To claim that the "'end of every political association is the preservation of the natural and imprescriptible rights of man" (Article II), argued Bentham, is nonsense. In fact, it was "dangerous nonsense ... nonsense upon stilts ... terrorist language" (Bentham 1987a: 52–3). The phrase "natural rights" was literally meaningless. Why? For Bentham, rights or duties could only be grasped in relation to positive law. They had no existence apart from law. A natural right, he argued (in another text dating from 1795) "is a son that never had a father", a "species of cold heat, a sort of dry moisture, a kind of resplendent darkness" (*ibid.*: 73). If you take away the law-giver and the various sanctions at his disposal you have no law, and with them you take the fictions of right as well. Natural rights are essentially fictitious entities. Laws and sanctions are real. Legal rights might begin as fictions, but our analysis of them ends up at real entities. If natural rights really did refer to a natural sovereign and his ability to induce people to act on their duties for fear of some tangible sanction, then perhaps they might exist, but that was often not an argument French and English radicals who invoked natural rights were willing to make.[26]

Another confusion promoted by natural rights talk was more political in nature. This involved implying that something contrary to nature cannot or should not take place. A perfect example of this, thought Bentham, was Article XVII of the Declaration of the Rights of Man and of the Citizen, which states that "property being an inviolable and sacred right, no-one can be deprived of it". But this is false. In politics, the literal inviolability of property is neither morally nor legally possible; property is regularly taken and people are deprived of it, sometimes for good reasons and sometimes for bad. The whole tendency of natural rights talk then, especially in the Declaration, is to make too many general claims absolutely, which is incompatible with the viability of any plausible political order. Or, when qualifications are made, they are done so vaguely as to undermine the whole point of making such a declaration in the first place.

Thus for Bentham, natural rights are ultimately a rhetorical device used to mobilize political action for personal or collective gain, without due awareness of the price:

> When a man has a political caprice to gratify, and is determined to gratify it … when he finds it necessary to get the multitude to join with him, but either stoops not to enquire whether they would be the better or happier for so doing … he sets up a cry of rights.   (Bentham 1987a: 73–4)

Since claims about natural rights are fundamentally empty, nothing can be said about their truth or falsity: "When we have said this much on either side, it is no purpose to say more; there we are completely at a stand, argument such as this can go no further on either side" (1962: vol. 2, 495). The political morality of the Declaration was thus "wild, unjustified, contradictory and potentially anarchic" (1987a: 40). To base political change on speculation about the origins of government in a state of nature, or on pre-political natural rights, was to invite anarchy.[27] Seeking absolute standards in politics, in general, was deeply problematic: to state them with any clarity entailed over-generality, and at the same time rigidity. Absolute principles tie the hands of future generations, preventing them from dealing effectively with changed circumstances (*ibid.*: 54). Appealing to natural rights also undermined the stability and determinacy of the rule of law, hampering its capacity to help coordinate human behaviour in complex societies. A society without the rule of law was not unimaginable, but that was precisely the point: a glimpse at the aftermath of the French revolution, and indeed the English revolution, demonstrated exactly what could happen. Bentham here echoes concerns about the value of the security and stability expressed with great force and clarity by Hobbes (see Chapter 2).

Of course Bentham still thought we could evaluate moral propositions about the law, and thus about legal rights, according to objective ethical standards, namely, utilitarian ones. Bad laws should be condemned on consequentialist grounds, not by appeal to natural rights:

> If I say that a man has a natural right to [this] coat or [this] land – all that it can mean, if it mean anything … is, that I am of [the] opinion he ought to have a political right to it: that by the appropriate services rendered on occasion to him by the appropriate functionaries of government he ought to be protected and secured in the use of it.　　　(1962: vol. 3, 218)[28]

It never makes sense to say of someone that they have a natural right independent of law, or that rights could exist somehow without it: "Reasons for wishing there were such things as rights", argues Bentham, "are not rights" (1987a: 53). It may well be that we can have moral duties in light of moral principles, just as we have duties in light of positive law. But for Bentham at least, rights are only correlative to the latter, not the former (see *ibid.*: 37–8).

A similar set of concerns about the plausibility of moral rights has been expressed more recently by Raymond Geuss (2001; 2005a), albeit from a radically different philosophical perspective. Geuss's particular target is the prevalence of human rights discourse, which we shall examine in more detail in Chapter 8. But the general argument applies here. Geuss argues that if rights can only be justified by appeal to moral reasons, and yet there is no evident or likely agreement on the kinds of moral fundamentals such justification requires, then claims about moral rights remain at best mere wishes or aspirations, and at worst "a kind of puffery or white magic" (2001: 144). Like Bentham, he suggests that the idea of absolute principles, such as natural or human rights, either betray the fact that they are regularly contravened, or (and sometimes at the same time) are used to "throttle the future" (*ibid*.: 154). His general point is that to be a genuine right, a claim must impose duties on others in ways that can be effectively enforced: "backed up by an effective method of implementation" (*ibid*.: 146). Otherwise they remain mere moral beliefs. Where effective enforcement is lacking, there is no right. For example, if I have a right to decent medical care, then it must be clear not only what we mean by "decent", but that there are the means for enforcing my claim *and* those charged with delivering it have the resources and motivation to do so (see also Darby 2001). The same holds true even for liberty rights. As a result, for Geuss, it is very hard to imagine that there are any universal rights at all, however much we might want there to be. We can, of course, continue to impress moral arguments upon each other in order to criticize existing states of affairs or provide alternative visions of politics. Also, since what we think should be effectively enforced involves different kinds of moral beliefs and judgements, moral criticism might well alter our conception of what rights people should have in the sense of what "effective enforcement" actually entails (see e.g. James 2003). But we should not confuse moral claims or judgements with rights. Rights may well involve moral claims, but they are moral claims attached to the effective conditions for their enforcement.

Wayne Sumner has summarized another variation of this criticism in the following way: a moral right exists "whenever the corresponding conventional right is morally justified, or simply … moral rights are morally justified conventional rights" (1987: 148). That is, the only moral rights that exist are those rights that are actually operative within a legal system or established social practice, and where the processes of recognition of those legal and conventional practices are morally justified. Furthermore, Sumner thinks that the kind of moral justification required is basically consequentialist. I have a moral right only if it has been conventionally recognized in some way and this recognition can be justified in an appropriately consequentialist way.[29] So, to return to an example we used in

Chapter 1, I have a moral right to vote, according to Sumner, just in so far as that right is conventionally recognized and provided for *and* my having such a right promotes greater utility (or "welfare") overall. The appeal to moral rights in itself, in other words, does not provide the requisite justification for the right, but rather is the outcome of a deeper moral justification for the validity of some way of acting or being acted on.

These are powerful and cogent criticisms. They will provide an important backdrop to our discussion of human rights in Chapter 8. They are also congenial to what I have called a "naturalistic" approach to theories of rights; that is, taking seriously the dynamic structure of rights, and the historical, social and political contexts in which they are articulated. For now, however, note the following about the general line of critique. First, Bentham's argument is aimed at a particular strand of the natural rights tradition, namely, one that is committed to a form of metaphysical realism. We have seen from our discussion above, and in Chapter 2, however, that the natural law tradition admits of great variation. We looked briefly at the voluntarist strand of that tradition, which was, in fact, deeply suspicious of many of the kinds of philosophical claims Bentham worries about. Haakonssen has argued very persuasively that this alternative voluntarist tradition has a trajectory that runs from the seventeenth century right up to (and feeds into) the work of David Hume and Adam Smith, both of whom were deeply sceptical of natural rights and yet retained a limited role for rights – historicized and socially embedded – in their respective political theories (see Smith, *The Theory of Moral Sentiments*, II.ii; for more discussion see Haakonssen 1981: 99–114). So the natural law tradition is not the "monolithic metaphysical monstrosity" that Bentham implied it was in his sweeping condemnation of "nonsense upon stilts" (Haakonssen 2004: 105). Geuss's criticism too seems to rest on taking aim at those theories in which one's "*final* political philosophy", or one's understanding of politics "in general" (2001: 152, emphasis added), is expressed in terms of a theory of rights.[30] But many liberal political theories – including some we shall discuss in later chapters – make no such claims. Rights play an important role in the work of Rawls and Habermas, for example, but they are also embedded within a wider theory of justice and discourse ethics, respectively, in which rights are the outcome of a constructive procedure, not one of its indubitable premises (cf. Geuss 2005a: 29–39, 92–4). Moreover, theorists such as Wayne Sumner and Richard Arneson, who are critical of thinking moral rights are foundational in any way, still see them as important and defensible, albeit on consequentialist grounds.

Secondly, although Geuss is correct to point out that our moral judgements about rights claims often conflict and are subject to deep disagreement, he is too quick to conclude that none are capable of being vindicated in moral and political argument. Political philosophy should not be thought of as contingent on first sorting out basic meta-ethical questions. It has to proceed in the face of uncertainty here just as politics has to. Rawls and Habermas, for example, set themselves a difficult but more modest task than Geuss implies. Starting from basic claims about human agency and our moral identity, they try to construct a common ground on which to argue about the rights people should have. Now it might well be that Rawls and Habermas fail to provide the common ground required to justify a coherent theory of rights, including human rights, but the further we move away from setting the bar for the justification of rights at the level of metaphysical realism, the less devastating are the objections mounted by Bentham and Geuss, important as they are. Another option is to move even further away from the juridical conception of rights altogether and embrace the recognition thesis implicit in Bentham's argument more wholeheartedly. Hegel provides one such example, although his philosophical system introduces a whole new set of challenges, as we shall see. Finally, Nussbaum's "justice as capabilities approach" (2000; 2006) offers a potentially interesting framework within which to take on board many of Geuss's criticisms, and yet at the same time retain some of the appeal of the Rawlsian attempt to recognize deep moral pluralism and defend robust principles of justice. She does this, in part, by appealing to a theory of the good to inform the capabilities seen to be most deserving of promotion and protection. We shall explore this approach when we discuss human rights.

Conclusion

The idea that rights are best understood as a kind of property of individuals – as the possessions or "controlling powers" of an individual – has been deeply influential in modern political thought. But it is not clear that believing that individuals deserve special respect in light of their fundamental freedom necessarily requires a belief either in self-ownership, or in the "choice" or "will" theory of rights. Nozick draws very strong conclusions about rights from claims about self-ownership. Before resources can be redistributed to help the less advantaged, for example, we first have to determine whether others have rights to those resources. If they do, then they can only be redistributed if they consent. This means that the talented – or even just the lucky – cannot be coerced into paying taxes to help the disadvantaged, since that would be to use them as a "means" to promote distributive justice. If others have a legitimate claim on my talents as a philosopher, and thus to the earnings I receive as an academic, then that amounts to a denial of my self-ownership: those others would seem to have partial ownership of my actions and my labour. Nozick thinks this is to fail to treat me as an equal. However, it is not clear that self-ownership yields such a strong form of exclusive property rights. Locke, arguably, offers a much more limited theory of property rights than Nozick suggests. Even some libertarians – so-called "left libertarians" – think that self-ownership is compatible with a much more limited theory of property rights, one that ensures that people are not excluded from an adequate level of resources required to enjoy genuinely equal freedom (see e.g. Otsuka 2003).

But more generally, it is not clear that respect for persons or equality is indeed best captured by the idea of self-ownership anyway. Are there other ways of capturing what it means to treat someone equally and to express the value of rights, that do not depend on claims about self-ownership? Does the emphasis on choice and control best capture the substance of rights, as well as who or what is the subject of rights? What happens when we begin to move away from the idea of rights conceived so closely in relation to choice? This will be the focus of Chapters 4 and 5.

4 Dignity

The debate is occurring because the Supreme Court's ruling that said that we must conduct ourselves under the Common Article III of the Geneva Convention. And that Common Article III says that there will be no outrages upon human dignity. It's very vague. What does that mean, "outrages upon human dignity"? That's a statement that is wide open to interpretation ...

(President George W. Bush, White House
Press Conference, 15 September 2006)

Introduction

Rights are connected to substantive views about the nature of persons. They are a way of expressing what it would mean to treat someone *as* a person, and as a citizen of a particular kind of state or political community. Rights also emerged in relation to a particular set of historical circumstances. They are associated with a concern about the kinds of threats that individuals face from the exercise of social and political power, by both the state and other powerful political actors. It is not just a matter of who should rule, but how there can be any legitimate coercive rule at all, given that individuals are supposed to be free and self-determining in the first place. The Grotian and Lockean emphasis on natural rights and natural law has been an influential language in which to make sense of these ideas. Here and in Chapter 5, I want to turn to two other ways of thinking about rights: dignity and recognition. The first is most closely associated with Immanuel Kant (1724–1804), and in many ways a direct continuation of some of the themes in the previous chapter. The second is most closely associated with the philosophy of G. W. F. Hegel (1770–1831) and represents an even more dramatic departure from the framework of natural law. Of course, the debate between Kant and Hegel is one of the grandest and deepest in the Western philosophical tradition and still shapes much contemporary political philosophy. I cannot hope to do any justice to it here. But I do want to explore their very different – and at the same time, in some moments, overlapping – approaches to the nature of rights, as well as the role rights play in their broader political theories.

Kant, in many ways, represents a view about the nature of rights against which the "naturalistic" approach I defended in Chapter 1 is most strongly opposed. His emphasis on the derivation of moral duty from pure practical reason, and the way this subsequently shapes his political theory, means that his approach is much less amenable to the historically informed and dynamic conception of rights I attempt to defend. This makes a close investigation of his work all the more important. But Kant has also had an enormous influence on contemporary political philosophers. John Rawls and Jürgen Habermas have been two of the leading political theorists of the late-twentieth century. Both are renowned for drawing on important themes from Kant's and Hegel's work, although both move well beyond them in significant ways too. Rights are central to both of their mature theoretical works and play an important role in their respective visions of a just society. We shall explore some of their arguments in the final section of this chapter and in Chapter 5.

Means and ends

One of Kant's most powerful ideas is that human beings possess an innate worth that can never be traded off against other ends, even ends we might find extremely desirable or valuable for all kinds of reasons. Human beings possess *dignity*;[1] or, in another formulation, human beings should never be treated as a "means" but always as "ends" in themselves. But what does this mean? How can it provide guidance for action in the complex and conflicted world of politics? One thing Kant's approach does is anchor claims about rights in what he calls "pure practical reason". People have rights, and others have duties to respect them, in virtue of a theory of justice that is derived from a particular account of the relation between reason and freedom.

In *Groundwork of the Metaphysics of Morals*, Kant writes that "What has a price can be replaced by something else as its equivalent; what on the other hand is raised above all price and therefore admits of no equivalent has a dignity" (1996: 4:434).[2] This he associates with our fundamental rational being, our *humanity*. And part of what distinguishes "humanity" from "animality" is the capacity to set oneself an end (6:392).[3] It is one thing to act out of fear, or to be constrained by others to act as a means to an end, but it is another thing to set an end for oneself: to act genuinely freely. The appeal to dignity here is not so much an appeal to a principle of action as it is to an *attitude* that we should take up towards others (see Hill 2000). Elsewhere in *Groundwork of the Metaphysics of Morals* Kant expresses it another way: "I say that the human being and in general every rational being exists as en end in itself, not merely as a means to be used by this or that will at its discretion" (4:428). Appealing to the fundamental dignity of human beings is now a familiar way in which we talk about rights. In fact, it is written into Article 1 of the United Nations Universal Declaration of Human Rights: "All human beings are born free and equal in dignity and rights". But what follows from it?

Let us take a step backwards before answering this question directly. Kant marks both the end of the kind of contractarianism we discussed in relation to Grotius and Locke, and a new chapter in its development. Like his seventeenth-century predecessors, he thinks there is a valid, universally binding principle of right, which is accessible to us and against which human action and human social and political orders can and should be judged. But unlike the natural lawyers, he does not appeal to any kind of empirical conditions for its justification – such as prudential self-interest or happiness – nor to any kind of traditional metaphysical teleology. Instead, he appeals to pure practical reason. We can derive our moral duties from reason. As *moral* agents, at least, we are subject to the laws of reason alone, not those of theology, or the traditional teleology of natural law, or even our passions. This is not to say that Kant is naive about what role the passions play in our *actual* behaviour, or that we are not shaped by our desires, inclinations, history and culture in all kinds of ways. In fact, quite the opposite; it is precisely because we *are* capable of being so influenced that we need to think about morality very differently.[4]

In *Groundwork of the Metaphysics of Morals*, Kant divides ethics into two parts: the *metaphysics* of morals consisting in principles valid *a priori* for every human being; and *practical anthropology*, an empirical study of human nature to which the principles are applied (4:388). As he makes clear, "the counterweight to all commands of duty, which reason represents to him as so deserving of the highest respect – [is] the counterweight of his needs and inclinations" (4:405). In particular, Kant thinks, we are prone to "self-conceit" (5:73), that is, to a desire to be superior over other human beings, and to use them as a means to our own purposes. (This is the same thing Hobbes referred to, among other things, as the desire for *power*, and especially the reputation for power, and is one of the many instances where Kant displays his acute reading of Hobbes; see *Leviathan*, xvii.8, x.5, viii.15).[5] It is also close to the difference Rousseau points out as between "*amour de soi*" and "*amour propre*" – between self-regard and pride – in the *Discourse on the Origins of Inequality*. In his "Idea for a Universal History with a Cosmopolitan Purpose" (1784), Kant argues that human nature develops in history through competitiveness; through our desire "for honour, power or property", which drives us to seek "status" among our fellows "whom he cannot bear yet cannot bear to leave" (8:21). In fact, it is through social antagonism and conflict that our rational capacities can develop to the point where we can recognize a moral law through which to govern our behaviour. Still, Kant thinks we need to keep discussion of the *a priori* or formal principles of morality separate from what he calls "empirical anthropology": a particular theory of human nature and history. His views changed about how precisely to integrate these two aspects, but he never ceased to think they were both necessary (albeit separate) parts of moral theory.[6]

For Kant, morality involves rational agents imposing a law on themselves that at the same time provides them with a motive to obey it. What does this mean? The basic idea is this: morality presupposes freedom. To think of myself as free is to think of myself as able to act according to self-legislated principles. To be self-governing in this way is to be autonomous (see Schneewind 1998). But what is the moral law and how can it show us what we ought to do (and not do)? In order to be consistent with our autonomy, the moral law must be formal, or *a priori*. Hence Kant's account of moral duties flowing from the "categorical imperative". To say that an imperative – a principle for action – is "categorical" is simply to say that its bindingness does not depend on the pursuit of some end set independently of it. I do not refrain from lying because I think by doing so I will go to heaven, or even for the sake of social cooperation. Rather, the bindingness of the norm is unconditional.[7] I do not lie, because that is what morality requires. Kant expresses this idea initially in the form of the "formula of the universal law": "Act only in accordance with that maxim through which you can at the same time will that it becomes a universal law" (4:442). In other words, obey only universal laws, that is, practical principles applying to all rational beings.

But this is only the beginning. Kant provides two further formulas: one that draws our attention to those affected by our actions, and another from the perspective of our being a member of a community that so wills. The second formula states: "So act that you use humanity whether in your own person or that of another, always at the same time as an end, never merely as a means" (4:429). This says that the ends of others, as long as they are morally permissible, set limits to our own and that we must respect them. In doing so we are respecting others as "ends in themselves", that is, not using them as "things" or coercing them for our own purposes. This is a good way of making sense of Kant's appeal to the inherent dignity of "humanity" with which we began above. The duties that the moral law will prescribe will – just given their form – coordinate with the rights of others (or at least, so he claims). The third is the "formula of autonomy": "the idea of the will of every rational being as a will giving universal law" (4:431), and that "all maxims from one's own lawgiving are to harmonize with a possible kingdom of ends" (4:436). This third formula instructs us to think of ourselves as members of a society of beings whose permissible ends are respected in the right way. We should act to help bring about such a community of harmonized ends.

None of these formulae are intended as moral algorithms that tell us how to act in each and every situation, whatever the context.[8]

But put together, they add up to a powerful set of rules or norms against which to test our actual or intended behaviour. In particular, they act as a set of constraints on our tendency to excuse ourselves from the demands of reason we expect of others. And they structure how we should think about our rights as well as the rights of others.

Kant makes another important but difficult distinction, this time between "right" (*Rechte*[9]) and "virtue" (*Tugend*). This is reflected in the structure of his most systematic statement of his moral and political philosophy, in *The Metaphysics of Morals*. The relation between these two parts is complex and subject to much scholarly attention.[10] For now, I want to focus on the kinds of duties that fall out of the distinction. We can think of various duties in relation to the maxims as "perfect" or "imperfect" (here Kant is drawing explicitly on the tradition we examined in Chapter 2). If a maxim cannot be conceived of as a universal law of nature without contradiction, then we have a perfect duty not to act according to it. Thus we have a perfect duty not to commit suicide, thinks Kant, and not to make false promises. If a maxim cannot be *willed* as a universal law of nature without contradiction (but can at least be conceived as such), then we have only an imperfect duty to act according to it (4:424). Thus we have an imperfect duty (to ourselves) to cultivate our talents, but this does not entail a requirement to become as perfect as we can possibly be. Similarly, we have an imperfect duty to give to charity, or help relieve others' hardship (4:422–4), but that does not entail that we have to maximize the happiness of others, or that our property can be expropriated from us on the basis of others' needs. Although we do indeed have a duty to act charitably, not everyone has a correlative right to charity from us.

For Kant, then, there is conceptual space between strict rights claims and purely supererogatory acts: that is, acting well beyond what duty calls for. This means that Kant can explain why we have duties to work not only towards a strictly rights-respecting society (which might be just, but also selfish and mean-spirited), but also to cultivate certain dispositions and act in ways that promote a more compassionate civil society (see e.g. O'Neill 1996: 143–5). This distinction between perfect and imperfect duties will be important for our discussion of human rights in Chapter 8. We shall soon return to the relation between rights, virtue and the state.

Kantian civil society

How does morality relate to the establishment of civil society and the rule of law: to politics? On the one hand, Kant is faced with a familiar question we encountered in our discussion of Hobbes and Locke. If human beings are fundamentally free and equal, how can they be legitimately subject to coercion? It should be clear now that Kant cannot help himself to the kind of argument Hobbes makes about the genesis and legitimacy of the state, namely, that it provides a solution to the assurance problem in the state of nature by creating incentives for people to act "morally". And this raises the very difficult question about the ultimate relation between morality and politics in Kant, or more precisely, between morality and *Right*.[11]

The political upshot of Kant's general moral view is something like this: if I am autonomous in the way Kant suggests, then no other external authority – whether the state, the church or "society" – has the right (or even could) impose *moral* obligations on me.[12] In principle, at least, I am both free and able to impose moral obligations on myself and in doing so provide myself with the motive to act in accordance with them. Freedom is conceived of as *independence*: I am free in the sense that I can set my own purposes, as opposed to having them set for me. Moreover, I am only truly independent when I am not dependent on others for granting or allowing me to possess what is truly mine. If I have to depend on the benevolence of others, at least with regard to what is mine by right, then my autonomy as a moral agent is undermined.[13] (Recall Baier's point, discussed in the Introduction, about the connection between the language of rights and a refusal to beg.) Kant thinks that it follows from this view of human agents as self-governing, autonomous moral beings that social and political arrangements have to be organized in a certain way. Each of us should have the freedom in which to determine our own actions. Others should not be allowed to interfere with our moral autonomy by telling us what morality requires. Nor should they be allowed to undermine our independence by using us as a means for their own purposes (for example, by defrauding us), or depriving us of our means (by controlling our person, or harming us). To do this is to treat someone as a means to purposes other than their own: to treat them as a "thing" instead of a person.

Ethics concerns how a human being regulates her own conduct according to self-given laws, as we have seen. The theory of right, on the other hand, concerns the rational standards for externally coercive laws and the framework within which laws are applied in society. On top of this, Kant (1983) has a philosophy of history that says that over time – a *very* long time – if human beings are able to act and speak freely, we have reason to hope that the ideal embedded in his moral theory can be realized.[14] But that development is neither linear nor guaranteed.[15] A crucial different between ethical duties and political duties (imposed by right), of course, is that the latter can be coercively enforced, but the former cannot. Why? Justice has only to do with *external* relations, not internal motives. The ethical and the political share similar ends, but different motives; they are continuous, but at the same time distinct (Riley 1983: 100, 173).[16] In other words, right concerns the concrete, observable actions taken by us that affect other agents. As Kant writes:

> in this reciprocal relation of choice no account at all is taken of the matter of choice, that is, of the end each has in mind with the object he wants … All that is in question is the form … and whether the action of one can be united with the freedom of the other in accordance with universal law. (6:230)

Thus, every action is "right" Kant declares, "if it can coexist with everyone's freedom in accordance with a universal law, or if on its maxim the freedom of choice of each can coexist with everyone's freedom in accordance with a universal law" (6:230). Kantian politics does not require so much the right kind of *willing* (as Kantian morality does), but rather the right kind of *acting*, which can be achieved through various means of coercion.[17] Still, respect for persons is supposed to provide a crucial limiting condition for politics. Part of the whole point of establishing public right is to create the conditions in which people will be treated as ends and not means in their unavoidable interactions with others. (The unavoidability of our interacting with others – the fact of human proximity – is one of the crucial empirical conditions that signal a discontinuity between politics and morality. I shall soon return to this important point.)

For Kant, each of us has what he calls an "innate right" of humanity: a "right of humanity in our own person". It is this aspect of Kant's moral and political theory – grounding law and politics in the innate rights of man – that is considered to be the core of Kantian politics for many readers today. In his own day, that would seem to put him squarely on the side of those who defended the French Revolution, and especially the First Republic. In fact, although Kant clearly welcomed the *spirit* lying behind the revolution, he deplored the means that were pursued. But what does Kant mean when he says we have innate rights, and how is our having them supposed to shape politics? Each of us has the right of *independence* from others (and equal to others) innately, that is, "by nature", independently of any affirmative act to establish it (6:236–7; see also 8:290). He summarized these rights into three general categories under the "General divison of duties of rights" in the *Metaphysics of Morals*:

(1) "Rightful honour", that is, "Do not make yourself a mere means for others but be at the same time an end for them";
(2) "Do not wrong anyone", even if, Kant says, "to avoid doing so you should have to stop associating with others and shun society"; and
(3) If you cannot help associating with others, "enter into a society with them in which each can keep what is his", that is, "Enter a condition in which what belongs to each can be secured to him against everyone else".

So we do not only have an innate right to our person, which is crucial to our setting and pursuing any kind of end in the first place, but also rights to usable things and to establish various kinds of rational relations. But if we are all equally free, then how can we interact in ways that do not compromise our independence? Since we are all fundamentally free and equal, nobody should have the power to interfere with or control how I set my purposes, except in so far as it is required to preserve the freedom of others. This is *private right*: the right to make something external one's own. Kant relates it to three categories: property, contract (i.e. our capacity to transfer our rights) and status (i.e. asymmetrical but rightful relations with others, e.g. masters/servants; parents/children; teachers/students; see 6.254–5). Let us examine these ideas more closely, since they allow us to grasp Kant's conception of rights more fully.

Property, contract and status

Consider for a moment Kant's theory of property. Free beings must be able to choose objects to use for their own purposes, as means toward their ends. Kant thinks of land as a common possession of all and believes that each of us has by nature the will to use it (6:261–2). To deny the possibility of exclusive possession would be to unjustifiably restrict the freedom of persons (6:251). Kant distinguishes between "phenomenal" and "intelligible" possession. The first applies to objects we are in immediate physical contact with and control, such as the computer on which these words are being written. When something I physically possess is taken away from me or damaged against my will, I am being coerced unjustifiably. But this is also true of objects that are not in my immediate physical possession, but that form part of my "intelligible" or rational possession (of "concepts of the understanding"; 6:253) – objects secured through a relation between rational wills. That is, when I say I own something I mean this to hold even if I do not now actually have physical control of it. Thus for Kant, ownership has to do with my intention to occupy land, for example, and to bring it under my will, not with my current actual possession, or the way I have used it, or the fact that I have invested my labour in it (as was the case for Locke).[18]

However, because we share the limited space of the globe, and live unavoidably side by side, we cannot help but affect each other's actions (6:262). This is a crucial point, which I referred to above as the "fact of proximity". Pure practical reason tells us how we should interact as rational wills: exercise your freedom in a way compatible with the freedom of all. But reason also tells us, given the fact that the world is finite, that some of our actions will unavoidably limit what others would otherwise be able to do. The principle of right provides a (supposedly) formal principle for resolving those conflicts, but one informed by certain empirical facts as well. Thus, even if it is the case that I can institute rational relations with others to secure non-physical ownership, I cannot do so on the basis of my judgement *alone* as to what should be the case. My possessing something will have consequences for your freedom. As Kant puts it, "a unilateral will cannot serve as a coercive law for everyone with regard to possession that is external and therefore contingent, since that would infringe upon freedom in accordance with universal laws" (6:256). This means we are necessarily subject to the principle of right, to justice. What is wrong with remaining in the state of nature, then, is that it is a state of indeterminacy about the boundary between mine and thine (in Pippin's [2006: 432–3] phrase). We know we have to respect each other's freedom and property, but we need a mechanism for determining what that actually entails. We cannot fulfil our duty to "harm no one" (see point 2, above) without the determinacy provided by a civil order. And we cannot, *in principle*, establish unilaterally the intelligible possession that is a necessary aspect of the exercise of our freedom in a finite world we share with other agents. Unilateral judgement is incompatible with the innate rights of humanity. It is not just that we are likely to disagree over property (*contra* Locke), but that we must already be in the right relationship for my act to have significance for you.[19] I need to acquire means for my purposes, but your rights must be respected in the process (6:250–51, 6:312). These two requirements can only be satisfied in a "rightful" condition (the same holds true for contractual and "status" relations).[20]

Interestingly, Kant does allow for an intermediate stage of possession, what he calls "provisional right". In a state of nature, something may be able to be seen as mine (or thine) but only *provisionally*, that is, "in anticipation of and preparation for the civil condition". Possession in the civil condition, on the other hand, is "conclusive" (6:256–7). This idea of provisional right recurs in other places too, for example, with regard to revolution and especially in his account of the state and relations between states. The idea of provisional right points to two interesting lines of thought in Kant's political theory. First, although the moral ideal of rational politics is impossible to realize on earth, we are still obligated to try to achieve it. Justice is impossible and yet obligatory (see e.g. discussion in *Perpetual Peace*, 6:347, 6:354, 6:491).[21] Thus, just as our property rights are not optimally realized in something less than an ideal state, the same applies to our autonomy in general. And since states exist in relation to each other in a state of nature (lacking a universal omnilateral will between them), the peaceful condition between them is only ever provisional until a cosmopolitan political order can be established. (This is the main theme of *Perpetual Peace*.) But states are still obliged, albeit not to the same extent as individuals in the state of nature, to work towards the establishment of those conditions.

The second thing that provisional right suggests (and return-ing to our earlier discussion of the relation between ethics and virtue) is a point at which Kant admits that one kind of status crucial to our nature as reason-responsive beings – namely "intel-ligible possession" – can only be "realized" in a distinctively social way.[22] What is mine and thine is only *really* settled when we move into a social condition in which the general will provides the back-ground against which we are in the right kind of relationship in which to genuinely claim rights against each other. A certain kind of liberal individualism is often read into Kant, which seems to fit not only with his practical metaphysics, but with his strong anti-paternalism and emphasis on man's innate rights. But with pro-visional right, some of the crucial parameters of the private are presented as only really existing *after* a process of mutual recogni-tion and settlement by the "omnilateral" will expressed through the rule of law. This does not make him Hegel (as we shall see!), but it complicates our sense of the Kantian inheritance in contem-porary political theory.

To remain in a state of nature, then, is to subject oneself to the potential interference of others, which is to live in a way incom-patible with one's autonomy (6:255–6). It follows from our being free that being subject to the right kind of coercive authority is not only permissible but required. Being so is the only way to make our freedom mutually compatible. Thus we have a duty to enter into the civil condition (6:256). The social contract grounds the "right of human beings under public coercive laws, by which what belongs to each can be determined for him and secured against encroachment by any other" (8:289). The legitimacy of the state flows from what it does (or should do), as opposed to our having literally consented to it. To use an abstract Kantian formulation, the state as an *idea*, not as embodied in any particular empirical or historical manifes-tation, is justified in terms of its role in enabling and coordinating our freedom and, over time, the promotion of moral ends (such as peace). Political right, in general, is grounded in the natural princi-ples of respect for autonomy. The enforcement of rights, in other words, has a distinctly public character in Kant's political theory. It is not just that the private enforcement of rights is inconvenient or likely to lead to conflict (as both Hobbes and Locke make clear), but that it is fundamentally incompatible with our status as free and equal. Even if it never did lead to conflict, private enforcement is wrong; the only imposition of force compatible with our freedom is one that issues from an "omnilateral" as opposed to unilateral will. The only rights I can have are those compatible with a system of rights in which your rights are guaranteed as well, including their mutual enforcement.

But Kant also says that we have a duty to establish not just any common authority, but rather a *republican* political order, one compatible with our innate rights. Formally he defines it as "the political principle of separation of the executive power (the government) from the legislative power" (8:352, 8:354). But it is also a regime in which the sovereign will of the people is represented to the ruling power, who are then charged with implementing it. Kant is often confusing here, because he seems to think that monarchy is, in fact, much more conducive to republican rule than either democracy or aristocracy (8:352–3).[23] Despotism has to do with the corruption of the general will, not a particular form of government. It is the "high-handed management of the state by laws the regent has himself given, inasmuch as he handles the public will as his private will" (8:352).

Our innate rights, thinks Kant, help explain the kind of powers the state has, as well as the nature of our obedience to it. For one thing, the justification has to be formal, in order to be universal. Free persons (ideally conceived), concerned to protect their freedom, can only ever agree (ideally, not actually) to enter a civil condition in which their freedom is secure.[24] So a state is never justified in seeking to promote the happiness of its citizens, but only their freedom (8:290–91). Nor is a state justified in appropriating the property of its citizens to help meet the needs of landless or poorer citizens. As we have seen, as a matter of private right, no one can be made to serve as the means for another, just as no one has a right to means that are not already their own. As a matter of public right, the state is not justified in using me as a means for promoting social justice or substantive equality, even if I can afford it and others are in genuine need.[25] (You can see why Nozick, whom we discussed in Chapter 2, is better seen as a Kantian than a Lockean.) However, the state still needs enough authority to make the division between "mine and thine" determinate and rightful, and this ends up justifying considerable state power.

Limits to freedom: rights against the state

One thing that follows from the justification of the state, Kant claims, is that there is no right to revolution. In one sense, to insist on a right to judge the sovereign creates a regress problem: who then has the right to judge your judgement about what the sovereign has done, and so on? Nor does Kant think it is useful to look too hard at the origins of states. All states are founded on injustices of one kind or another, and it is hopeless to think that the right historical pedigree matters for evaluating legitimacy (6:299; 6:318). Kant's main point is that living in a rightful condition provides the grounds for being able to make relevant judgements about justice in the first place (6:355). To claim a right to overthrow the legal order is thus to be caught in a kind of performative contradiction; you are asking to undo the very thing that enables you to make claims about justice in the first place (6:320). More seriously, it involves retracting into the state of nature, and insisting on the unilateral imposition of your will on others, which violates their freedom. A rightful constitution is an "Idea of reason", a regulative standard against which to judge existing politics. But for it to be applied to particulars there must be procedures that respect the innate rights of all, and Kant thinks this rules out any kind of violent overthrow of the existing order (which usually ends up in disaster anyway; 8:36). Non-ideal regimes are thus forms of provisional right. We have a duty to leave open the possibility of them developing into a more rightful condition then they currently are (see Ellis 2005: ch. 4). Thus we should use our "public reason" to try to persuade the sovereign (and each other) to rule in a more enlightened fashion (8:35–42; and see below).

Does that mean that Kant thinks we are stuck with not only moderately bad rule, but really terrible rule? Do people never have the right to withdraw their consent and seek a new political order, even if they are being brutally repressed? On the one hand, Kant is simply pointing to the fact that revolutions often go terribly wrong, however noble the sentiments inspiring them. Reason can tell us what an ideal constitution consists in, but it cannot tell us how to get there (8:370). But it does not follow that *every* regime, *however* it exercises power is, *ipso facto*, legitimate. Remember that we have a duty to enter the civil condition, a duty that can be coercively enforced by others if we refuse. Although Kant does not spell it out in this way, it might be that a state that is systematically oppressing its citizens exists in a state of nature in relation to *them*, and therefore the oppressed have not only a right but a duty to bring that state or ruler into a "rightful condition".[26] In really terrible circumstances, even provisional right might be absent, and individuals would be justified in acting to protect themselves against violations of their innate rights. (States cannot do this to other states, of course, since the international sphere, for Kant, is a state of nature that lacks the conditions for a genuinely omnilateral will.) However, at this point we have probably reached the outer limits of Kant's form of social contract theory. Unlike Locke, as we saw in Chapter 3, Kant does not see political power as something delegated by individuals, acting collectively, when they establish civil society. The sovereign and the people do not mutually subject themselves and then hold each other accountable. Rather, power is instituted when the civil constitution is created, and it is only against this background that people can make effective judgements about their rights in the first place.

It is striking how, despite his strong anti-paternalism and his explicit support of freedom of expression (what he calls the "public use of reason"), Kant still allows for considerable interference with and limits on people's civil liberties.[27] The state is justified, for example, in restricting the expression of various aspects of people's "private" reason. And for Kant this includes not only private firms, but most public institutions as well, for example, the military, religious institutions, schools and universities. The public realm involves only those interactions between citizens free of necessity and arbitrary differences. The public use of reason – as a kind of ideal form of judgement on earth – is "as a scholar before the entire public of the world of readers" (8:37). In other words, the public use of reason must be as impartial as possible, and at arm's length from all those particular interests and inclinations that can be an effect of one's position or affiliations in society. And for this to be so, certain conditions must hold. Hence the notorious distinction he made between "active" and "passive" citizens. The former are entitled to full citizenship rights, and the latter to civil but not political rights (i.e. rights of participation). Passive citizens are those least able to exercise public reason because they lack the capacities and means to do so; Kant includes women, farm labourers and manual workers among them.[28] The ideal state, at least in principle, is open to anyone who achieves active status, and some passive citizens might yet become active over time. But some, including women, can never do so, however much their basic needs may be taken care of. Once again we find Kant admitting that an aspect of our status as reason-responsive beings is in part a social achievement, that is, it relies on our having the right kind of opportunities and conditions in which to exercise our reason.

Kantian liberalism

The Kantian emphasis on treating human beings as ends and not means, and the accompanying idea of human dignity are today closely associated with the appeal to moral rights, and especially to human rights. Kantian liberals tend to be strong defenders of the relevance and importance of moral rights in politics. They have also continued to make use of the idea of a social contract to help generate an account of basic rights. The basic gist for these philosophers is that contractarianism provides us with a way of modelling the kind of procedure that would itself be justifiable to individuals assumed to be free and equal. In this section I want to turn to two of the most important recent examples of work in this vein, by Rawls and Habermas. I cannot hope to do justice to their immensely complex theories here, nor to the voluminous secondary literature that has grown up around them, but I do think it is useful to have a general sense of how they go about justifying rights in the context of their overall philosophical framework. Both draw on Kantian philosophical resources, albeit each in their own way. And both depart from Kant in significant respects as well. Let us begin with Rawls.

Rawls (1999b: 11) states explicitly that his theory of justice is an attempt to revive and extend social contract theory in a way that draws on Kant's philosophical framework (among others). In adopting a contractualist approach, Rawls sets up his approach against utilitarian and consequentialist arguments. Recall that consequentialism, as a meta-ethical approach, says that we should seek to maximize, or at least promote, good consequences. Utilitarianism is a particular version of consequentialism, and says we should aim to maximize utility (or desire-satisfaction, or "welfare", etc.).

One general problem for this approach is that the goal of promoting good consequences overall might license deeply problematic actions. What if, for example, welfare was increased for society as a whole if a small group of citizens were regularly humiliated or stigmatized? What if acts that harm one group of patients entail a larger group of worse off patients being better off? There are ways around some of the most egregious examples of these kinds of problems, usually by adapting various forms of "indirect" and "rule" consequentialist strategies (which we shall discuss in Chapter 6). But the worry is that even these more sophisticated approaches still do not, at some fundamental level, take the equality and freedom of each and every individual seriously enough. This is the kind of worry Rawls seeks to exploit. For him, the kind of universal-impartial-spectator view that utilitarianism requires offers the wrong kind of view about the nature of society. We cannot approach the problem of what is right for society as a whole from the perspective of an impartial spectator who considers society as if it were a single agent for whom the satisfaction of its own desires should be maximized (*ibid*.: 23–4). To think of people in this way is to fail to "take seriously the plurality and distinctness of individuals" (*ibid*.: 26).

What Rawls takes over from Kant, then, are two very broad themes: first, the regulative idea of our moral personality as fundamentally free and equal, as well as "reasonable" and "rational";[29] and secondly, the idea of the social contract as an ideal procedure for identifying universal norms of justice, including basic rights.

Any set of social and political institutions to which we might be subject must be compatible with the common moral identity human beings share as free and equal. And thus, just as we saw with Kant, the justification of the exercise of political power must be compatible with it too. Of first importance for Rawls is paying adequate moral attention to the "higher-order" interests people have in being able not only to form and pursue a particular conception of the good, but also to stand back from, revise or even abandon that conception in favour of a new one. When we are thinking about justice what matters is protecting the capacities people have for making choices at all, as opposed to the content of the choices themselves (although they will have to be exercised always within the context of just social institutions). Having said that, Rawls recognizes the enormous impact society and its institutions have on what we are able to do with our lives, even when we are acting freely. In fact, the whole reason why we *need* a theory of justice in the first place is to help regulate what Rawls calls the "basic structure" of society (see Rawls 1999b: 6–10): that complex of social, political, economic and legal institutions that shape our lives in all kinds of significant ways. So the kinds of rights a theory of justice will promote and protect will be those shaped by the "Kantian conception" of the person Rawls adopts, as well as the enormous influence the basic structure of society has on our prospects for living a decent life.

Rawls (1993: Lecture III) refers to the process whereby we determine what principles of justice would be compatible with individuals so conceived as a form of "Kantian constructivism", and later "political constructivism". We do not have access to an independently knowable and verifiable order of moral value, and so we need to construct our principles on the basis of certain conceptions of the person and society. But this does not mean giving up entirely on the idea of there being an objective set of ethical principles in the first place (at least in relation to justice and politics). Instead, a moral conviction will be objective on this view "if reasonable and rational persons who are sufficiently intelligent and conscientious in exercising their powers of practical reason would eventually endorse those convictions, when all concerned know the relevant facts and have sufficiently surveyed the relevant considerations" (2000: 245).[30]

Rawls thinks principles of justice are constructed out of both the rational and the reasonable. The "reasonable" for Rawls is a complex (and often confusing) notion, but involves, basically, our not only accepting inevitable disagreement over the ultimate nature of the good (which is the product of the free exercise of human reason), but also having a sense of justice.[31] The reasonable is prior to the rational in the sense that any principles of justice that might emerge from a constructivist procedure will involve something more than being simply the product of rational choice or bargaining. That is, Rawls is not trying to derive principles of justice from the idea of rationality itself. Thus substantive ideas about the person – as free and equal, rational and reasonable – structure the design of the process through which the principles of right (of justice) are supposed to emerge.

The key innovation Rawls offers within the social contract tradition is using the thought experiment of the "original position" to model the consequences of our taking seriously the moral identity of persons as free and equal. This device is used to justify the principles of justice, including identifying basic moral rights.[32] It is "procedural" because justice is whatever emerges from suitably designed procedures, as opposed to mapping some independently established order of value. The idea is by now familiar: imagine yourself stripped of basic information about, for example, your social position (rich or poor?), natural talents (Pete Sampras or Homer Simpson?), and even your conception of the good (Catholic, atheist or aesthete?). In seeking to regulate the basic structure of society according to principles of justice, participants – acting as representative citizens – must choose from behind this "veil of ignorance". Rawls argues that, given these constraints, the participants would choose two principles of justice: one guaranteeing equal basic liberties (including basic civil rights of freedom of speech, movement, association, etc.), and a second (the "difference principle"), which allows for inequalities, but only if they are required for improving the situation of the worst off. Moreover, they would make it so that the first principle has "lexical priority" over the second (1999b: 53–4). The basic liberties of the first principle are accorded special priority, according to Rawls, because they constitute important goods that we all require whatever (reasonable) conception of the good we might have. They should never be traded off against other goods, even other "primary goods", including economic well-being.[33]

What Rawls actually writes is this:

> Each person has an equal claim to a fully adequate scheme of equal basic rights and liberties, which scheme is compatible with the same scheme for all, and in this scheme the equal political liberties, and only these liberties, are to be guaranteed fair value.
> (1993: 5)

So, first, Rawls is defending the importance of a basic *scheme* of rights and liberties, not liberty as such.[34] And he is marking out a specific core of rights and liberties that deserve to be protected, not just individual rights as such. Still, in *A Theory of Justice*, Rawls aligns his defence of the basic liberties with the idea of natural rights along one dimension. Each member of society is thought to have an inviolability founded on justice. And this status is not something contingent on social recognition or legal norms. The capacity for a moral personality is sufficient for being entitled to equal justice, and this also explains the weight accorded to basic liberties in the theory: "Thus justice as fairness has the characteristic marks of a natural rights theory" (1979b: 442–3 n.30; cf. 2001: 42–50). But Rawls's conception of the core or scheme of basic rights and liberties is still very broad, especially given the general basis on which they are justified and his acceptance of pluralism as an avoidable condition for any conception of justice applicable to a modern democratic society.

It is interesting to note what Rawls *does not* include in this list of basic rights: private property (1999b: 242; 1993: 298, 338). Although people clearly have the freedom to own property, property rights are not themselves accorded the same status as freedom of speech, worship or even freedom to choose one's employment. As Thomas Nagel (2003: 68) has crisply summarized it, individual property rights are the consequence, and not the foundation, of the justice of economic institutions.[35] This is in part because Rawls does not think people are necessarily entitled, on account of some kind of pre-institutional conception of desert, to the product of their own labour. You are entitled to the fruits of your efforts, of course, but only in the context of a just set of rules arranged so as to benefit the worst off and not just you (Rawls 1999b: 88–9). You do not deserve your natural advantages or talents any more than you deserve the disabilities or incapacities you inherit; they are, as Rawls puts it, "arbitrary" from a moral point of view (*ibid.*: 104; see also *ibid.*: 74). Thus Rawls is very far removed from the kind of libertarian fundamentalism about property rights we explored in Chapter 2.

Finally, Rawls says that in relation to the first principle, all citizens should be "confident in the possession and exercise" of their basic liberties, and that the basic *political* liberties are to be guaranteed "fair value" (*ibid.*: 194–206; 1993: 327–9). What does this mean? It is not enough that the basic liberties are legally recognized, but they must also be secure. Rawls never really spells out what would constitute adequate security for the overall scheme of basic liberties, but he does have more to say on the "fair value" of the political liberties. The political liberties only have fair value if their worth to all citizens – their usefulness – whatever their social or economic position, is "approximately equal", or "sufficiently equal", in the sense that everyone has a fair opportunity to hold public office and influence the outcome of a political decision (1993: 327; 2001: 149). Where the political liberties have "fair value" for only a few, just background institutions are unlikely to be created or sustained. As an example, Rawls mentions the problem of campaign finance in the United States (1993: 328; 2001: 149–50). The vast amounts of money given to and spent by political candidates distorts the ability of citizens to exercise their political rights effectively because of the enormous influence fundraising exerts on the political process. To deliver the "fair value" of the political liberties in this context may well require restricting the amount of money that can be donated by individuals or groups in a political campaign, or raised by the political parties. Here we see a potential clash within the scheme of liberties between, say, freedom of speech or the press (given the need to restrict donations, etc.) and certain political liberties, something that Rawls accepts will require balancing (2001: 250).[36]

So the basic liberties identified in the first principle are linked to the particular conception of the person and its two moral powers outlined in the "Kantian conception of the person". As Rawls puts it, "these liberties and their priority are to guarantee equally for all citizens the social conditions essential for the adequate development and the full and informed exercise of [their moral powers]" (1993: 332; 2001: 45). These include freedom of thought and expression (in relation to the first), and liberty of conscience and freedom of association (in relation to the second). The significance of these liberties is explained by reference to the two "fundamental cases" of the moral powers. To deny or restrict them would, thinks Rawls, make social cooperation on the basis of mutual respect and recognition of the basic freedom and equality of citizens impossible (1993: 337). They are crucial to the process of developing a just political procedure, which will then result in further specifications and elaborations of other liberties and rights (including concerning property and the ownership of the means of production) (*ibid.*: 339–40). Rawls is clearly Kantian in his insistence that social institutions are to be judged from the perspective of their compatibility with protecting and advancing what Kant called people's "rightful honour" (see § "Property, contract and status, above) and what

Rawls calls their moral powers.[37] Taking up the perspective of the social contract – a distinctly public perspective – is supposed to enable the exercise of state coercion to be made compatible with citizens' freedom and equality, for citizens are then bound by laws of which they are, in some significant sense, the author.

In setting up the derivation of principles of justice in this way, however, including the justification of moral rights, Rawls is also moving away from Kant in at least three ways. First, as Brian Barry (1989) has pointed out, Rawls ends up trying to marry two different senses of justice present in the social contract tradition: justice as impartiality and justice as mutual advantage. These represent two ways of capturing both the unconditionality and conditionality of justice.[38] For Kant, the just person relates to the requirements of justice in the spirit of the categorical imperative. But for Rawls and other social contract theorists, justice is also conditional; people should be ready and willing to act justly, but only when they can be reasonably assured that others are so willing to act as well. Rawls defines one of the main ideas of his theory as when people engage in a:

> mutually advantageous cooperative venture according to rules, and thus restrict their liberty in ways necessary to yield advantages for all, those who have submitted to those restrictions have a right to a similar acquiescence on the part of those who have benefited from their submission.   (1999b: 96)[39]

In fact, the willingness to form conditional relationships of mutual benefit and restraint is part of what Rawls calls a "reasonable moral psychology" (1993: 86). This acceptance of conditionality in relation to the disposition to act justly moves us some way from Kant's views. Modern theories of justice tend to hover much more explicitly than Kant ever did between the hypothetical and the categorical when it comes to the motivation to act justly.

Secondly, Rawls's theory is not a comprehensive account of morality, but more narrowly what he calls a political conception of justice. Nor is the account of practical reason meant to appeal to all possible audiences everywhere. Instead, it is specifically an account of *public* reason, aimed at those who are "ready to propose principles and standards as fair terms of cooperation and to abide by them willingly, given the assurance that others will do likewise" (*ibid.*: 49). Those "others" are fellow citizens of a democratic society, and the kind of reason appealed to are those "characteristic of a democratic people" (*ibid.*: 213). But democratic societies are also characterized by "reasonable pluralism" and that means we cannot simply appeal to shared social norms, or to what Rawls calls "comprehensive views", that is, a comprehensive set of moral ideals meant to inform how people should live their lives in all of its aspects, both public and private.

Thirdly, Rawls's appeal to our shared moral identity as free and equal (and rational and reasonable) is not grounded in transcendental idealism, but rather in the "shared fundamental ideas implicit in the public political culture" of a liberal democratic society (*ibid.*: 100). Rawls thinks that his conception of justice is "political, not metaphysical" in this sense. So instead of appealing to our "*nature* as a moral person" (1999b: 503), he appeals instead to those "fundamental ideas viewed as latent in the public political culture of a democratic society" (1993: 175). And it is here that we find the idea of *citizens* as free and equal on which to construct our now *political* conception of justice. The political conception of moral personality need not, thinks Rawls, involve questions about the ultimate metaphysical doctrine of self. It might well be that we do not need agreement on the ultimate metaphysical story about persons to construct an adequate theory of justice for modern societies. However, it is no small irony that in turning to those ideas latent in the public political culture in order to avoid the problem of metaphysics, Rawls might have actually made things harder for himself rather than easier. For it is not clear that support for his conception of the moral identity of democratic citizens, or the content of the two principles, can indeed be found "latent" in the public culture of modern liberal democracies.[40] One is certainly hard-pressed to find his views about the difference principle, or the "fair value" of the political liberties (and especially his scepticism about desert) deep in the cultural DNA of Western liberal democracies today.

The general effect of Rawls's increasing constriction of the scope and range of the principles of justice, and of practical public reason itself, has been to also make the justification of moral rights more restricted, and tied more closely to particular historical and cultural conditions. In the absence of those ideas central to the political conception of justice being latent in the public culture of a political community, it is unjustified to impose on it a political conception of justice.[41] This makes Rawls's overall approach "more Rousseauian than Kantian, more civic than cosmopolitan" (O'Neill 2003: 353). This has interesting consequences for his approach to human rights. We shall return to this problem in Chapter 8.

Habermas: discursive rights

Consider, finally, the work of Habermas. Like Rawls, he too seeks to socialize and make less abstract the universalizability test embodied in the Kantian categorical imperative.[42] For Habermas, valid norms are those *intersubjectively* constituted norms that participants in an "ideal speech situation" would converge on. In one sense, Habermas is arguing that deep in the structure of our conventional modes of communication lie the (intersubjective) grounds for redeeming our moral claims on each other. This is a striking combination of Kantian and Hegelian insights.[43]

Habermas's great innovation is thus to tie the emergence of valid moral norms, including claims about rights, to a sophisticated account of discourse theory. Very briefly, for Habermas, the discourse principle ("D") states that "just those action norms are valid to which all possibly affected persons could agree as participants in rational discourses" (1996: 107).[44] Valid norms are those that can be freely accepted by all those affected by them.[45] The deeper claim he is making is about the relationship between morality and what he calls "communicative rationality". The foundations of morality, such as they are, are actually located deep in the structure of "communicative action"; they are built into the structure of practical discourse. "D" sits, as it were, prior to both law and morality, and is meant as a model of legitimization that cuts across the whole range of discourses Habermas identifies (moral, ethical and "strategic") (see Habermas 1993; on societal rationalization see 1987: 153–97). The minute I commit myself to engaging in open and rational communication, I am committing myself to a set of basic norms to do with equality, impartiality and universality. This is why morality is said to be implicit in the transcendental conditions of rational communication. Communicative action involves our coordinating our actions and plans with others on the basis of consensus rather than force, claims that all concerned could accept as valid and binding.

It is distinct from "strategic action" in so far as the latter involves my simply trying to get you to do what I want so I can achieve my aims. If I want to buy your house for less than its market value than I might try to trick you into selling, say by fabricating some rumour about an impending highway to be built nearby, or by threatening you with heavy-handed tactics if you do not agree to my offer. In acting communicatively, on the other hand, I seek to harmonize my plans with yours on the basis of our coming to have a common understanding of the situation we are in.

The notion of our coming to a common understanding is crucial. To reach this involves my being willing, when challenged, to provide a warrant for the claims I am making (*ibid*.: 302). The idea of normative validity is implicit in communicative action. This validity can only be redeemed, Habermas argues, through "practical discourses" among the social actors concerned; that is, through an actual discourse among the affected parties (see Habermas 1990). Thus every valid norm must fulfil the condition that "all affected parties can accept the consequences and the side effects its general observance can be anticipated to have for the satisfaction of everyone's interests" (1984: 65, 93). This principle of universalization (U) is implicit in moral argumentation itself. By engaging in communicative action at all I am presupposing, if only implicitly, the validity of certain norms that can only be tested through argumentation.[46] Principles U and D thus provide Habermas with a powerful set of tools with which to approach basic questions in moral and political philosophy. They offer a distinctive synthesis of a Kantian emphasis on universalizability and a Hegelian and pragmatist emphasis on the relation between normativity and intersubjectivity.

What does this mean for a theory of rights? Well, the rights we have will be those that are the product of deliberation between individuals who see themselves, first of all, as free and equal. Habermas wants to avoid making any presumption about there being a set of pre-political moral rights that are imposed on, or preloaded into, the mutual justification of our political arrangements. Here he echoes some of the remarks we made in the Introduction and Chapter 1 about rights being tools constructed by people committed to addressing particular problems or threats. First, it is not clear how moral rights conceived as sitting independently of the discourse principle could be justified. And secondly, to appeal to such a notion would be to pre-empt what Habermas calls the "public autonomy" of citizens, taken as authors of the laws to which they are subject. It would make the legitimacy of the law far too removed from the processes of democratic forms of will-formation that Habermas thinks are required as a source of legitimacy in complex, pluralistic societies such as our own. (This was a problem, you will recall, that we encountered in our discussion of Kant's rational idea of the social contract.) Democracy is not subordinate to a system of rights, but nor are rights simply whatever a particular group of people thinks they are. How does Habermas balance these two claims?

To begin with, like Rawls, Habermas is concerned to show how the norms and rules that govern human interaction not only can be justified to individuals conceived as free and equal, but also are stable. Rawls, as we have seen, turns to the forms of "overlapping consensus" available, to varying degrees, in the public political culture of a liberal democracy. Habermas, on the other hand, turns to law. In complex modern societies, it is the institutionalized procedures of legitimate law-making that mediate between the products of the diffuse networks of "discursive opinion formation" in civil society, and the collectively binding decisions of the state. Legal norms are supposed to supplement moral norms by helping to overcome the inherent indeterminacy and motivational uncertainty that accompany the latter, all the while remaining "reflexive" and open to moral argumentation. The question, then, is how can the law be legitimate in light of the account of communicative ethics outlined above? In *Between Facts and Norms*, which provides his most complete response to these questions, Habermas introduces a principle of democracy alongside his principle U: "Only those juridical statutes may claim legitimate validity that can meet with the agreement of all legal consociates in a discursive law-making process that in turn has been legally constituted" (1996: 110).

Parallel to this interdependency between legitimate law-making and the discourse principle is the claim that democracy and the system of rights are also complementary or, as he puts it, "co-original" (see e.g. *ibid.*: 88–9). What does this mean? The basic idea is to try to explore the conceptual presuppositions inherent within the idea of a legitimate rule of law, which means exploring the nature of rights. First, Habermas claims, rights do not presuppose social atomism: the view that society is made up of self-sufficient individuals who have contracted with each other for mutual advantage. In fact, for Habermas, the upshot of his discursive approach is that individual rights rest ultimately on *inter-subjective* foundations, not atomist ones: rights "presuppose collaboration among subjects who recognize one another, in their reciprocally related rights and duties, as free and equal citizens" (*ibid*.: 88).[47] In other words, basic rights are not best understood as *natural* rights independent of any legal or social form. They are something we mutually confer on one another in so far as we decide (a) to regulate our common life via positive law, and (b) in so doing, recognize each other as free and equal. Rights are not "given", in other words, prior to the self-determining practices of citizens. However, the discourse principle *is* given, just in so far as it is built into the conditions of communicative association in general and into the legal medium as such (*ibid*.: 128). It is the "inter-penetration" of the medium of law and the discourse principle that explains the (logical) genesis of the system of rights, and in which "public and private autonomy" is brought into a relation of mutual dependence (*ibid*.: 119–21).[48]

We can get a clearer sense of what this means by looking briefly at the kinds of rights or, more precisely, the kinds of *categories* of rights Habermas thinks are implied by this logical genesis (*ibid*.: 126ff.). There are five: (i) equal individual liberties; (ii) rights determining the status of political membership; (iii) rights to equal protection under law; (iv) rights to equal political participation; and (v) social and economic rights. The first three are close to the standard set of basic liberal rights, similar to what Rawls has covered in his first principle of justice. These rights, such as the freedom of speech, religion and association and to legal protection and due process, refer to what Habermas calls the *private* autonomy of citizens. These rights are conceptually presupposed in the attempt to generate a legal system compatible with an association of citizens taken to be free and equal. Category (iv), on the other hand, points to our *public* autonomy as authors of law, and helps to secure it by protecting and promoting our access to political participation. This category is required in order to institutionalize the democratic elaboration of the specific content of the others, which Habermas thinks will always be required. The last category, thinks Habermas, is implied by the first four as providing for the conditions required for the effective opportunity to exercise our rights.

This system of rights is thus constitutive of the legal medium, and yet will always have to be specified and elaborated by citizens in a politically autonomous manner in light of their own particular traditions and history. It is the complementarity between U and D, and the interdependency between "public" and "private" autonomy, that enables Habermas – or so he claims – to avoid the perils of embracing either legal positivism or natural law, or choosing between human rights and popular sovereignty. So the particular content of the system of rights will vary considerably across time and space. When we attempt to justify discursively a particular scheme or system of rights, what we are doing is claiming that the legal enactments of rights x, y and z are morally valid, that is, acceptable in principle to all those affected by them. We need both moral argument (via the discourse principle) and the medium of law (via the principle of democracy) to realize rights. The legal positivists and the natural lawyers are both wrong in claiming to explain wholly the nature of rights; our basic rights are not pre-political, nor are they exclusively the product of an effective sovereign. You cannot have rights without an effective legal order. But that legal order will lack legitimacy without the effective participation of those subject to it. And effective participation by citizens will be lacking not only without the right to participation, but also without the protection of citizens' basic individual liberties to make such participation effective. Finally, we could argue that the legitimacy of the democratic procedures will also depend on citizens enjoying certain substantive rights not only against state interference (hence the importance of rights to private property, freedom of speech and privacy, etc.), but also to the material means to exercise their rights effectively, for example, to welfare, or to a basic income.[49] Although Habermas (and Rawls) would not necessarily put it this way, the rights central to a democratic order are thus both procedural and substantive.

Conclusion: two problems

Contractarianism and discourse ethics provide two powerful frameworks for thinking about the kinds of rights people should have, as well as about justice more broadly. I want to conclude by pointing to two broad criticisms of these frameworks that look forward to the chapters to come, and back to some of the issues raised in earlier chapters.

The first criticism is that social contract theory presupposes atomism: the view that society is nothing other than a means for individuals to realize their particular desires, whatever they happen to be. A belief in the importance of individual rights is often taken to signal the acceptance of this kind of atomist ontology (see e.g. Taylor 1985e[50]). Such a critique has been an important theme of political "communitarianism". Can contractarianism and its justification of moral rights account for the social dimension of our political experience? Must it be saddled with the thin gruel of methodological individualism and rational choice theory? The short answer is no, and I think we have provided enough above in our discussion of Kant and Rawls to see why. But we shall explore some more sophisticated versions of this worry in Chapter 5. The purpose is not entirely critical. One important outcome will be to explore an account of the nature of rights that does not rely mainly on the conceptual tools of contractualism, Kantian or otherwise. Here the claim will be that in order to treat persons adequately *as persons*, it is not enough to appeal to the Kantian idea of mutual justification, as important as that is. We need a richer conception of the good that can help explain the point of the rights we ascribe to each other, as well as the goods we seek to distribute.

The second broad set of concerns lies with the presumptions that contractarian thinkers make about the parties to the contract, or exactly who participates in practical discourses. This returns us to some of the themes we explored in Chapter 2. What is distinctive about modern social contract theory, as we have seen, is its proceduralism. Most of these arguments start from an initial choosing situation that is structured in such a way that principles of justice, including rights, can be justified. The most influential forms of modern contractarianism have also been constructivist; that is, principles of justice are valid not according to some independently established order of value, or as against a set of pre-political natural rights, but emergent from procedures that start from certain basic premises widely shared, out of which more determinate principles are "constructed". Now there are important differences between the various modes of contractarian thought. Some are more Hob-

besian than others, focused as they are on deriving political principles almost exclusively from mutual advantage. Others are more
Kantian, in so far as they seek to derive political principles from
claims about fairness or impartiality. And finally, some involve a
mixture of both impartiality and mutual advantage, as we find in
Rawls and Habermas.

The problem lies in the extent to which any such theory presupposes that the parties to the contract, or participants in the
discourse, are actually able to offer the kind of reciprocity that
contractarian arguments require. The purpose of social cooperation
is said to be mutual advantage and reciprocity. Rawls's fundamental
question, remember, is: "what is the most appropriate conception
of justice for specifying the terms of social cooperation between
citizens regarded as free and equal, and as normal and fully cooperating members of society over time?" (1993: 20). But what exactly
does it mean for a participant to be "normal and fully cooperating", and why should our principles of justice, and the ascription
of rights, depend on such an assumption?

Hume once suggested (1973: 190–91) that if there were a "species of creatures" intermingled with us, we being radically inferior
in strength ("both of body and mind") and unable to offer anything
by way of reciprocal exchange, then it was not clear what *justice*
had to do with our relations with them, as much as other "laws of
humanity" and "gentle usage" might apply.[51] For Hume, justice
arose only where it was mutually advantageous to the parties, and
the alternative of not having rules of justice was much worse than
having them. Justice has a point, in other words, only where what
he called the "circumstances of justice" obtain: namely, "the selfish-
ness and confin'd generosity of men, along with scanty provision
nature has made for his wants" (Hume 1978: 495; see also 1973:
188). But it would be very odd, not to say deeply disconcerting, if
it turned out that one of the most influential ways of thinking about
justice was not applicable to the scenario Hume describes (see Barry
1989: 162–3). However, Rawls takes Hume's claim about the relevance of the "circumstances of justice" very seriously indeed. And
both Rawls and Habermas see the disposition to act justly as conditional on others being willing to act in similar ways. The worry
is that the presumptions they make about what is required to be a
genuine participant in the construction and interpretation of justice

ends up privileging norms and rules – including the ascription or interpretation of rights – that are insufficiently inclusive or acceptable to all those subject to them.

What are these assumptions? For Rawls, as we saw, persons are assumed to be "rational and reasonable", that is, capable of pursuing their own conception of the good and having a sense of justice. They are also presumed to be capable of engaging in relations of mutual advantage. And finally, they are presumed to be capable of justifying their moral and political beliefs to others in particular ways. Although Rawls claims the capacities required for equal citizenship are of a sufficiently minimal kind, they still establish a certain threshold and idealization of rationality. It means, for example, that non-human animals are excluded from relations of justice proper. And it may mean that human beings with severe mental impairments, or severe physical disabilities, are marginalized in the process too.[52] How can a severely disabled person be expected to engage in relations of mutual advantage if there is no way they can engage in productive activity that would be commensurable to that of the non-disabled?[53] If the capacity for rights – my right to have rights – is tied to capacities associated with my participation in a "mutually advantageous cooperative venture", then this suddenly looks like much more than a minimal threshold of competency ascribable to all. This is a problem for those with severe disabilities, but not just them. All of us are subject to variations in our capacities over time; we get sick, we age, our capabilities diminish and we struggle with unexpected events and misfortune. But the larger point has to do with the way we conceive of the basic conception of human agency shaping our theories of justice and rights. Kantian liberals put autonomy at the heart of their political theory. Autonomy is a complex ideal. It need not entail heroic self-sufficiency, or acting only on the grounds of beliefs, the formation of which is also strictly autonomous (see e.g. Wall 1998; Appiah 2005). But the assumptions we make about the capacities of citizens matters. They shape Rawls's list of basic primary goods, for example, in the way that they are supposed to be those goods that all normal (politically) autonomous adults require in order to exercise their moral powers and cooperate for mutual advantage. And they shape the way the basic liberties are protected, lexically, in relation to addressing social and economic inequality.

If we were to modify our assumptions about the Kantian conception of the person – for example, by admitting greater variation in the equality of capacity of the parties to the contract, or by dropping the assumption that the purpose of social cooperation is mutual advantage – then the conception of justice would change along with our conceptions of rights. We might think that greater attention needs to be paid to the variation in capabilities of individuals to act in meaningful ways over time, given the kinds of frailties that human beings suffer from, as opposed to measuring equality in terms of Rawls's narrower list of primary goods. And we might think that the moral and legal rights people ought to have should be justified in relation to the nature of these capabilities. Finally, we might think that both of these moves will require offering a different political conception of the person altogether, and yet one that still captures the ascription of dignity that remains a powerful legacy from Kant in modern political thought (see Nussbaum 2000).[54]

Similar concerns have been raised about Habermas's emphasis on communicative rationality. One set of worries has to do with the underlying logic-of-development arguments that Habermas (1990) makes about the nature of modernity and the emergence of the "decentred" worldview as the highest stage of individual and social development. If the decentered subject is posited as the universal subject, and yet the criteria whereby its universality is determined are not impartial, then the validity of the claim is in question (see Tully 1999). Other critics have argued that in emphasizing communicative rationality as the main currency of moral and political discourse, Habermas discounts other perspectives and forms of communication that are also important politics.[55] This is connected to another set of worries about the distinction between communicative and strategic rationality, as well as between normative and evaluative discourses (between the language of the right and the good). These distinctions not only privilege particular perspectives on justice (as opposed to being genuinely impartial), but are also unsustainable given the complex intertwining of strategic, symbolic and rational modes of communication in politics. Relations of power suffuse communicative interaction such that even a formal distinction between "communicative" and "strategic" communication seems misguided.

Feminist critics have suggested that the assumptions about autonomy that lie at the heart of discourse ethics are gendered, often relying as they do on a separation between public and private, and an overly abstract conception of the establishment of the validity of norms through discourse.[56] Seyla Benhabib (1992) has summarized this tendency as taking up the perspective of a "generalized other" as opposed to "concrete others". This prevents a suitably rich and interactive form of universalism from emerging that would reflect more genuinely the experiences and views of those subject to the effects of the "basic structure" of society. One aspect of what equality involves is that each individual is owed an effort at "seeing the world from his perspective", and this is certainly one way of making sense of the force of Habermas's discourse principle (Williams 1973b: 236–7). But there are different ways of realizing this commitment. One way is to abstract from our particular identities, as well as those of others, and imagine ourselves as subject to the kinds of rules and norms we are proposing or evaluating. But another way is to try much harder to imagine how our conceptions are perceived from the perspective of "concrete others", given their particular social and historical positions. This might expose hitherto unnoticed exclusions or partialities built into dominant perspectives, just in so far as we become more aware of what we are actually asking others to do. More radically, it might entail that achieving the moral point of view itself not only requires abstraction, but also involves engaging more directly with particularity and remaining open to deeper reformulations of the underlying claims of validity and normativity (but see Habermas 1995).

Recall, for a moment, the example of the rights of indigenous peoples mentioned in Chapter 1. One way of interpreting what the recognition of their claims entails is not only an appeal to the extension to their case of general principles such as equality, non-discrimination and self-determination, but also a profound reinterpretation of the grounds of those principles, and the introduction of new conceptual schemes and frameworks. The assertion of their rights in this way consists of an exercise – however limited and constrained – of their self-government and capacities for agency that were previously denied. In so doing, the "we" of Canadian or Australian popular sovereignty is radically pluralized. If popular sovereignty and innate right are "co-original", as Habermas argues, then the pluralization of one cannot help but pluralize and reshape the other. The interests and perspectives of the participants are not simply enlarged, as if the previous interests of Canadians are held constant and then added to, but fundamentally reshaped (*pace* Benhabib 2002: 140–41).[57]

Thus John Borrows, in the course of a discussion of the impact on Aboriginal self-government of the Canadian Charter of Rights and Freedoms, argues that the underlying principles of the Charter could help First Nations. More specifically, Borrows argues that the Charter might help to create a "conversation" between the forms of equality embodied in the European languages of rights and those within indigenous traditions (1994: 170). What is striking in Borrows's argument is the alignment of three distinct modalities of politics that are often kept apart: conversation, rights and tradition. Borrows suggests that by exploiting the conjunction of the wide acceptance of rights language in the broader Canadian community, along with the conceptual and justificatory indeterminacy of rights claims themselves, they can be put to work in contributing to the emancipation as opposed to the domination of indigenous peoples. It will be no easy task, as he makes clear (1994; 2000a). But, as he argues, "retranslated and transposed by [indigenous peoples]", the language of rights can be used to "convey our meanings" (1994: 23). His specific example is the debate over sexual equality, but the general point is this: the language of rights, just like the language of citizenship (see Borrows 2000b: esp. 329–30),[58] can be retranslated and redescribed through a (genuine) conversation with tradition, and a living tradition can be reinvigorated by, and some of its vulnerable elements even gain strength from, a suitably transformed discourse of rights and citizenship (1994: 174–5).

One question is whether or not Habermas's scheme allows for such a degree of pluralization and contestation. But a more interesting question is what it means for a political theory of rights. I think it lends itself to the naturalistic analysis of rights I offered in Chapter 1. Changing the subject of rights – in this case, introducing the idea of "indigenous peoples' rights" – not only generates a demand for inclusion into an established register or discourse of rights, but can also change our understanding of the nature of that discourse more generally. I shall return to this point in Chapter 8.

5 | Recognition

I was in bondage in Missouri, too. I can't say that my treatment was bad. In one respect I say it was not bad, but in another I consider it as bad as could be. I was a slave. That covers it all. I had not the rights of man.

(Benjamin Miller, former slave, quoted in Darby 2006: 430)

Introduction

So far we have been concentrating on theories of rights that are closely aligned to the notion of law, which is not unsurprising. Right and law are indeed closely related. But there are different modes of juridical thought. We have been exploring some of these differences in our discussion of Grotius, Hobbes, Pufendorf, Locke and Kant. The differences between these philosophers are as significant, I think, as their shared commitment to the centrality of law to the language of rights, and to politics more generally. I also noted that civic humanism and republicanism (especially the neo-Roman conceptions of freedom) offered an alternative set of frameworks within which to make sense of rights, or even to displace them in favour of an emphasis on civic virtue. In this chapter we turn to yet another approach to rights, this time embodied in the philosophy of Hegel. Why read Hegel on rights? Well, for one thing, he is an important source for an influential set of critiques of modern liberalism that take aim at the centrality of individual rights (and the social contract) in their accounts of state, society and the self. We shall explore this critique below. But Hegel's arguments – as daunting as they are – are also well worth considering in their own right. He offers a comprehensive attempt to reconcile the standpoints of the individual and community, and thus to take seriously the conception of freedom lying behind our commitment to individual rights, as well as our "thicker" communal attachments. The key to his approach is his emphasis on the role that mutual *recognition* plays in the process of rights ascription. The rights we have are, in part, a function of our being recognized by others like us. On the face of it, this sounds worrying. Does this mean the only rights I have are those that others will recognize? Does a slave only have a moral right to be free, for example, if enough people in his society (or the institutions therein) "recognize" that right? The short answer is yes. But Hegel has a very long answer about why we should believe it.

Like Kant, Hegel associates freedom with *autonomy*; with the capacity to follow laws one gives oneself. And he associates personhood with the capacity for rights. Above all, like Kant, freedom is central to Hegel's political theory. The will's freedom consists in its ability to will for itself universalizable principles and norms. But there are deep differences between Kant and Hegel about the way these basic ideas are elaborated. One crucial difference is that for Hegel freedom is not something that is ultimately gained independently of our social and political embodiment in the world. In fact, it already lies before us, if only we can grasp it in the right way. Political philosophy is the attempt to comprehend the structure of institutions and norms before us in thought. And if we can do this, we can become reconciled to our social world; that is, we can come to see the social and political institutions it contains as expressive of our essence as free *persons* (which includes our capacity for rights).

Hegel's philosophical system is dazzlingly complex, and it is hard to make sense of his political thought without keeping the load-bearing structure of the wider system in mind. However, the crucial idea I want to explore is the role that *mutual recognition* plays in Hegel's account of right. It provides us with a genuinely distinctive view about the nature of rights.

Another thing Hegel offers us, perhaps surprisingly, is a distinctive way of understanding some of the key components of modern liberalism. Hegel tries to reconcile and integrate the different ways human beings conceive of their interests and their membership in various different institutions and society as a whole. As we have seen, one powerful strand of liberal thought conceives of individuals as bearers of rights antecedent to the formation of political society, which then structure and help explain the purpose for which political power is established. A liberal political order, on this account, exists as a medium for individuals to realize whatever particular interests or goals they happen to have, and political power is justified to the extent that it helps create the conditions in which those interests or desires can be realized, consistent with the freedom of others to do likewise. Now Hegel does not think this account is necessarily wrong so much as radically incomplete. Our subjective freedom is vitally important to us, and any political order we live in must recognize and protect it. In fact, this is what makes modern life fundamentally incompatible with that of antiquity: "the right of subjective freedom, is the pivot and centre of the difference between antiquity and modern times" (Hegel 1991: §124A).[1]

But rather than argue, as some liberals do, that this means that there is a fundamental conflict between the individual and community, Hegel goes on to try to show how they can be reconciled, How can we recognize the value of individuality at the same time as acknowledging its social bases? For Hegel we must be able to reconcile the individual and community, because otherwise man is fundamentally cut adrift from society, and this has serious political consequences.[2] Social contract theory and utilitarianism, two distinctly modern ways of conceiving of social and political order, take up a fundamentally instrumentalist stance towards it. That is, they conceive of society as basically a means for realizing the particular desires or interests of individuals. This approach lacks the resources, argues Hegel, for being able to explain how men can genuinely identify with their society.[3] Why does this matter? As traditional norms and institutions break down under the pressure of the demand for subjective freedom, men can end up turning to revolutionary ideology (e.g. Jacobinism), or to nationalism, or to various founding myths, as a way of helping to explain the ends of that new society and why they should be committed to it. But these alternatives are insufficient, and in many cases (e.g. Jacobinism) lead to political disaster. They do not provide the meaningful differentiations and institutions that modern society requires for modern people to identify with it. They are not, in Hegel's complex sense of the term, *rational* (*vernunftig*) enough. Thus Hegel can be seen as trying to provide an account of how we can overcome alienation that is rational and therefore compatible with our freedom, and yet also embodied in the world. We have to preserve differentiation – all the particular ways in which men identify with their families, cultures, professions, faiths, and so on – and yet also integrate these differences into a larger whole, what Hegel calls "unity within difference". He locates the emergence and meaning of rights within this broader logical and historical argument.

Spirit, freedom and right

If for Kant the primal moral scene is the self-legislating will, then for Hegel it is only one moment in a larger and more elaborate drama. Famously, this involves the working out of "spirit" (or "mind") in the world. Now, whatever spirit ultimately is,[4] it is closely related to freedom (freedom is its "essence" or "substance") (Hegel 1987: 172–3). For, on the one hand, Hegel makes it clear that individual thinkers, and philosophies as a whole, are products of particular forms of society, and in some sense conduits of spirit reconciling itself with the world (using a phrase from Guess 2005a: 46). Indeed, for Hegel the history of the world just is the progress of freedom. Spirit cannot "reconcile" itself to the world, it cannot be at home in the world (and here, crucially, Hegel means both the natural and social world), without freedom. Spirit can only realize itself in the world if certain objective conditions hold; namely that social and political institutions are organized in such a way that spirit can be at home with itself: can be free. This means that the social world actually has to have been made over in a spirit-friendly way by human action, albeit not necessarily on the basis of intentional actions by any particular group of human agents. The kinds of changes involved happen over time through the combined effect of both intended and unintended human action. *Elements of the Philosophy of Right* presents an outline of the structure of this "objective spirit", with its account of the movement between "abstract right", "morality" and "ethical life", and within the latter, between family, civil society and the state. Objective spirit is the realm of human action guided by will, wherein we pursue and realize our projects in the world. Note, however, that ultimately it too is deficient, or at least incomplete, compared to "absolute spirit", which is realized in art, religion and philosophy. This is where spirit gains its final substance and warrant. Spirit requires not only that the social world be made over in a certain way, but that it is represented to itself in the right way.

Now it is in the realm of objective spirit that we find Hegel's account of "Right": of reason being actualized in the structures of will that make up the social world. For Hegel, the basis of right lies ultimately in the development of spirit: "its precise location and point of departure is the will; the will is free, so that freedom constitutes its substance and destiny and the system of right is the realm of actualised freedom, the world of spirit produced from within itself as a second nature" (Hegel 1991: §4). Hegel is talking of the *concept* of the free will here, which is an aspect of spirit, actualized in the world over time, taking on a more appropriate expression of freedom in each case. Early on in the *Philosophy of Right*, Hegel tells us that the Idea of right involves the concept of right together with its actualization (*ibid.*: §1). "Actuality" is a technical term for Hegel, which means, basically, the achievement of a potential disclosed by reason, or the conditions that will exist when reason is fully realized in the social world (think of actuality as distinct from *reality*). For our purposes, what Hegel is suggesting is that social institutions, very broadly understood, are structures of thought and will. This might be hard to imagine in relation to the natural world, but not with regard to social and political institutions and practices. The system of right – the whole normative life of a society, including the moral beliefs, attitudes, emotions, practices and institutions that make up that particular form of life – just is "actualized freedom", a realm of freedom made actual. That is, the normative structures examined in the *Philosophy of Right*, concerning individual rights, property, the family, civil society, the state and so on, are all structures of freedom. If a system of right is justified to the extent that it can be shown that it is necessary for the expression of the free nature of the will, then this is what the *Philosophy of Right* is purporting to show about modern institutions (or, at least, those found in nineteenth-century Prussia!).

Note that this means that Hegel's conception of reason is very much material and concrete, as opposed to abstract and formal. It manifests itself in the concrete way of life – the ethos – of a particular society. And it is the job of philosophy to grasp the rational in terms of the "actual"– as a phase in the development of spirit (*ibid.*: 20–21). What Hegel means by "rational" here is important. He does not mean that something is rational if it enables us to satisfy our desires, whatever they happen to be. Something is rational when we have grasped its purpose and meaning in relation to the exercise of our freedom. When we grasp the meaning of our social institutions in this way we become "reconciled" to them. They are not real to us – they are not actual – until grasped self-consciously in this way. This also explains why political philosophy is unavoidably an *ex post facto* exercise. It can only grasp what is rational once it is actualized in a concrete form of life. It does not look to a world that ought to be, but rather tries to grasp the one in front of us that actualizes our freedom. This is (partly) what Hegel means when he writes in the Preface to the *Philosophy of Right*, that when philosophy "paints its grey in grey, a shape of life has grown old" (*ibid.*: 13). Or as Robert Brandom (2002: 45) has succinctly summarized it: tradition is lived forward but understood backward.

But where does this leave the individual subject? Are we *merely* conduits for the working out of spirit? How we answer this question will depend, in part, on what we understand spirit, ultimately, to mean, which (thankfully) is not my task here. But in many ways, Hegel's whole political theory can be seen as trying to get to grips with the nature and value of human individuality and freedom. Hegel makes clear that modern societies are different from ancient ones, and so we cannot simply adopt an ideal from ancient Greece or Rome as our own. One of the key differences between modern societies and ancient ones is the role of the market (Hegel 1991: §46R, §185, §185R, §206). The market enables people to pursue their own interests and provide for themselves. Of course it also generates serious problems, especially to do with the division of labour and poverty. A major theme of the *Philosophy of Right* is placing the economy into a wider context within civil society (see esp. §184, §185A); then civil society within the state as a whole; and then the state into an even larger historical context. But Hegel also points to another crucial difference between ancient and modern polities: modern societies acknowledge the "*right* of the subject's particularity", or the "*right* of subjective freedom" (§124R, §138A, emphasis added; see also §185R, §§260–61R). What does he mean?

"A human being counts as such", argues Hegel, "because he is a human being, not because he is a Jew, Catholic, Protestant, German, Italian etc." (§209R).[5] Freedom, ultimately, is the basis of right.[6] In fact, Hegel ties what it means to be a person in general with the capacity for rights: "Personality contains in general the capacity for right and constitutes the concept and the (itself abstract) basis of abstract and hence formal right. The commandment of right is therefore: *be a person and respect others as persons*" (§36).

Since rights are so central to my (private) personality, it follows that there are certain rights that are inalienable: my personality as such, my freedom of will, my "ethical life" and my religion (§66).[7] Hegel claims that the "alienation of personality" lies behind practices such as slavery, serfdom and disqualification from holding property. And that "alienation of intelligent rationality, of morality, ethical life, and religion", is exemplified in "superstition": that is, "when power and authority are granted to others to determine and prescribe what actions I should perform" (§66R). To claim a right is, of course, also to make a claim on others. Hegel thinks this means that the logical form of a right is restricted to the negative: do "not violate personality and what ensues from personality" (§38). Persons are ends not means, and should be treated as such (see §107). So far so Kantian. On this account, right has to do mainly with our external freedom in relation to others. But lying behind this idea of the capacity for rights is a deeper story, and one that ties our personhood to our being *recognized* by others in a particular way. And this links what Hegel calls "abstract right" and the realm of negative freedom to a larger story within which freedom acquires richer and more determinate content.

After the discussion of the inalienability of personality in the *Philosophy of Right*, Hegel writes:

> The right to such inalienable things is imprescriptible, for the act whereby I take possession of my personality and substantial essence and make myself a responsible being with moral and religious values and capable of holding rights removes these determinations from the very externality which alone made them capable of becoming the possessions of someone else. When their externality is superseded in this way, the determination of time and all other reasons which can be derived from my previous consent or acceptance lose their validity. (§66R)

What is involved in my *making myself* a responsible being, one capable of possessing rights? The previous quote (from §36) suggests that personality *just is* the capacity for rights. In what sense, then, is the capacity for rights an *achievement* of some kind? Of course, the main discussion of "personality" occurs in the section entitled "Abstract Right", which is distinguished from the domains of "Morality" and "Ethical Life". We cannot elaborate Hegel's full argument here, but we need to try to understand how rights-bearing agents are to be understood in relation to these other domains. To put it very generally, Hegel is arguing that if you accept the value and importance of personality, then you should see as justified (i.e. be reconciled to) those practices and institutions that must exist in a world that contains persons so described. But at the same time, he also thinks that it will follow that you will see that a world in which only personality exists and is recognized would be radically incomplete, and indeed self-undermining.

First, what are those institutions and practices that the world must contain if the agents in that world are *persons*? In §§5–7 of the *Philosophy of Right*, Hegel describes three fundamental moments of freedom: universality, particularity and individuality. They specify three ways in which I can be free. In the first instance, *universality*, I am free in the sense of being able to abstract from particular situations and be aware of myself as apart from them. Without this, I have no sense of my own agency, and thus no capacity for assessing rationally what I should do. In the second instance, *particularity*, I am free when I choose particular options and act in a particular situation. If I do not choose or act, and do not choose or act to do something specific, then I cannot be free. The third moment, *individuality*, involves the synthesis of the other two and here I detach myself from all the various options and, in reflecting on them, choose one with which I can most fully identify. Hegel describes this as the will determining itself and yet at the same time binding itself together with itself (§7). I accept certain commitments, but I do so on the basis of reflection and deliberation. In short, to be free, and to be a person requires that you have a sense of independence from your given situation and your ends (§35). Freedom is fundamentally something we realize *in* the world, as opposed to apart from it.

One example of this is the fact that persons require property (for helpful discussions see Ryan 1874: 116–41; Knowles 1983; Patten

1999: 139–62). Recall our discussion of property in Kant (and Locke). If I am free then I must also have access to the means to realize my projects. But it must also be the case that others are not able to coerce me to become part of theirs. For Hegel too, (private) property is intimately connected to our freedom and our status as persons.[8] Possessing an object is a specific instance of the general phenomena, as Alan Ryan (1984: 122) has put it, of the permeation of the noumenal by the mental, of the object by the subject: "I as a free will am an object to myself in what I possess and thereby also for the first time am an actual will, and this is the aspect which constitutes the category of property, the true and right factor in possession" (Hegel 1991: §45). In other words, I externalize myself in my property and see myself in it. In doing so – in becoming an "actual will" – I am developing the very capacities that enable me to be a person in the first place, involving as it does the capacity for independent reflection and agency (the capacity for rights). I am also manifesting my independence from the object; by possessing it, working it and reshaping it according to my needs and desires and so on; I am declaring my supremacy over it.[9]

A crucial aspect of Hegel's discussion of property is the role of recognition and, as I mentioned above, recognition is central to his political theory as a whole (see esp. R. Williams 1992; 1997b; Wood 1990). In externalizing my will in property, I not only relate the object to myself, but to others as well; my will becomes recognizable by others. Property, then, is a medium through which I can be recognized by others. It is not enough that my "inner idea and will" make something mine, since property is the embodiment or "existence of personality": "the existence which my willing thereby attains includes its ability to be recognized by others" (Hegel 1991: §51). Recognition is thus central to the "existence" that property gives to personality. In manifesting the activity of my will, property mediates between my self-recognition and that of others, who can see the effect of my agency on the object. This helps develop and sustain the self-understanding required to be a person.

A similar argument applies to the idea of contract. The sphere of contract is made up of this "mediation whereby I no longer own property merely by means of a thing and my subjective will, but also by means of another will, and hence within the context of a common will" (§71). That is, we will a mutual exchange, but with different ends in mind: you want my portable media player, I want your $200. But what contract presupposes is that the parties entering "recognize each other as persons and owners of property" (§71R). In giving each other something in exchange for what each of us wants, we are mutually recognizing each other as the owner of the value of the thing we possess. And through this, our personality, our capacity for making rights claims, is acknowledged and at the same time developed. Hegel does not appeal here to the consequences that private property or contract generate, either for the individual or society as a whole. Private property is not valuable because it promotes greater welfare overall than some other way of organizing property. The justification of a system of right is based not on consequentialist reasoning, but rather in terms of its appropriateness as an expression of freedom. This is a crucial aspect of the way Hegel goes about making sense of the rationality of social and political institutions. And in some ways it makes him more liberal than many readers initially suppose.

Recognition

But how does recognition actually do this? For Hegel, I am only really free when *self-consciously* free, that is, when I make freedom the object of my actions in the appropriate sense. You cannot be accidentally free. You cannot be free when your "objective condition", as Hegel would say, entails that you are actually a slave. But nor are you free simply because you are *not* a slave. If I act according to my desires, whatever they are and in whatever circumstance, then I am not free. If I act simply on the basis of someone else's authority (whether my church, my tribe or my nation), or out of fear of punishment, or on the basis of mutual advantage, then I am not acting freely in the full sense of the term. So like Kant, Hegel thinks we act freely only when we have the ability to set our own ends and will independently of external authority. But unlike Kant, he does not think our ability to will independently entails that real freedom is acting exclusively on the basis of self-legislated duty alone, in terms of the categorical imperative. What a free act requires will involve desires, for example, but the actual content of those desires will matter. To be fully free I must will, and have as my end, what Hegel calls the "universal" (1991: §258A, §20). The institutions and norms within which I live and act must be shown to have "rational form".

What is the content of the universal, and what are the conditions for the realization of this capacity? Well, that is ultimately what the *Philosophy of Right* sets out to answer. One overarching element of the story involves mutual recognition. I am only really free when, among other things, I receive objective confirmation from my surroundings that I am indeed free – including when I am recognized by *other* self-conscious beings. The most explicit discussion of this thesis comes in a famous (and very difficult) section of Hegel's *Phenomenology of Spirit* (1977: ¶¶178–200) but it plays an important role in the *Philosophy of Right* too.[10] This is an unusual conception of freedom to be sure, at least when compared to the others we have examined so far. To borrow a phrase from Robert Pippin (2000), it is a (social) "state" as opposed to "voluntarist" conception of freedom. Freedom for Hegel involves a certain sort of self-relation and a relation to others: "it is constituted by *being* in a certain self-regarding and a certain sort of mutually related state [that involves] deeds and practices, but are understood to be free by being undertaken in certain ways, not by having special causal conditions" (Pippin 2000: 156). That is, Hegel does not define free agency in terms of the possession of a particular faculty or property by human agents as such. Nor does he appeal to a particular philosophical anthropology. Rather, free agency is an *achievement*, and a social and historical one at that; it is the product of social interaction over time, and of living in a particular kind of society.

To fully grasp the connection between recognition and freedom would require diving deep into Hegel's philosophical system, but here is the basic idea. One way I can achieve self-consciousness is by identifying an object as "other" in the course of desiring it, since in order to desire something I have to distinguish myself from it. But this form of self-knowledge is far too incomplete and transitory, since it vanishes the moment the object of desire is consumed (or "negated"). I cannot maintain a sense of myself if the object that is supposed to help deliver self-awareness is a nothing. So in order to achieve self-consciousness, two conditions must hold: first, that the object is independent of me and not simply negated; and secondly, that I can see my identity in the object somehow, so that it is not completely alien to me. If that does not happen then

I lose any sense of independence, since I would be dependent on something completely outside myself. So I need to recognize myself in an "other" that is independent and enduring. Hence the claim that "self-consciousness achieves its satisfaction only in another self-consciousness" (Hegel 1977: ¶175); that is, mutual recognition between equal and independent persons. I need to experience others like me, and through my interaction with them, come to recognize myself. In recognizing them, they recognize me; an "I that is a 'We' and 'We' that is 'I'" (¶177).

Of course, to achieve this kind of insight the self has to proceed through a series of stages of experience, dramatized by Hegel in his discussion of the life–death struggle and the famous master–slave dialectic in the *Phenomenology*. This is a kind of idealized developmental story: an attempt to identify the logic of recognition. On the one hand, to achieve recognition from others, the self has to engage in a life and death struggle with them. Both you and I will struggle to achieve our independence and recognition as a rational being and that means, Hegel thinks, that we must be willing to risk our lives to do so, in order to demonstrate our power over mere biological life and the desires that accompany it (¶187).[11] It is precisely because I am not driven solely by my animalistic desires – including the desire for mere self-preservation (*contra* Hobbes) – that I am willing to risk death. But this is deeply unsatisfactory as a means of achieving recognition; if I do manage to kill the other then my source of recognition has vanished and if I lose, I am dead (¶¶188–9)!

Thus Hegel offers another scenario. Here, since killing my opponent does not secure recognition, and yet granting him freedom threatens mine, I enslave him. We are now in a relation of master and slave. This is a step up from the stage of desire, since the self has to restrain its desires and acknowledge that it cannot consume the slave. But I do not recognize the slave as an *equal* rational being, however much I let him live and therefore recognize his animal needs (the slave has foregone his rational status by accepting his status as slave anyway). And therefore I get not recognition in return, but rather submission; the relation is thus "one-sided and unequal" (¶191; see also ¶185). This means that I am simply using the slave as a means for my ends and, worse, I eventually come to depend on his labour to satisfy my desires. In an ironic twist, it is the slave then who, through working on the world and transforming it through his labour, comes to "rid himself of his attachment to natural existence" as opposed to the master (¶¶194–5). Mutual recognition requires recognition between equals; otherwise, it is deeply unstable. The upshot of this story is that to be a free agent is to be recognized as one by another whose recognition is freely given. And this can only occur if I, in turn, recognize the other as a free individual. But for this to occur we need the right kinds of social and political institutions, as well as a proper grasp of the sense in which they are rational.

Rights, morality and "ethical life"

As I mentioned above, Hegel claims that individuals have the "right to subjective freedom", or the "right of subjectivity" (1991: §124R). Property and contract are clearly part of the elaboration of this notion, but just that; only part of it. He elucidates the principle in the section of the *Philosophy of Right* entitled "Morality", which concerns the internal motivation and principles of action of individuals. If "Abstract Right" focuses on my external freedom and relations, then in "Morality" the scene shifts inside, to the internalization of principles of action (§104A, §105). And it is here that we find the principle of a right to subjective freedom: "The right of the subjective will is that whatever it is to recognize as valid should be perceived by it as good" (§132). This means that for Hegel the individual can only be bound by laws and policies to which he could consent if thinking rationally (although as we shall see, political obligation should not be conceived in contractual terms). His views and interests should be represented in government (§301), and he should enjoy a degree of religious and intellectual freedom (§270R).[12] Our acquisition of this right, Hegel thinks, is part and parcel of (our) subjective education, but ultimately is too abstract (§132R; §§136–8). We need to understand the subjectivity of the will, that is, how our willing seems to us, but also the objectivity of our will, that is, how it actualizes itself in the world (§132). Morality and abstract right deal with individuals on their own, apart from their place in society and in the state. Hegel insists that we need to reconcile individuals and their rights with the "right of objectivity", that is, with the proper content to be willed and acted on. And this can only occur in "ethical life" (*Sittlichkeit*). Ethical life consists of the whole ensemble of rational social and political institutions that makes our freedom possible.

The discussion of ethical life takes up half of the *Philosophy of Right*, and is the domain in which the synthesis between individuality and community is supposed to occur. Today we often use the designations "moral" and "ethical" behaviour interchangeably, as meaning basically the same thing. Although ethical life includes moral action, for Hegel it has a much more specific sense. It is closer to the Greek root of *ethos*, which refers to not only the morality, but the whole way of life of a particular community. For Hegel, ethical life consists of three fundamental moments: family (immediate unity), civil society (difference) and state (unity in difference). In the family, we are absorbed into an immediate unity that prefigures the unity of the state, but it is one-sided and incomplete. Participation in civil society, which involves the pursuit of our self-interest and our recognition by others as bearers of rights and property, enables us to grasp ourselves as distinct individuals, but it too is one-sided and requires further elaboration in the state, which is literally the "actuality of concrete freedom" (§260). So in the family and civil society, we have two opposite but interlocking forms of social existence, and they help explain the overarching structure of the rational state, whose role it will be to mediate between and reconcile the one-sidedness of each to the other.

The great strength of the modern state, argues Hegel, is its capacity to enable the realization of subjectivity, but at the same time bring it back to "substantial unity". The crucial idea then is that ethical life is the domain in which the one-sidedness and abstraction of morality and abstract right are overcome, and freedom is made concrete. It is made concrete because living in the state enables individuals to realize their interests beyond those developed within the family and civil society. But Hegel also says that these interests "pass over of their own accord into the interest of the universal, and on the other, knowingly and willingly acknowledge this universal interest even as their own substantial spirit, and actively pursue it as their ultimate end" (*ibid.*). What does this mean? The state is not merely a *means* for the realization of my particular interests, but is held together by a commitment to the universal good of all members of society in virtue of its making our freedom possible. When I willingly and knowingly acknowledge the universal as my own and give it priority, then I am not living simply as a private person in civil society, but as a *citizen,* and guided by the common good.

The reason why ethical life can do this is because it provides *content* to our reason, as well as an objective set of norms for our conscience. Recall Hegel's criticism of the abstraction and formality of Kantian ethics. We overcome this by reasoning within the concrete ethos of the ethical community. Ethical life is substance. It provides the material inferences required for my practical reasoning. To put it another way, the norms of ethical life are implicit in the practical inferences of its members. Others hold me responsible for my actions by demanding reasons for them. The question of what we ought to do and what duties we have is answered with reference to the laws and customs of the institutions and practices of the ethical community (§150).[13] The laws and norms of the community are objective in the sense of existing independently of my will, and as authoritative for me (§144). But they are also subjective in so far as I have internalized them through education and reflection, and act on them as if they were my "second nature" (§151). Hegel is clear that although ethical life overcomes or transcends morality, it does not dissolve it. The whole point is to help make sense of it, by placing the basic "right of subjectivity" in a wider context (§154).

Still, conflicts can occur between different role-specific responsibilities and duties embodied in ethical life. Sophocles' account of the conflict between Creon's upholding of the laws of the city and Antigone's loyalty to her brother is one such famous example (see Hegel 1977: ¶437). Hegel makes it clear, however, in this particular case, that the conflict actually derives from the fact that Greek ethical life was essentially pre-reflexive. Men (and women) identified far too completely with the law: "Antigone proclaims that no one knows where the laws come from; they are eternal" (1991: §144A). But we moderns are not like that. The laws that Creon or Antigone take as simply given are for us grasped more reflectively. We are capable of reflecting on the norms and laws that bind us and, given such understanding, act in accordance with them. Conflicts will occur, but a developed form of ethical life, along with proper understanding of it, provides the background against which to make sense of these conflicts and minimize the damage they can do. Genuine ethical dilemmas will be rare (§150R). And yet, whenever there is a conflict between subjectivity and objectivity, the latter takes priority. At one point Hegel explains that "the right of the rational – as the objective – over the subject remains firmly established" (§132R). The good is the "substance" of the particular will, and has "absolute right in contrast with the abstract right of property and the particular aims of welfare" (§130). In fact, I can never declare my right of subjectivity *against* the state.[14] For Hegel, this is to engage in a kind of performative contradiction; that is, to assert my freedom against the very conditions that make it possible in the first place. *Sittlichkeit* has priority over morality and abstract right just because it is only within ethical life that we can be free in the way that matters most to modern human beings.

We arrive, then, at a deeply contested point in Hegel scholarship: what is the nature of the Hegelian state? Is it a conservative or even authoritarian theory of the state, or does it offer an attractive account of social and political freedom? We cannot adjudicate this dispute in any depth here. One crucial question is *why* are the customs and norms of ethical life reasonable for me to adopt and live by? And *how* does living in accordance with them make me freer than I would be in other circumstances? In other words, why should I adopt the disposition and act according to the duties expected of someone who is a son, or a member of a guild, or as a citizen of a constitutional monarchy? Hegel's answer seems to be that you should so act because this is what is expected of you, given the practices and customs you find yourself in, and that in doing so self-consciously you are acting freely. You must still act on rational grounds, and not on the basis of mere authority or habit; this is an important difference between the ethical life of moderns and that of the ancient Greeks (1991: §185A). But this is not the same thing as asking for a rational grounding "all the way down" for every duty one has, as if one could give an account of those reasons in terms of some absolute or non-inferential value independent of "inclination" or social forms. One danger is that an overemphasis on conscience leads to the idea that whatever is good or right is a function only of what is compatible with my conscience, and that entails subjectivism (§§137–40). So reflection, deliberation and conscience are crucial for my acting freely, but only in so far as they help me grasp the universal embodied in ethical life.

Therefore the state – understood in the rich sense as the embodiment of substantive "ethical life" – helps *constitute* free human agency, not merely protect it. Moreover this is what is wrong with Kant's moral and political philosophy. The price of the radical freedom of the will, argues Hegel, is emptiness and arbitrariness.[15] Kant was right to try to separate freedom from the realization of whatever desires we happen to have, or the realization of some external order of ideas, but the purely formal character of the categorical imperative means it is essentially empty. And Hegel thinks this has serious political consequences. Referring to Kant's account of "right" in the "Doctrine of Right" (Part I of *The Metaphysics of Morals*), he argues that it results in only a "negative category": "Once this principle is accepted, the rational can ... appear only as a limitation on the freedom in question, and not as an immanent rationality, but only as an external and formal universal". This produces phenomena in men's minds and in the actual world "whose terrifying nature is matched only by the shallowness of the thoughts on which they are based" (§29). The desire for absolute freedom, in other words, without any way of grasping the kinds of institutions and norms required to realize it in the world, can lead to disaster.

Having said this, Hegel is also very clear that the state, as the embodiment of ethical life, is not *just* a unity, but also a "unity-in-difference"; it has a unified but differentiated structure. There is the unified structure of the state, consisting in the monarch, parliament and bureaucracy. But there is also the differentiated structure of civil society, consisting of the market and the freedom people have to hold property and contract with each, as well as the complex range of sub-state entities, such as guilds, trade groups, associations and local councils, with which individuals can identify (§§182–256). It is these sub-state entities that mediate between the freedom provided by rights and property, and the overarching identity of membership in the state (§289). They provide a source of identification and belonging beyond abstract right (§252), and yet also help preserve freedom in so far as they are independent (relatively speaking) of the central control of the state (§290). Civil society is a crucial manifestation, then, of the principle of subjectivity (§185), albeit incomplete, since the content of our ends therein is given by our desires and inclinations, now worked over and extended by our participation in the market, but still not yet fully "objective" (§195, §236R). Without the overarching rule of law that applies universal rules of justice, and without the intervention of the state to regulate the consequences of economic competition, the atom-ism of civil society would dissolve itself.[16] So although the whole – the state – is prior to the parts, it also exists as much *for* the parts (§272). And each part, in seeking to preserve itself and pursue its own self-interest, also promotes the interest of the whole (§184). In other words, the state needs to promote and protect the interest and rights of its citizens. And yet citizens must also identify with the state in the right way – as universal and as necessary for the maintenance of their freedom – and thus will to act for it as an end in itself.

The critique of atomism

This brings us to Hegel's critique of social contract theory (§75, §258A). Hegel's specific criticisms only really apply to those social contract theorists for whom political society is literally a product of the actual consent of those who join it. Or, more broadly, those social contract theorists for whom the state really is nothing else but a means of protecting pre-political rights: of life, bodily integrity, liberty, property and so on. As we shall see, this means that it is less telling against those such as Kant or, more recently, Rawls, for whom the social contract is a very different kind of device.

Why does Hegel think social contract theory entails atomism? This has to do with Hegel's political ontology (in a phrase bor-rowed from Pettit 2005). Every political theory presupposes a polit-ical ontology of some kind. That is, every political theory makes assumptions about to what extent the members of a polity form a distinct kind of group, whether as a "multitude", "people", nation-state or "assemblage". At one extreme would be to see the people, or the state, as constituting a unified corporate entity; at the other, a mere aggregate, or heap of individuals. As we have seen, Hegel is not vulnerable to the charge that he defends a conception of the state as a single, unified entity, given its differentiated structure. But he does conceive of it in holist terms. At one point he writes, for example, that there are only two possible viewpoints on the ethical realm:

> either one starts from substantiality, or one proceeds atomisti-cally and moves upward from the basis of individuality. This

latter viewpoint excludes spirit, because it leads only to an aggregation, whereas spirit is not something individual but the unity of the individual and the universal.   (1991: §156A)

The problem with the atomistic view, thinks Hegel, is that it means that the state exists only as an instrument or a means for the realization of the desires of its members. But what is wrong with that?

Hegel's basic criticism of social contract theory is that it takes the principles and ethos of civil society and extends it to a theory of the state: "The intrusion of this relationship [of contract], and of relationships concerning private property in general into political relationships", he argues, "has created the greatest confusion in constitutional law and in actuality" (§75R). Transferring contractual relations into a theory of the state is a total distortion of the appropriate way of conceiving of it. It grounds the state on the arbitrary will of individuals, which grounds it in the choice, and therefore discretion, of the individual. This makes it seem as if it is up to the individual to decide whether or not to enter into or leave the state. But membership in a (rational) state is not optional: "It is the rational destiny of human beings to live within a state, and even if no state is yet present, reason requires it be established" (§75A).

All of the classic social contract theorists – Locke, Rousseau and Kant – accepted that there is a difference between arbitrary freedom and moral or civil freedom. But they also still attached equal importance to a more open-ended conception of freedom – to do with freedom of choice – that is hard to find in Hegel.[17] Freedom for Hegel is much more closely aligned to membership in a substantive ethical order in which I act on the basis of reasons that emerge from the institutions and customs of that way of life. Hegel insists that men cannot actually be conceived of as independent agents possessing all the necessary capacities for reflection and deliberation prior to their entry into civil society. There just cannot be agents like that in the state of nature. The capacities, attitudes and forms of self-understanding required for rational freedom can only be developed and sustained within a framework of social and political institutions and, more particularly, those of the rational modern state and ethical life. Why are these specific institutions required? Well, as we have seen, they provide the appropriate structure of recognition required for self-conscious freedom. They enable the right kind of development of the capacities and self-understanding required for freedom, as well as helping to maintain and support it. I can only *manifest* my agency in ways that attract your equal recognition by fulfilling the various roles that are found in the rational state. And others can only express recognition through the institutions of property, contract, the family, civil society and ultimately the state as a whole.[18] By grasping how the social and political institutions in our world help make a community of mutual recognition possible, we become reconciled to them.

Hegel's critique of social contract theory and atomism has informed one strand of a set of criticisms of modern liberalism known as "communitarianism". This label is actually quite unhelpful, since it tends to be applied to disparate philosophers often making very different arguments about the nature of liberalism (for discussion see Mulhall & Smith 1996; Kymlicka 2002). Nevertheless, we can identify a certain line of communitarian critique that stems out of the Hegelian themes we have been exploring and that has a direct bearing on how we should understand the nature of rights.

One problem communitarians have emphasized is the weight accorded to rights claims in liberal politics. An over-emphasis on individual rights leads people to misunderstand the extent to which their freedom is also dependent on various collective goods, and especially duties to maintain them. Our obligations to sustain the common good(s) of society are as important as our duties to respect each other's rights. Individuals can only realize their true freedom in a certain kind of community (or, more accurately, certain kinds of *communities*). Our capacities for being able to form and pursue our own ends, as well as stand back and revise them, depend on our living in certain kinds of societies (Taylor 1985c,d). Taylor argues that we do not simply have preferences that we pursue, whatever their content, but that we also engage in "strong evaluation" (1985c; 1989: chs 1–2). That is, as moral agents we are capable of second-order reflection on our extant desires, and where this form of practical deliberation draws on moral sources that stand independently of those desires. These moral sources provide us with standards of value and they help constitute the goods that matter most to us. In fact, we cannot help but reflect in this way, thinks Taylor; it is part of what it means to be a human agent in the first place.[19] The concepts and frameworks we use to do this come to us through language, which in turn comes to us via the traditions and intersubjective understandings of the communities in which we live. Our articulation of these goods, as Taylor puts it, direct us not only towards certain ends – as we struggle to make them more perspicuous – but also (re)shapes the very desires and preferences we form in the first place. "[T]he good", Taylor argues, "is what, in its articulation, gives the point of the rules which define the right" (1989: 89). If individual rights are taken to be morally primary then, according to this analysis, any duties we have to help maintain the common good(s) of society – those institutions and shared understandings through which our capacities are developed and exercised – will remain presumptively suspect. This can end up undermining the very conditions required for the meaningful exercise of our freedom (*ibid.*: 72–88).

However, in his interesting lecture notes on Hegel's *Philosophy of Right*, Rawls (2000: 349–71) addresses this challenge. Recall our earlier point about political ontology. Hegel thinks there are two possibilities: substance and atomism. And he thinks that atomism is untenable. Rawls disagrees. He rejects the idea of conceiving of society, or the people, as a single agent with a single mind, which rules out, he thinks, the kind of impartial-spectator type reasoning often found in utilitarian thought (Rawls 1972: 187–8). But he rejects atomism too: that society is nothing more than a heap of individuals, a "multitude" as Hobbes put it. Instead, there is a third alternative, and one he associates with Kant and Rousseau. First, the social contract is not simply analogous to a commercial contract, but rather involves the union of many individuals for a common end they share, and moreover *ought* to share. Secondly, the contract is an idea of reason, a regulative ideal, not dependent on actual consent or some particular historical pedigree. For Rawls this means it obliges legislators to frame their legislation in such a way that it *could* have been produced by the united will of all, which is the "touchstone" of public law (Kant 1996: 8: 297). These two features of the Kantian social contract, thinks Rawls, distinguish it from atomism and the idea of the state as substance and individuals as mere "accidents'" of its substantiality. The state is that domain within which "individuals can pursue their ends according to principles each can see are reasonable and fair" (Rawls

2000: 365). Citizens share the end of securing for themselves, and others, their basic constitutional rights and liberties, and this end is itself "reasonable and fair". This means the state is not merely a means for the realization of private ends, but has the publicly shared common end of promoting and securing freedom. And so even though, for example, reasoning within the original position is "purely procedural", the reasoning that leads to it – the appeal to a particular conception of moral agency, and to a conception of political society with a set of shared (political) ends – is not.[20] These goods, to paraphrase Taylor, provide the point of the rules that define the right.

Taylor himself, in fact, has offered a helpful way of mapping the different possibilities between holism and atomism (Taylor 1995b).[21] Ontological questions are distinct from "advocacy" ones. There might well be an overlap between the ontological stand one takes and the particular advocacy position one defends. Maybe defenders of Quebecois language legislation, which restricted the use of English in order to preserve the French "face" of Quebec, are, by and large, social holists, and maybe their critics are, by and large, atomists, but I doubt it. In fact, the really interesting terrain, both in terms of ontology and public policy, lies between these two poles. A social holist can defend individual rights, as Hegel clearly does. And there are other non-atomist forms of political ontology that fall short of Hegelian holism that can be combined with the language of rights. Indeed, this is the space in which we find most interesting liberal political philosophy, including that of Mill, Rawls and Taylor himself.[22] Liberal rights of freedom of association, speech and assembly, for example, enable people to form, pursue and deliberate about collective goods in a range of different ways in civil society. And Will Kymlicka (1989) has combined a strong commitment to individual rights with an acceptance of what he calls the "social thesis". Individuals need a secure cultural structure within which to make sense of the choices they make. When such a structure is lacking or access to it is insecure, through no fault or choice of their own, liberals can and should support policies that enable particular groups to preserve those frameworks, up to and including, at least for some groups (such as indigenous peoples) self-government rights (*ibid.*; 1995).[23] Tensions and conflicts between individual and group rights are, of course (for the liberal), inevitable. But that in itself does not undermine the ability of liberals to accept the importance of collective goods.

Recognition and rights

Finally, what does this emphasis on recognition ultimately mean for a theory of rights? As we have seen, for Hegel personhood is a status concept, but it is a status constituted by mutual recognition. I am a person in so far as others treat me as one, and vice versa. Recall that part of what it means to be a person is to be an agent who has the capacity for rights. So, the rights people have are constituted by mutual recognition too. They are not justified by an appeal to autonomy, as they are by Kant. And they are not justified by an appeal to some fundamental faculty or property that persons are said to possess (such as reason, or "humanity"), or on the grounds of our being the workmanship of God. Individuals are not conceived as possessing pre-political natural rights that condition the establishment of social and political institutions. Nor is their freedom and independence thought to lie in the formal and universal demands of the categorical imperative. Instead, the rights we have are those that others recognize us as having; and those others are people like us – free and equal. In other words, others recognize and respond to our claims as rights-bearing agents, and the norms and institutions we appeal to in making those claims are recognized as providing justification for us to do so. In coming to adopt the normative status as persons (and then also as sons, daughters, fathers, mothers, workers, bureaucrats and citizens) we are provided with reasons for acting that others can hold us accountable to, just as we do for them.

The idea that rights are constituted by recognition was also defended by the English political philosopher T. H. Green (1836–82), who was an important figure in British idealism and the development of what has been called "social liberalism".[24] In his *Lectures of the Principles of Political Obligation*, Green characterizes a right as a "power claimed and recognized as contributory to the common good" (1986: §99).[25] In fact, "rights are *made* by recognition", and to be a rights-holder requires living in a society in which men see each other as equals (*ibid.*: §136, emphasis added). We need to be clear about exactly what this recognition thesis says. It is not just that in claiming my rights I need to recognize that you too have rights to claim against me. The point that Green is making is much stronger: the very existence of a right depends on mutual recognition. To put the point another way, Green holds that there is a *very* strong correlation between rights and duties. "Rights do not begin until duties begin", Green argues, and it is the cardinal error of theorists such as Hobbes, Spinoza and even Rousseau to fail to appreciate this point (*ibid.*: §116). It is not just that if I have a duty to Φ then you have a correlative right against me, or that if I have a right to Φ then you have a correlative duty to perform, or not perform, some action.[26] Rather, correlativity holds only if I recognize that I have a duty to Φ. If I do not recognize that duty, then the right does not exist. Now it requires some work on Green's part to show exactly what duties I ought to recognize myself as having, an argument we cannot examine here. It is tied ultimately to a thesis about our desiring the good of self-realization, whatever other things we might desire (see Green 1990).[27] It is not simply the case that if I do not desire the good then I do not have any moral duties. That would make moral obligation (and thus rights) vulnerable to the ignorant or wilful immoralist, or hostage to extant social norms, rational or otherwise. Green seems to think that I can recognize what morality requires internally (i.e. desire it), even if in the end I do not actually act morally. Moreover he also ties the recognition of duty to society in general. The obligations I have are also ones that are generally recognized by society although, again, they are not just any obligations that happen to be socially recognized. Both of these moves, however, lead directly to some general worries about the rights-recognition thesis.

It is one thing to recognize something that is there already, and another to speak of recognition as *constituting* something. When I recognize you in the queue at the cinema, I am recognizing something that is already there, independently of my action. So it may well be that recognition is a crucial feature of our rights talk, but just in the sense that we can fail to recognize the rights of others because of partiality or moral weakness. In this case, those denied their moral rights have always had them, whether or not we saw or acknowledged them. However Green's recognition thesis (and Hegel's) is much stronger than this. It says that mutual recognition *constitutes* rights; it creates something that was not there before, a status that each of us can now claim in virtue of mutual recognition.

But if rights depend on mutual recognition, then one of the key aspects of the whole point of rights seems lost: their ascription to individuals independently of what others may think or do. As Loren Lomasky has put it, "If I have rights, it is because of something about *me*, not something that resides in the messy world outside" (1987: 153, emphasis added). The whole thrust of the argument from natural rights, for example, is that there are certain facts or moral claims about me that entail my status as a rights-holder. This means that the natural rights theorist, or the defender of moral rights more generally, can claim that the rights people have stand independently of the extant social institutions and norms of their society. That is the point of appealing to rights in the first place, so this line of argument goes: they provide critical standards against which to judge existing social norms, including those constituted by mutual recognition. Should we say of a slave, for example, that he has a moral right to be free only if enough people in his society, and its main institutions, recognize him as free and equal and thus deserving of such a status?[28] Do we not need the language of rights (and especially human rights) precisely where they are not embedded in law or in the existing social norms? The Kantian appeal to the fundamental dignity of human beings, and the Lockean appeal to natural rights, deny the conditionality of the recognition thesis. Rights presuppose the basic freedom and equality of individuals, as opposed to being the product or achievement of some social and historical process.

Here we return to one of the fundamental debates in the literature on rights, which we saw in the Introduction and Chapter 1. Are rights best understood as referring to the fundamental status of individual human beings, independent of their membership of any particular culture or society or their participation in some particular practice? If people have moral rights, then do they have them whether or not they are actually defended or respected?

According to the recognition thesis, I am only a genuine rights-holder if there are established social and (or) legal practices that recognize and enforce certain ways of acting to which the (moral) claim refers. Thus a morally valid claim is a necessary but not sufficient element for rights-ascription. The missing element is confirmation that actual recognition and enforcement of the moral claim is present, or at least reasonable to expect. The naturalistic approach to rights I have defended in Chapter 1 leans heavily in the direction of the social recognition thesis. To be sure, we do not want to say of the asylum seeker held indefinitely in a prison camp, or on a remote, dusty island in the South Pacific, that he has no rights, full stop. He does indeed have moral rights, among other things, to humane and equitable treatment, both during his incarceration and in relation to his claim for asylum. But unless there are some means of ensuring that his guards do not abuse him, and that the relevant government and international authorities will actually hear his claim impartially, then the promise of rights risks becoming essentially an empty one.

Rights, consequences and terrorism

6

The war on terrorism is a war for human rights.
(Donald Rumsfeld, 12 June 2002)

Introduction

In Chapter 1 I suggested that we look at rights in three ways: as statuses, instruments and conduits. Up until now we have been exploring at least four different ways in which rights can be understood to refer to the fundamental *status* of persons, whether as the workmanship of God, as possessing some crucial moral faculty, as possessing inherent dignity or as constituted by mutual recognition. In Chapters 6 and 7, we turn to the notion of rights as *instruments* and *conduits*. Of course, they can be all three of these things at once, as we shall see, and part of my argument is that a political theory of rights must especially try to capture the sense in which that can be true. But for now I want to treat these ideas separately.

I also argued in Chapter 1 that we should approach rights "naturalistically". In turning to the idea of rights as instruments and conduits it is hoped that the distinctive nature of this approach will become apparent. If rights are instruments, then they are not primary, but rather derivative of some other valuable moral end or goal. And if they are conduits for the distribution of responsibilities and powers, and yet also for forms of "government" more broadly understood, then they do not only help explain the legitimacy of political power but are implicated in various relations of power themselves. This is part of what I referred to (borrowing a distinction from Habermas) as seeing ourselves from the perspective of being both authors and yet also – simultaneously – "addressees" of the law. We are self-governing and yet always subject to a variety of forms of government.

To bring some of these issues more sharply into focus, later on in this chapter I turn to the vexed question of to what extent our beliefs about rights should be affected by the threats posed by transnational terrorism, highlighted recently in the terrible events of 9/11, Madrid, Bali, London and the ongoing conflict in Afghanistan and Iraq. If rights are importantly shaped by our perception of the threat the state and other political agents pose to us (as I have argued they are), then what are the consequences of terrorism for our practices of rights today?

Rights and consequences

An important idea lying behind rights is that they provide reasons to act (or not act) even when the aggregated interests or benefits of other people might point in another direction. In other words, that they signal that the costs of protecting the right are worth bearing, even at the expense of promoting better consequences overall for many others. Rights are seen as constraints on the pursuit of even good consequences. Liberal rights also protect actions that are clearly not other-regarding; they give people power to organize their relations and act in ways that have costs for others, and indeed give people power over others that does not always optimise their interests. As Baier has shrewdly noted, our increasing unwillingness to beg has also been accompanied by an increasing unwillingness to give to beggars. This fundamental idea is at the heart of Dworkin's famous book *Taking Rights Seriously* (1977): if we have moral rights against our government and against each other, then this places serious constraints on what the state, and a democratic majority, can ask of us (and we of them).

In Chapter 1 I outlined two broad approaches to liberal rights at work in modern philosophical debates that lead us in different directions when thinking about their relation to politics. The *interest* approach, which sees rights as promoting and protecting certain crucial interests people have, tends to depict rights as *instruments* for achieving some optimal distribution of interests (which might or might not be understood in terms of maximization).[1] This can make rights seem derivative of the value of the benefits to be gained. The other general approach is what I have called the *status-based* approach, in which rights are tied to the moral standing individuals have, often connected to the possession of certain basic capacities or attributes. This seems to make rights primary, in the sense that they are intended to constrain, *a priori*, any action or policy aimed at generating aggregate welfare. Nozick called rights understood in this way "side-constraints". A specific instance of this approach is the *choice* theory: rights are fundamentally about a set of protected choices that individuals ought to have. As we shall see, rights are also *conduits* through which different powers and capacities for action and being acted on are distributed. In other words, although rights can often be used to criticize existing relations of power, they also sit within them in various ways, just in so far as they presuppose various conceptions of the person, practices and institutions, and are shaped by and help underpin social and political norms. (A right to privacy, for example, involves both a protected choice and the alignment of behaviour with certain social expectations and norms.)

Although there is no logical incompatibility between the choice and interest accounts, discussions of liberal rights often end up as a face-off between these two views. This mirrors, to some extent, a larger meta-ethical debate between consequentialist and deontological approaches to ethics. But political theory is not simply applied meta-ethics. It has its own concepts and questions, especially with regard to power and legitimacy, that need to be taken seriously and related to moral theory in the appropriate way. However, I also think that the best account of liberal rights must weave together the key theoretical insights offered by the interest and status accounts. The interest approach provides a suitably flexible, empirical and historically sensitive approach to the practice of liberal rights, and helps to explain their complexity. The status-based approach helps us explain the underlying urgency and importance of the interests at stake. Let me elaborate on this further.

The interest approach emphasizes the extent to which claims about rights are linked to beliefs about the important interests people have. But these beliefs are also shaped by historical and empirical considerations. I argued above (§ "The distinctiveness of rights") that our beliefs about rights are shaped by beliefs about the kinds of

threats we face in societies such as ours. Many such threats change
across time and are highly specific to cultural and social frameworks.
But some threats are general enough that they are faced by just about
all human societies. Even these more general threats, however, still
depend on certain background conditions and beliefs about what is
likely to happen in a society such as ours given a certain distribution of power and the patterns of motivation of our fellows, if certain rights were absent. This is true of even our most basic rights. A
belief in religious freedom, for example, depends, in part, on beliefs
about the likelihood of people developing the appropriate patterns
of motivation that are required to make toleration possible. A belief
in due process of law depends on the likelihood of an independent
judiciary, or at least the possibility of the realization of virtues commonly associated with what we call the "rule of law". The degree of
institutional specification presupposed by rights claims will vary –
some rights are associated with more particular institutional arrangements then others – but the connection with institutional authority
and responsibility is crucial.[2]

At the same time, rights are not merely goals. To claim a right
against torture, for example, is not only to point to a state of affairs
in which people are not tortured as a good thing, or an appropriate
goal for any society to pursue, or to condemn the pain, suffering,
and humiliation inflicted by torture. It is to do all these things, but
it is also to point to the particularly *political* character of the harms
involved. Torture involves the infliction of pain and humiliation to
which the state and its agencies (as well as non-state actors too) are
particularly prone, especially in times of war, heightened national
and international insecurity and fear: in other words, in times like
these. Torture, as David Luban (2005: 1430) has put it, represents
a microcosm, raised to the highest level of intensity, of the kind of
tyrannical political relationship liberals should hate most (see also
Scanlon 2003: 116–17). The rules against torture found in international law, in the main human rights instruments of the past sixty
years and in most democratic constitutions, represent a particular
kind of "legal archetype": we oppose torture not only in and of
itself, but also because of the deep repugnance it represents to the
rule of law (see Waldron 2005: 1718–50).

But if our aim is to interweave the interest and status accounts
of rights, then this will inevitably mean the need to balance rights,

and that means rights will conflict and trade-offs will have to be made. This is unavoidable in politics. But how should we think about these kinds of conflicts and trade-offs? Is there any time, for example, in which we should consider relinquishing some of our repugnance towards torture? If the current "war against terror", for example, depends as much on good intelligence as it does on effective military action, and extracting good intelligence sometimes requires treating interrogatees "roughly", would it ever be justified to modify the rules? We shall return to this particular question. But is there something more general that can be said about the kind of weighing of interests that goes on in generally consequentialist approaches to rights?

One worry is that consequentialist approaches offer a less than persuasive explanation of some of the fundamental intuitions at work in our commitment to rights. For example, utilitarianism, which is one kind of consequentialist theory, holds that the right moral action is that which best promotes utility overall.[3] But what if restoring feudalism would, in the long run, generate the greatest amount of utility? What if allowing various forms of rights-violating behaviour – in part because it was so intensely satisfying for the perpetrators – promoted greater utility overall (Sen 1982a)? These are familiar worries.[4] On the one hand, they rest on complex and unreliable empirical considerations that render any firm judgement about the probable outcomes highly suspect. They also rest on the assumption that consequentialism is focused mainly on utility understood as subjective preference satisfaction. But that is a mistake. For one thing, utility can be understood in different ways. One can appeal, for example, to what *objectively* makes a person's life go better and thus, in any evaluation of alternative states of affairs, discount the subjective utility or pleasure that people achieve in acting in various ways (including in rights-violating ways).[5]

J. S. Mill famously thought there was no necessary opposition between the idea that there were moral non-legal rights and a consequentialist political morality. "To have a right", he argued, "is to have something which society ought to defend me in the possession of ... If the objector goes on to ask why it ought [to do so], I can give him no other reason than general utility" (1962: 309). In other words, the protection of the interests involved in relation to individual rights represents an "important and impressive kind of utility", including security from harm inflicted by others and wrongful interference with the pursuit of his own good (*ibid.*: 310). Moreover he claimed that an equal distribution of these basic rights is vital to realizing the special utility attached to them. *Every* individual is to be protected in these ways (*ibid.*).

Many have thought Mill was too quick to assume there was no contradiction, or at least serious tension, between an appeal to general utility as the basis of moral and political evaluation and the defence of basic individual rights. He never really shows that general utility would be maximized by an equal distribution of basic individual rights. It is surely at least logically possible that it might not be, and that is enough to fuel the kind of scepticism entertained in the previous paragraph.

However, a consequentialist can also recognize the importance of moral rights more directly. Sen argues that we should count the fulfilment of basic individual rights in the evaluation of states of affairs and in determining what we should do. He provides an elaborate example in which Ali, a shopkeeper, is menaced by thugs (Sen 1982b). He stipulates that if Ali is allowed to be beaten by the thugs, total utility, average utility and the utility of the worst off will all increase, compared with the alternative in which the beating does not occur. If we are committed to utilitarianism, Sen suggests, we have a problem; the moral value of protecting Ali's right not to be physically harmed must surely be outweighed by the aggregate utility gained in allowing him to be bashed. Sen further stipulates that a friend of Ali's can prevent the bashing, but only by inspecting Ali's therapist's files, therefore violating his right to privacy. The upshot of the story for Sen is that, first of all, basic human rights – like the right not to be bashed – should trump utility, understood as subjective preference satisfaction. We should seek to maximize, in other words, the fulfilment of basic human rights, understood by Sen as involving rights to basic "capabilities" (Sen 1982b; 1985; 1999). Secondly, however, Sen is also pointing out that conflicts and trade-offs between *rights* (as opposed to between rights and utility) are inevitable for both the deontologist and the consequentialist. If we adopt a strong deontological view about moral rights, then Ali's friend will not violate his therapist's right to privacy in order to prevent the violation of Ali's right not to be bashed. If she adopts Sen's consequentialist view, on the other hand, she will violate the right to privacy in order to maximize the degree of rights fulfilment (understood in terms of basic capabilities), given the judgement that it is worse for Ali to be bashed then for his therapist to have his privacy violated.

Sen's story might be fanciful, but the questions it addresses are not. If we think of rights as intrinsically valuable and absolute, then it is hard to make sense of the difficult choices we often have to make – especially in politics – between pursuing or promoting different but equally valuable goals. On the other hand, pure rights-instrumentalism risks leaving many of the crucial interests that rights protect vulnerable to consequentialist calculation. Rights are importantly *protective* in nature, and not just things to be promoted. Just as the love my children feel for me might be undermined if they came to realize that, as an unrelenting consequentialist, their emotional and physical well-being is only one consideration among many that I deliberate about in trying to maximize probable value overall, so too might those whose rights are at issue feel uneasy about the consequentialist who says he respects their rights. Given different circumstances and different probabilities he might not.

There is another way, however, of thinking about the relationship between consequentialism and rights. If the worry is that consequentialist approaches to rights undermine their protective function because, ultimately, what matters is optimising or maximizing welfare then one response is to adopt indirect or "restrictive" consequentialism (Pettit 1988: 45). This has a slightly paradoxical air about it, but the basic idea is this. Sometimes the best way of getting people to act in ways that generate the greatest amount of well-being is to restrict the extent to which they are supposed to think they should act in every instance so as to maximize or optimize welfare. Thus we should recognize moral rights because restricting people from engaging in consequentialist calculation is itself a way of maximizing probable value.

Phillip Pettit has suggested an ingenious response to the general worries I outlined above about consequentialism and rights that draws on this idea of indirect consequentialism. If the benefit that accrues to the rights-holder is genuinely a *by-product* of respecting rights, and not something that is vulnerable to consequentialist calculation, then the consequentialist can recognize rights.[6] That benefit, suggest Pettit, is *dignity*. A person only realizes dignity in his interactions with others when he retains some "dominion" over his actions and plans; when he is not merely a pawn in the consequentialist's "beneficent scheme" (Pettit 1988: 53). An unrestricted consequentialist cannot guarantee dominion to those with whom he interacts. Even if he is restricted by the rule of law, for example, those around him may still fear that there will be some circumstances in which the sanctions imposed by law will be outweighed by the possible gains of interfering with their dominion. So the only way of guaranteeing that those with whom he interacts will accrue the benefits associated with dignity will be if his consequentialist calculations are restrained in the appropriate circumstances. In other words, if the consequentialist really cares about dominion and dignity, "then the consequentialist will have reason to impose upon himself an appropriate sort of rights-restriction" (*ibid.*).

This returns us to the whole question of the relation between dignity and rights, which we explored in Chapter 4. One criticism of Pettit's argument is that it simply begs the question: why assume that recognizing rights at the fundamental level delivers dignity, as opposed to recognizing rights in more derivative ways? Why can moral rights understood exclusively as instruments not do the same, or at least deliver an alternative, but nevertheless morally adequate sense of dignity or self-worth (see Arneson 2001: 192–5)? And if special relationships really do generate value, then consequentialists have good reason to act to promote them and make room for them in any society organized on the basis of consequentialist principles.

However, instead of pursuing these questions in more detail in the abstract, I want to turn to recent debates over the threats posed to liberal democracies by global terrorism. Here the language of balancing and trade-offs has become prominent in the most dramatic way imaginable. Some have argued that unless we are willing to think about our rights in radically different ways, the future of liberal democracy itself may be at risk.

Rights and necessity

If my claim is that we should try to combine the interest and status approaches to rights, as opposed to seeing them as fundamentally opposed, then how would this actually work? And if I am arguing that we should embrace a historically and empirically sensitive approach to the interests at stake in claims about rights, then how should we think about the challenges to liberal democracy posed by transnational terrorism?[7] How empirically sensitive should we be?

One response might be: *necessitas legem non habet*, "necessity has no law", or perhaps more interestingly, "necessity creates its own law". The saying is an ancient one, but is also discussed by Aquinas in the *Summa Theologica*. There he relates it to both the sovereign's power to grant dispensation from the law, and the emergence of a "sudden danger", the very necessity of which "carries a dispensation with it" (*Summa Theologica*, q. 96, art. 6). It is clear for Aquinas, however, that necessity only releases a particular case from the application of the norm; it does not threaten the very basis or foundation of law, or suspend its operation in its entirety. It does not mark what we might call an existential threat to the juridical order as such, one that might call for special consideration and thus, literally, extraordinary measures in response.

It is this latter idea which has garnered much recent attention from political and legal theorists in thinking about the threat of terrorism for liberal democracies today. The basic mantra, repeated by many in both the United States and Australia (and elsewhere), is that the world changed after 11 September 2001.[8] The idea is that the threat faced by liberal democracies today is literally one of survival, and one parasitic, in part, on the general openness of liberal societies. To fight such terrorism means that the risks that always accompany rights and civil liberties – here understood broadly to include not only basic political liberties of freedom of speech, movement and religion, but also those procedural rights and norms associated with the right not to be detained without a fair trial, to counsel, to due process and so on – have to be re-evaluated in light of the new circumstances. Consider this passage in an essay by Harvey Mansfield:

> [T]he rule of law is not enough to run a government. Any set of standing rules is liable to encounter an emergency requiring an exception from the rule or an improvised response when no rule exists .... We need both the rule of law and the power to escape it – and the twofold need is just what the Constitution provides for .... Much present day thinking puts civil liberties

and the rule of law to the fore and forgets to consider emergencies when liberties are dangers and law does not apply. But it is precisely difficult situations that we should think about and counsels of perfection that we should avoid.   (2006: 12–13)

Indeed, many major initiatives taken by the US, British, Canadian and Australian governments since 9/11 (and subsequently Madrid, Bali, London, etc.) reflect such a judgement. For example, in all of these countries, new legislation defines "terrorism" very broadly and empowers security agencies to monitor, interrogate and detain citizens and non-citizens in new and intrusive ways, without charge and with extremely limited judicial scrutiny. The US government created the Guantanamo Bay detention camp, where it detains, indefinitely, so-called "illegal non-combatants", outside the jurisdiction of both the US Constitution and the Geneva Convention governing treatment of prisoners of war (since the prisoners are defined as falling outside the application of the conventions).[9] Until recently, these prisoners were to be tried by specially designed military tribunals, without the protections normally offered by US criminal courts, or even US courts martial, including a basic right to *habeas corpus*, the right to challenge their detention in court. At one point the US administration argued that some forms of interrogation, up to and including what amounts to torture (at least as defined by international law) were justified, given the threat that terrorism presented.[10] "Special rendition" of prisoners to countries where torture regularly occurs has regularly been used. Although the by now notorious "torture memos" justifying such policies have been repudiated, and legislation has been passed in Congress to stop US officials from engaging in torture, "aggressive" interrogation techniques just short of "grave breaches" of the Geneva Convention continue to be justified and used (Zernike 2006).

In Australia, recent anti-terrorist legislation (Anti-Terrorism Act [No. 2] 2005) includes the capacity for the government to detain Australian citizens and others for long periods of time without charge or legal representation, as well as severely restricting any reporting of their treatment in detention. It also includes vast discretionary powers awarded to intelligence agencies and police without judicial scrutiny. And finally it includes measures that would make even "indirect" association with someone who urges "terrorist" acts liable for criminal prosecution. In so far as the Australian government has also officially sanctioned the legality of the American military tribunal system, it can be said to have endorsed, among other things, the denial of *habeas corpus* and the admissibility of evidence gained under torture from prisoners held in Guantanamo Bay and elsewhere, including (until recently) some of its own citizens.

Two ways of framing these kinds of policies have become common. The first is the appeal to *balance*: that we must re-adjust the balance between liberty and security that always exists in liberal democracies.[11] Individual liberty, even in normal circumstances, must be balanced with the need for society to protect itself. Absolute liberty is not political liberty, since civil society requires that we all constrain our actions in various ways so that each of us has equal opportunity to pursue our own projects. But if threats to the safety of society escalate, then the balance between liberty and security must be reset. When terrorists are willing and capable of causing massive death and destruction, the normal balance is no longer acceptable. Even Nozick and Rawls, for example, admit that in certain extreme circumstances it may be justified to restrict or even violate fundamental liberties.[12]

The second way of framing these concerns is less quantitative and consequentialist and at least sounds more high-minded. Here the claim is that we have a conflict between two sets of basic rights: liberty and security. Individuals have a basic human right to security, just as they do to equal freedom. I am unfree in just about every sense of the word if I am blown up on a bus by a terrorist. Now one way to deal with rights conflicts is to propose a hierarchy or lexical order between them (recall our discussion of Rawls). For example, one might argue that right X is a necessary condition of the fulfilment of rights Y and Z, or, that fulfilling right X has lexical priority over rights Y and Z. Thus, some argue that a right to security – understood in the broadest sense as "human security"– is lexically prior to civil liberty, or at least a necessary condition of civil liberty.[13] Indeed, in recent debates over anti-terrorism laws in Australia, the current Australian Attorney General, Phillip Ruddock, has rejected the suggestion that Australia's most recent anti-terrorism legislation is incompatible with civil liberty.[14] He writes:

Unfortunately the debate on counter-terrorism issues has been dominated by traditional analysis of protecting *either* national security *or* civil liberties, as if the protection of one undermines the protection of the other. This discourse is unhelpful as it implies that counter-terrorism legislation is inevitably at odds with the protection of fundamental human rights.

(Ruddock 2004: 113)

For Ruddock, national security and human rights are not mutually exclusive: "Human security, in other words, is a necessary precondition to the exercise of our most valuable rights" (*ibid.*). This shifts the argument from one between rights and social welfare or utility to one about choices between *rights* and in which it seems less clear that civil rights loses in the battle against terrorism. But it matters crucially what we take to be required to provide the right to human security. If all it meant was more intrusive procedures at airports, more television commercials encouraging us to be vigilant and more frequent, vigorous singing of the national anthem, then the reconciliation between security and civil liberty would not be an issue. However we know that is not only what is at stake, given the legislation on offer.

So the notion that there is a straightforward reconciliation between security and liberty here is deeply misleading. What we have, potentially, is still a conflict between two kinds of rights. And although seeing it in these terms signals at least that there are rights at stake on both sides of the equation, we still have to justify how best to handle the conflict, and which right deserve priority over others. One argument would be (reaching for the distinction between act and omission) that there is a big difference between a government violating your civil liberties in order to protect you, and failing to protect you because they did not want to violate your civil rights (as opposed to through negligence). Which is worse? There is no obvious answer, or at least people's intuitions and considered judgements go in radically different directions. Others reject the distinction between act and omission and argue for something along the lines of what Nozick called (unflatteringly, for him) a "utilitarianism of rights": that some rights infringements can be justified if, overall, greater rights protection or promotion results as a consequence. This is basically

Sen's position, as we saw, and in some cases one that even Rawls appears willing to endorse.

Yet another approach would be to try to *specify* the rights at issue more carefully (for an impressive defence of this approach see Steiner 1994). We discussed this strategy above in § "Rights as self-ownership", when discussing various neo-Hobbesian theories of rights. A right to freedom of speech is not, after all, a right to speak freely at all times and in every circumstance. A right to equal protection of the laws is not a right to be treated equally in each and every respect in every instance. If these rights conflict – as they do, for example, with regard to hate-speech or pornography – then we can try to specify the claims factually or normatively (or both), such that the conflict dissolves. Freedom of expression is freedom to express non-hateful speech. Equal protection under the law is a right to non-discriminatory treatment, excluding protection against hateful expression. Furthermore, we can specify that these freedoms, as rights claims, are exercisable only where others are not in a position to exercise any competing rights.

There are a number of problems with this analysis, as we saw, but for now I want to point to two. First, the detail of specification would have to be so extensive that our rights would be almost unknowable, or at the very least, unworkable. My right to freedom of religion would have to be specified in detail in terms of my being free to practise my religion in *this way*, at *this time*, in *this particular place*, completely free of interference from others. But secondly, and more importantly, what drives the specificationist is the effort to explain *away* conflicts of rights; for them, rights must be fundamentally compossible. Each right, so specified, is supposed to be absolute within its domain, such that conflicts with other rights cannot occur. I, on the other hand, have argued that we are faced unavoidably with genuine conflicts of rights, in part due to the unavoidably controversial premises that any claim to moral rights involves, and that we need to accommodate and address these conflicts, as opposed to explaining them away. In particular, we need to try to explain the moral traces – as Judith Thomson (1986: 253–4) calls them – that certain acts leave when rights are unavoidably infringed. The inevitability of disagreement in modern, plural societies means that democratic will-formation will always entail that some will lose.

A genuinely political theory of rights must grapple with the consequence of this fact.

To summarize, if there is no easy reconciliation between security and liberty and often a conflict of rights, then we need some way of making sense of that conflict. The specificationist tries to explain it away, but this is not always possible. What should we do? A straightforward rights instrumentalism is equally unpromising for reasons I mentioned above: rights do not only express goals but also entail constraints on the pursuit of goals, however worthy. So that leaves the idea of balancing. But we need to treat this metaphor with care. First, we need to keep in mind the *distributive effects* of rights infringements (just as we do about which rights deserve greater protection and promotion over others) (a point well made by Waldron 2003b: 198–204). Since it is *rights* we are dealing with, we must care about the effect of any infringements or derogations on individuals taken one by one. If protecting the security of the majority entails consequences for one particular group more than any other – for example, not just the actual terrorists and their supporters, but others who happen to share their ethnicity or religion – then those consequences need to be carefully evaluated in light of our commitment to rights in the first place.

Moreover, we also need to face up to the difficulties presented by uncertainty and imperfect knowledge that plague judgements about the relation between security and liberty. The so-called "ticking time bomb case", which has become a kind of litmus test for civil libertarians about the permissibility of what has been called (improbably) "liberal torture", conveniently avoids these realities.[15] In the example we are supposed to know that there *is* a ticking bomb, and that the guy we have in our clutches *has* information that can, if we can extract it, help us to prevent the terrorist act. But if, as is usually the case, we rarely know all of these things at the same time, or even some of them at all, then what does the case actually show? Moreover, we know a lot about how torture works in the real world, and the messy, brutal and often uncontrollable ways in which it is carried out (see Rejali 2007). To abstract away from these realities, and to assume they can be easily regulated (as Alan Dershowitz's notion of "torture warrant" presumes) entails a form of political naivety that is far worse that the rights romanticism that the hypothetical seeks to question. The aim is to get the civil libertarian to admit that torture may be permissible in some cases and therefore his rights absolutism is impossible. But the hypothetical shows nothing, except that some people will justify anything. As I have argued, one need not be a rights absolutist to be a consistent defender of the normative force of the rights we care about. We know there will be conflicts and we know that people disagree over the interpretation of rights as much as their philosophical foundations. We also know that moral judgements change over time and are subject to social and political developments. And we know that emergencies might well require restricting certain liberties as a means of preserving the political order itself. But it does not follow that every right we are committed to is therefore up for grabs in the same way. History shows us that individuals regularly face threats from the state and other powerful political actors. The nature of the threats may change, but the presence of such threats – given the way human beings are and the world is – is constant. Rights are one of the tools we have developed to address them. And the idea of there being certain basic rights – to basic liberties, to freedom from torture and arbitrary arrest – has a special weight that manifests itself in arguments for the idea of human rights. One does not need to believe in natural law to think that some rights are more important than others.

Moreover, the ticking time-bomb case suggests that torture itself can be isolated to the exceptional case without any danger to the wider legal system. But it is not clear that it can. The permissibility of torture can give rise to its regularization – to what Luban calls a "culture of torture" – as norms about the treatment of detainees or prisoners shift and decision-makers are required to construct and implement policy around it. This (arguably) is precisely what happened in the United States in the aftermath of 9/11 and the build up to the "war on terror", as revealed in the various memos discussed above and the exposure of the abuse and torture of prisoners by US forces in Abu Ghraib and elsewhere.

Thus the justification for "balancing" basic civil liberties against the kind of necessity posed by terrorism should be treated with extreme care. This is especially true if it means either directly or indirectly endorsing torture, the suspension of *habeas corpus*, as well as severe restrictions on basic political freedoms.[16] These rights are aimed, in particular, at the potential arbitrariness of the exercise of state power in relation to the interests they protect and promote. If the price we pay for not being willing to abandon these basic rights is that we all go up in flames, then perhaps it is one that liberals should be prepared to pay.

But as I said above, democratic conversation proceeds in the absence of agreement about the interpretation of even shared values, and especially about the ranking of such values. Many today think that necessity does indeed entail a change in the structure of our basic rights. I want to try to make sense of this impulse in our culture as seriously as I can. If a naturalistic approach to rights means taking the historical and material circumstance in which rights claims are made seriously, as well as assuming that the structure of rights is fundamentally dynamic, then how should we think about these challenges? The law, for example, can exhibit dramatic shifts in emphasis and interpretation; think, for example of the US Supreme Court decision in *Brown v. Board of Education of Topeka* (1954), or the *Mabo* land rights case in Australia. Could a similar kind of change occur not only in our legal thinking, but perhaps in our moral and political thinking too, with regard to terrorism and our practice of rights?

Rights and emergency

It is clear that even the strongest supporters of rights do not think of them as *completely* impervious to necessity. And the evolving practice of liberal constitutionalism and the international law of human rights include the recognition of the force of necessity, even with regard to some very important human rights.[17] The susceptibility of the rule of law to the forces of necessity has become, not surprisingly, a key theme of post-9/11 legal and political theory. In addition to the kind of arguments appealed to in the ticking time-bomb case, many argue that democratic self-government, limited as it is supposed to be by various checks and balances, struggles to deal with emergencies. When public safety is seriously threatened, and the need for quick and decisive action is required, the deliberative pace of ordinary legislative procedures and institutions can hamstring the capacity of the state to protect itself.

For some, however, this is not merely a point of institutional design. It points to a deeper issue within liberal constitutionalism and the rule of law more generally. For Carl Schmitt, liberal legal formalism, along with its predominantly normative approach to legal and political problems, robs liberal democracy of the capacity to deal with the problem of the exception: a threat or emergency that imperils the very survival of the political order itself. Liberals are either unwilling to face this fact, or naively think they can anticipate and control for it through constitutional and legal means. For Schmitt, this is a doomed strategy. Dealing with the exception might require the exercise of absolute authority, and how can anyone predict what will be required to save the political community in extreme circumstances? Hence Schmitt's famous declaration that "he who decides on the exception is sovereign" (1988: 1): that is, the highest power in a political order is he who can determine and act in relation to an emergency, including suspending the operation of the normal legal order itself. For Schmitt, this means we are faced with a deep paradox, as William Scheuerman has summarized it: "The actor outfitted with the power to grapple with the emergency must belong to the legal order since it must name him, while simultaneously standing outside of it since he alone decides whether the constitution in its entirety requires suspension" (2006: 63).[18] Schmitt's analysis has been remarkably influential since 9/11. Scheuerman points to three main Schmittian themes that have emerged: (i) the ubiquity and unavoidability of emergencies; (ii) the impossibility of legal norms constraining or containing those emergencies; and (iii) the possibility that emergencies may require absolute power, or at least significantly unrestricted power, in response (*ibid.*). If most recent commentators reject Schmitt's ultimate conclusions, many seem to accept that greater authority and discretion must be granted to the executive.

Perhaps the most dramatic extension of Schmitt's analysis has been offered by Giorgio Agamben (1998; 2005). For Agamben, the "state of exception" has been transformed into "the dominant paradigm of government in contemporary politics". It has involved the transformation of a "provisional and exceptional measure into a technique of government", that has already altered the "structure and meaning of the traditional distinction between constitutional forms" (2005: 2). For him, the state of exception is fundamentally a space devoid of law, "a zone of anomie in which all legal determinations ... are deactivated" (*ibid.*: 50). This means that any attempt to regulate the state of exception through law is fundamentally confused. And yet this space devoid of law has a "decisive strategic relevance for the juridical order and must not be allowed to slip away at any cost" (*ibid.*: 51). Thus law and the exception are intimately connected and yet also distinct. The juridical order has a "double structure": one that is normative and juridical, the other anomic and meta-juridical (*ibid.*: 86).[19] One needs the other and yet, just because of this, as Agamben puts it, "the ancient dwelling of law is fragile". The state of the exception is the device that tries to hold the two parts together.

Agamben's argument is tied to a wider thesis about sovereignty, which, following Schmitt, he locates not in the will of the people, but rather in the power to declare the state of exception. Law is ultimately the expression of sovereignty then, not in terms of a relation between the general interests of the majority and the rights of individuals, but rather ultimately in terms of brute force: of violence. To put it crudely, the state is not the institutional expression and guarantor of democratically constituted law, but the enforcer of legal violence. And the subject of law is not the citizen as bearer of rights, but rather "bare life", something far less then a fully human "form of life". What the political response to 9/11 ultimately exposes is the real ground of the liberal rule of law. And so for Agamben, following Hannah Arendt (1966: 276), it is the concentration camp, where fact and right are indistinct, that is the definitive "*nomos*" of modernity, not the Universal Declaration of Human Rights. For Agamben then, the state of exception is a legal black hole, and the trouble for liberals is that this black hole lies at the heart of their normative commitments to human rights and the rule of law. It is a relentless and depressing conclusion, and Agamben resists any easy solution. The "task at hand", he writes, "is not to bring the state of exception back within its spatially and temporarily defined boundaries [or to] reaffirm the primacy of a norm and of rights" (2005: 87). We have crossed the Rubicon into the state of exception, and there is no easy return to the rule of law and respect for individual rights.

For all of its suggestiveness, Agamben's analysis blurs too many historical differences and conceptual distinctions that we need to reconstruct rather than abandon. For one, the assimilation of liberal democracy to authoritarianism and especially the blurring of Nazi concentration camps with Guantanamo is unhelpful. We need the conceptual tools to make distinctions between certain pathologies of liberal government and the breakdown of rights protection and outright fascism. The association of rights with struggles against authoritarian political rule and social and political emancipation is not without its ambiguities, but nor are they cancelled out by their implication in the exercise of state power. (This is an important implication of my claim that rights must also be understood as conduits through which capacities for action are distributed.) It was Arendt, after all, who pointed out that although the Holocaust showed that the universal rights of man broke down precisely when and where they were needed most, this made clear that they could only be effectively realized when each and every individual had an equal and effective right to *political* membership as a necessary condition of the "right to have rights" (Arendt 1966: 299–302).

Responding to necessity

How, then, do we theorize necessity in relation to the justification of rights in an age of global terrorism? How can the liberal defender of civil liberties and human rights square them with the facts of a post-9/11 world? Well, first, we should not rush to agree with the judgement that "everything has changed" after 9/11. As I have been trying to show, the emergence of our various conceptions and practices of rights has been a slow and painful process, born as often as not in the midst of sectarian conflict and civil war. It is not clear that the threat posed by terrorists such as Osama Bin Laden, with delusions of establishing a new Caliphate and so on, really represent the kind of existential threat to our way of life that powerful politicians want us to believe. It is true, of course, that if "weapons of mass destruction" – a phrase unfortunately debased in the lead-up to the Iraq war – were to get into the wrong hands, terrible destruction could ensue. And governments clearly have a duty to protect their citizens as far as possible against such possibilities. But responding effectively to these threats does not automatically entail giving up on hard-won freedoms.

Consider two models for thinking about the relation between rights and necessity: (i) the exercise of "eminent domain" or compulsory acquisition with regard to property rights; and (ii) war.

The problem with the first model is that the best justification for property rights is overwhelmingly instrumentalist. Even someone like Nozick has to accept that existing holdings are so far removed from what a pre-institutional account of rights would justify, given the intervening facts of force and fraud and so on, that any legal principle blocking disturbances based on such grounds would be deeply suspect (see Waldron 1992). Moreover, consider the principle of eminent domain. Although it varies between different legal systems, the basic idea is that the ultimate power of the sovereign can be applied, as the sovereign sees fit, to override property rights. Still, our legal systems have generated norms that govern the application of this force. Section 55(1) of the Australian constitution, for example, empowers the government to make laws with respect to the compulsory acquisition of property on "just terms". And this has been determined over time to mean something like that the state must clearly derive some public benefit from the acquisition, and due compensation must be paid.[20]

In moral theory too we have ways of thinking about the force of necessity, especially with regard to war. Just war theory attempts to set the conditions in which something that is normally totally unjustifiable is permissible; namely, the mass killing of human beings, including even non-combatants. Very generally, the rules for just war theory fall into two broad categories, one concerning whether or not force is justified in the given instance (the cause for which war is proposed – the *jus ad bellum*), and the other concerning the means to be pursued (the *jus in bello*). Among the traditional list of causes that trigger just war include the right to retake something wrongfully taken, to punish "evil", to defend against an attack in progress or indeed to prevent an imminent attack. The means to be pursued are to be governed by three basic conditions: that there is a reasonable chance of success; that there are no other, less costly means available to achieve the desired end; and that the costs of war must be proportional to its benefits (see Walzer 1977). Under these principles, some of which have been codified in the International Humanitarian Law of Armed Conflict (including the Geneva Conventions), while civilians and their property cannot be directly targeted, they may be killed as a result of indirect and unintentional actions, subject to military necessity (see Byers 2005).[21] Civilians in war are thus subject to a utilitarian calculus driven by military necessity, but the hope (often forlorn) is that it is at least a *restrictive* one.

Note that the common law, as well as the criminal codes of common law countries, also allow for a claim of necessity and self-defence. Sailors can dump cargo if it will save their ship, and hikers can break into a cabin to escape a storm (examples from Feinberg 1978). If I stumble across a burglar in my house and he attacks me, I can fight back and possibly even kill him if it can be shown that I had reason to fear for my life. The right of self-defence, and the claim of necessity, is also often ascribed to states. There is a strand in the history of natural law theory, as we have seen, that allows a state to take action not only against enemies who actually attack it, but also preventive measures against potential violators of the natural law (see Tuck 1999).[22]

So although just war doctrine and the common law allow for the infringements of even some of our most basic rights, it is not supposed to be a *simple* "balancing" or "weighing" of costs and benefits.

Let us now turn to the third example, that of the *emergency*, and more specifically one generated by the threat of transnational terrorism. What is difficult about this category, however, is that it fits awkwardly into our existing frameworks for thinking about derogations from basic rights and norms. Emergency powers that would significantly alter our basic civil liberties cannot be justified along the lines of eminent domain, since that presupposes that *all* of our rights should be conceived of in a generally instrumentalist fashion. I am not saying that some people are not willing to justify rights in this way. But the price of doing so is too high. Honouring rights will only be justified when it contributes to the long-term aggregation of welfare, such as, for example, greater security. This subjects *all* of our rights, including, for example, those against torture or indefinite detention, to a utilitarian calculus (and a deeply uncertain one at that), independent even of the usually extraordinary conditions of war. But this will not do. We need to maintain the more complex picture of liberal rights with which I began.

So that leaves the analogy with just war doctrine. But this is also deeply problematic. Wars happen between states and peoples, and usually after a build-up and series of interactions over time. As Bruce Ackerman has argued, to say we are at war against terror is, on the face of it, to declare war against a general technique, not a particular enemy. And to declare war against a technique opens up a "dangerous rhetorical path" (2006: 13). It invites: "an aroused public to lash out at an amorphous enemy ... makes it easier for the president to fight real wars against real countries [and] it encourages the public to grant powers that threaten grave and permanent damage to our civil liberties" (*ibid*.: 15, 18–19). Transnational terrorism is a product not of overwhelming state power, but of the free market and proliferation in destructive technologies combined with extremist ideology and political instability. Framing the issue in terms of war misstates the kind of threat we face. We do not face the "shattering forces mobilized by major nation-states" (*ibid*.: 14–15), but rather the possibility of non-state marginal groups engaging in everything from targeted, "conventional" bombings of civilian and industrial targets, to the possible detonation of "dirty bombs" (albeit aided by "protector" or "sponsor" states). This is scary enough. But it is not helped by analogies to the fight against Hitler or the Soviet Union. Strategies pursued in those wars are not necessarily the best in this one.[23] The question now is: what kind of response does this threat justify in terms of our basic civil rights and freedoms? We find ourselves in between normal law and war, and thus in the realm, it seems, of the law of the exception.

Conclusion: other models

Agamben is wrong to think that the law of exception *in itself* poisons the rule of liberal law, but the question he is pursuing is a good one: how can we prevent the force of necessity from undermining civil liberty without simply ignoring necessity? How can we recognize the force of this kind of necessity without thereby undermining the force of rights?

The models associated with rights instrumentalism and war are plausible, but inadequate, for the reasons canvassed above. There is another model, what we might call the *crime model*, but it too has problems, at least if pursued on its own (see Ackerman 2006: ch. 2). The crime model says that just as we think it justified for a political community to pursue and try to punish someone who has violated our laws, as long as those laws and procedures are justified and have been adhered to in the appropriate way, the same set of principles and norms should govern our pursuit of terrorists. Due process and respect for the rights of the defendants should govern the procedures and means used to pursue and prosecute terrorists. However, already labelling defendants "terrorists" indicates that we are dealing with a different process than the criminal law. And yet we have precedents for dealing with these kinds of cases too. Indeed, one of the key principles of Anglo-American legal systems, the writ of *habeas corpus*, emerged out of attempts in the seventeenth century to limit its effectiveness due to the perceived heinousness of the acts involved (i.e. regicide).[24]

If the acts for which terrorists today are to be tried are particularly horrific, and yet also complex given their transnational nature, then we have international criminal models to draw on, too, including the Nuremberg trials and the various international criminal tribunals set up over the past few years. These include the International Criminal Court (which the US has opposed); the international court set up in the Hague to deal with crimes against humanity in the former Yugoslavia; the tribunal in Tanzania set up to deal with the aftermath of the Rwandan genocide; and the Special Court in Sierra Leone set up to deal with the aftermath of its civil war. All involve a mixture of local and international judges and lawyers applying procedures and norms meant to be consistent with basic human rights, but focused on dealing with the extraordinary crimes that took place in those countries. They are imperfect, of course – too slow, too expensive and subject to political infighting – but they give us something to work with. They certainly offer a more legitimate way of dealing with terrorists, once caught, then the model adopted by the United States in Guantanamo Bay, where suspects are held in indefinite detention and denied many basic legal safeguards.[25]

However, it is true that the transnational terrorists currently at the centre of attention are not quite like the brutal nationalist leaders, ethnic cleansers or alleged war criminals being put on trial through the auspices of the International Criminal Court and the United Nations. They are motivated by very different beliefs and have very different ends. Terrorist actions of the kind practised by Al-Qaeda and its followers are a distinctly political challenge to liberal democratic norms and institutions. They aim to destabilize the political order in various ways, including what Ackerman calls

RIGHTS, CONSEQUENCES AND TERRORISM 177

the "expectation of effective sovereignty": that is, the ability of the state to maintain basic security. Police action is a necessary but insufficient means of combating these threats, since some kinds of terrorist actions might threaten the very possibility of effective police action. Moreover, the threat is dispersed both within and across borders, and includes some states who provide support to terrorists, either directly or indirectly. So although multinational counter-terrorism policing is superior to unilateral military intervention, it will require new levels of cooperation and transnational institution-building than ever before to become truly effective. And it confronts an enemy that is very different from the typical transnational criminal.

Assuming this analysis is correct – and I accept that for many it is not (see e.g. Smith 2004)[26] – what should be done? To conclude, I want to return to the problem of how a political order can be designed to deal with the kind of necessity that transnational terrorism presents, and to think through the consequences for our theories of rights. The crucial question is the extent to which taking these threats seriously entails modifying our commitment to a full schedule of basic liberal rights.

If neither the crime nor war model quite fits, then some argue that we need a different constitutional and political structure to work with, albeit building on these historical and normative resources. One model that has emerged is the idea of *constitutionalized* emergency powers. This contemplates something Agamben and Schmitt (along with many other contemporary legal theorists) deny, namely, that one can contain any moral and political spillovers from emergency powers into the ordinary legal system. The source of one possible model here comes from republican political theory and can be found in Machiavelli's *Discourses on Livy* (ch. 34), as well as in Rousseau's *Social Contract* (bk IV, ch. vi). I shall not summarize the detail of the discussions to be found there, but the fundamental features of this neo-Roman approach are threefold: (i) the aim of any emergency powers should be fundamentally conservative, that is, to preserve the existing political order, not to transform it; (ii) the institution recognizing the emergency should be separate from the creation of the specific powers called on to deal with it; and (iii) the regulation of these powers should be fixed constitutionally. The idea is to try to recognize the force of necessity and yet contain its consequences, even when faced with circumstances that even Machiavelli – and certainly the American founding fathers – could not possibly imagine.

The greatest danger, however, is that the open-ended threat of international terrorism transforms temporary measures into permanent ones, and thus instead of helping to protect our free way of life, fundamentally transforms it. Interestingly, the very strength of democratic political orders can sometimes work against itself in these circumstances. Unlike the republican model, which relies, in part, on the virtuous character of the person chosen to exercise the emergency powers, in modern democracies the executive requires at least the impression of democratic approval for any such measures. And this leads to familiar problems to do with the relation between popular sovereignty and human rights. In a parliamentary system such as in Australia or the UK, governments have taken a legislative approach to dealing with this necessity. The risk is that extraordinary measures, without built-in constraints such as judicial or parliamentary oversight, or various forms of procedural safeguards (such as sunset clauses or super-majoritarian escalators; see Ackerman 2006: 80–90), get normalized into the existing constitutional structure. The neo-Roman model seeks to block these developments and bring emergency powers out into the open in order to be corralled by public institutions. The crucial question is: can they be so corralled? I am not so sure. This will be a fundamental challenge for liberal democracies over the next few years.

Democracies are indeed faced with threats that demand different kinds of responses. But our democratic values and identity should always shape the means through which we respond. It follows, therefore, that certain means will be unavailable to a democracy to pursue its ends – even if used by its enemies – given the need to exercise its authority in ways compatible with the freedom and equality of persons. The kind of security liberal democracy offers, after all, is not that purchased at any price, but one constituted by a commitment to certain basic freedoms and the rule of law. Rights conflict and they have to be balanced against each other. Necessity inevitably shapes our moral and political judgements when it comes to evaluating these conflicts and trade-offs. But the fact of necessity should not be confused with the reasons we have for justifying the rights and the institutions that protect them in the first place. It is not in the least paradoxical to think that fighting and exposing the inhumanity of terrorism requires that we extend to its perpetrators the very same basic rights they denied to their victims, and that they seek to deny to us.

7 Rights as conduits

Coercion is natural. Freedom is artificial.   (Menand 1996: 1)

Introduction

So far we have seen how rights are used to mark the moral status or standing of agents in various ways. We have also explored how they can be understood as instruments to promote certain goals, whether "utility", equality of resources or welfare. But they can also, I shall argue, be understood as *conduits*, that is, as modes for distributing capabilities and forms of power and influence and thus shaping behaviour as much as constraining it. The key idea here is that rights are often implicated in various relations of power as much as they are a means of criticizing them. Part of this is due to the fact that if rights are to be enforceable, even in principle, then they require infrastructure: laws, rules, effective social norms, bureaucracies; all manner of institutions. Even negative rights require positive enforcement. So rights are implicated in relations of power not only because power must be exercised to enforce them, or that one can possess all manner of rights (including basic civil and political rights) and still be subject to various forms of power, but also because rights themselves represent a distinctive relation of power. It is this cluster of ideas that I want to explore in more detail in this chapter.

It is important to notice that although there are clear differences between each of these different ways of conceiving of rights – as statuses, instruments and conduits – in any particular instance they will often overlap. The appeal to interests helps us make sense of the complexity and dynamic nature of rights claims, and especially of the particular systems of rights that emerge historically and in different contexts. The appeal to status pushes us towards fundamental principles and conceptions of human agency (and even beyond), and thus towards debates about foundations and the philosophical grounding of rights. Seeing rights as conduits, on the other hand, orients us in the direction of power. Although we can find many different sources for looking at rights in this way, two of the most influential come from the work of Marx and Foucault. Marx offers a comprehensive critique of what he calls "bourgeois" rights and the ways in which they actually reinforce deep inequalities and forms of domination, as opposed to protecting us from them. For Marx, liberal rights do indeed require specific social, political and economic institutions in order to be realized. But this is the problem: they are the product of the development of liberal, capitalist societies, and as a result express – rather than provide critical leverage against – some of the deep injustices and inequalities of such societies. Foucault, on the other hand, offers a very different framework, one in which rights are constitutive of various relations of power and a tool for both extending and criticizing them. What is interesting about Foucault's discussion is that he is arguing not that we should abandon moral or liberal rights altogether, but rather take up a very different perspective about their nature and function.

Against bourgeois liberal rights

Although having rights and claiming them requires our having certain dispositions and attitudes, many philosophers see them as focused above all on our *external* conduct in relation to each other. Since it is not a logical mistake to talk about someone having a right to do wrong, rights seem to stay on the surface, so to speak, of morality and politics. If I have a right to vote then I can vote for a frivolous or even racist candidate. If I have legitimate title to my property, then I have a right to dispose of it how I wish (within the rules governing property), even if I do so in a way that you might disapprove (leaving it to my rich mistress instead of my impoverished children). In both instances, I have a right to act in ways that

I see fit, even when it might well involve acting immorally. Having the right means that others are free to criticize me, but my freedom to so act is protected. My neighbours may shun me once it gets out that I voted for the racist candidate, but they cannot strip me of my right to vote. My children may resent me for spending their inheritance, but as long as the property was mine alone they have no grounds to interfere. The alternative is to say that we only have those rights entailed by our moral duties, and that we are only genuinely free to act in relation to morally indifferent matters. (Recall the different ways of interpreting Locke's theory of rights in Chapter 3.) But this restricts the scope of rights far too dramatically and undermines their role in diverse societies in which people disagree about the nature of morality.[1]

This focus on the external conducts of agents, along with protecting people's choices to act immorally (at least in some instances), can make rights seem rather shallow. They protect choice but leave the object and content of our choices unchallenged. They purport to protect individuality, but leave unaddressed questions about the nature of individuality, and thus the kind of community in which valuable forms of individuality can flourish. More radically, rights can be seen as the expression of deeply problematic social relations, as opposed to offering a solution to their resolution. This kind of worry about liberal rights finds one of its most potent formulations in Marx's critique of liberal rights in his essay "On the Jewish Question".

In "On the Jewish Question", Marx was reviewing and responding to an argument made by Bruno Bauer about the struggle of Jews to achieve political recognition and emancipation. The crucial distinction Marx makes is between "political" and "human" emancipation. Political emancipation is indeed great progress, but it is "the final form of human emancipation *within* the framework of the prevailing social order" (1978a: 35). With regard to religion, for example, Marx writes: "To be politically emancipated from religion is not to be finally and completely emancipated from religion, because political emancipation is not the final and absolute form of human emancipation" (*ibid.*: 32). Although we never really get a sense of what human emancipation ultimately entails – it will involve, at least, overcoming alienation and living in a communist society – we do get a clear sense of the limits of political emancipation: that a state can be a free state (liberated from a state religion, for example) "without man himself being a free man" (*ibid*.). How is this so?

Man emancipates himself politically from religion by expelling it from public law to private law, where it becomes the "spirit of civil society". But that sphere, argues Marx, is one "of egoism and of the *bellum omnium contra omnes* [the war of all against all]". It is an expression of the "fact that man is separated from the community, from himself and from other men" (*ibid*.: 35). The reference to Hobbes gives us a clue to what Marx thinks is the ultimate character of civil society. Why would we want to seek the freedom to live in that kind of world? And yet this is what we get with the entrenchment of the rights of man and citizen, those general rights to equality, liberty, property and security, as well as political and civil rights to freedom of worship, speech, thought, assembly and the right to vote and stand for office (*ibid*.: 41–2). These rights entail genuine political emancipation, but they also mean we are now split between being members of the political state and civil society. We are all equal as citizens; however, in civil society the situation is very different. In civil society we are at each other's throats, constantly seeking to take advantage of others and to protect our property against encroachment. Since these material and economic relations are, for Marx, the more basic – they are the conditions of our *real* existence, as it were – left unchanged, we remain unfree.

Thus we can be politically free and yet bound to material inequality. We can act in ways that respect the basic rights of our fellow citizens and yet still undermine many of their most important interests and needs. Underlying material inequality can also shape the ways in which different citizens can exercise their rights. Greater wealth enables you to purchase better legal advice and protection; it enables you to build bigger walls and hire more security guards to keep others out. Moreover, the protection and exercise of basic liberal rights can help entrench and perpetuate social and economic inequality, instead of helping us to address it. Property rights enable wealth accumulation and the fulfilment of basic needs, but can also block wealth redistribution. The freedom to exercise my rights as a property-owner and to become economically successful further entrenches my ability to protect the exercise of those rights, often at the expense of those without property.

So for Marx and his followers, civil and political rights are symptomatic of a deeper division between not only political and civil society, but also within man – between egoistic man and his true "species being", his fundamentally communal nature.[2] But, worse, liberal rights actually *perpetuate* these divisions and deepen the separation between each of us and between our external selves and our true human nature. Rights both presuppose and reinforce the idea of human beings as isolated, egoistic agents. And it will not do, on the Marxian analysis, to counter this by seeking to add to the list of basic liberal rights new rights to work, food, shelter, a basic income and healthcare. This does not get at the root of the problem. Just because rights serve to separate us from each other and our social essence, no amount of tinkering with the content of rights will do. One has to address the whole system of production and organization of labour – meaning overcoming all the divisions and inequalities inherent in civil society that liberal rights protect and promote – before *human* emancipation can genuinely be achieved: "Human emancipation will only be complete when the real, individual man has absorbed into himself the abstract citizen; when as individual man, in his everyday life, in his work, and in his relationships, he has become a species-being" (*ibid.*: 46).[3] And you cannot get there by incremental change either; social and political revolution is required.

There have been interesting attempts by socialists to reconcile rights talk with this critique of capitalist social relations (Campbell 1983). Moreover, the egalitarian impulse at the heart of Rawlsian theories of distributive justice tries to reconcile a strong commitment to liberal rights with an equally strong commitment to equalizing the resources and capabilities people require to live decent lives (but for a perceptive analysis of the relation between Marxism and liberal theories of egalitarian justice see Callinicos 2000). Moreover, as we have seen, although rights undoubtedly do express a commitment to protecting individual agency, this need not entail promoting egoism. Rights connect individual interests to duties, for example, in so far as they require others to take my interests seriously, as I hope they will take mine. And the way we exercise our rights can vary too. By not standing on my rights, or waiving them in certain situations, I signal my commitment to building trust or engaging in cooperative ventures with others. Yet the fact that they remain in the background in these situations also signals a certain realism about human behaviour and the always present possibility of the breakdown of social relations. The legal rights associated with no-fault divorce, for example, do not necessarily encourage marriage break-ups, but rather provide protection and support for individuals who find themselves in the difficult situation of a relationship breaking down (see Waldron 1993: 1–34). The strong commitment to individual rights in Rawls's theory of distributive justice attempts to reconcile a commitment to social justice with a recognition of pluralism and a wariness about the exercise of state power. So one response the defender of liberal rights has to his Marxist critic is: I am with you when it comes to seeking genuine equality, but whatever your social aims, whatever your political goals, you must act within *these* constraints with regard to the basic agency and well-being of the individuals involved (Waldron 1987: 173).

Still, the Marxist critique of rights (as opposed to its proposed alternative) is disconcerting for the liberal. It asks difficult questions about the complacency of liberal democratic societies. Do rights really protect people from the kinds of harms societies generate? For example, despite all the signing of human rights treaties, the entrenching of basic rights in constitutional charters and Bills, along with the general promotion of "rights consciousness", women are still paid less then men for similar work in almost all of the leading liberal democracies today. More generally, poverty and racism still shape the life-chances of too many people to a disturbing degree. The Universal Declaration of Human Rights and its accompanying treaties have emerged alongside colossal and devastating global poverty, including the recurrence of state torture and genocide. No one is naive enough to think that simply appealing to rights will solve these terrible problems. But the Marxist critique reinforces the sense that rights alone guarantee almost nothing (Wolff 2002: 107–8). They have to be effective, and to make them effective we have to ask difficult questions about the deeper changes that need to occur in order to realize the values underlying them. And we have to admit that even if we are able to make the most important of our rights effective, we shall still be left with much more work to do in order to overcome the unjust inequalities and asymmetries of power that continue to blight many societies. The history of the struggle to entrench social rights into liberal democratic constitutions seems to bear at least some of this worry out. Close analysis of the increasing reliance of liberal democratic states on the courts to sort out our disagreements over rights – what Ran Hirschl (2004) has called the rise of "juristocracy" – raises serious questions about the links between an emphasis on rights and the promotion of social justice.

Rights and power

If the Marxist critique of liberal rights is that they mask and perpetuate deeper inequalities constituted by capitalist relations of power, the analysis we turn to now both generalizes this point and departs from it in radical ways. Foucault is famous for saying that, with regard to understanding power, "We need to cut off the King's head; in political theory that has still to be done" (2000b: 122). What does he mean? And how does it relate to an analysis of rights?

The most interesting aspect of Foucault's analysis is the way he locates rights as always existing *within* relations of power instead of by definition external and opposed to them. This might seem to entail rejecting rights – especially liberal rights – altogether. He is certainly often read this way. But I think this is far too quick. For one thing, especially in his later work, Foucault made numerous appeals to the language of rights itself, and not simply in a critical vein. So, he is offering a rather different and more complex analysis than simply reducing all claims about rights to power. What he does is show us how rights can act both as tools or instruments for resisting power, and, often at the same time, as themselves conduits for power or, more precisely, *relations* of power. This is a helpful way of thinking about rights, or so I shall try to show. It reminds us that normative principles or rules manifest themselves in the context of complex institutions and social practices, all of which have a history that shapes how those rules and norms are interpreted, perceived and applied. As Bernard Williams (2005a: 28) has put it, no political theory can by itself determine its own application. Moreover, Foucault also emphasizes the extent to which those norms or rules we think of as universal, or at least regulative, are often the product of a particular history and context that is much messier and contingent than we think. Just because power suffuses almost all human relations, we should not think that we can transcend or neutralize it through an appeal to certain universal features of human nature or reason. Each of these moves, along with each claim about nature and reason, has a history, including especially the way we think about ourselves. Foucault, as Ian Hacking (2002: 83) describes it, is an extreme nominalist; nothing is either this or that but history made it so. We might well want to defend particular ways of conceiving of ourselves, or particular institutions and ways of life, but we should not confuse that with claims about their intrinsic universality. This does not rule out the possibility of there being political universals. But they will be much more hard won and contingent then many political philosophers have been willing to admit.[4] Where does this leave claims about the nature of rights? Let us turn first, briefly, to Foucault's basic claims about the nature of power.

Power involves, at one level, the capacity to do essential things: to climb the stairs, to get food, or to vote in an election ("power-to"). But it also involves, especially in political analysis, the power to get *others* to do what you want, whether or not they want to ("power-over"). One standard way of explaining both the source and exercise of power in political theory, as we have seen, is to refer to sovereignty and consent. Locke, for example, partly defined political power as the "right" to make laws and enforce them for the public good (*Two Treatises*, II.3).[5] The source of this right (and capacity) is said to be the consent of those subject to it; the right to exercise power is directly related to the individual rights of those subject to its exercise. Foucault's point, however, is that referring to sovereignty and consent can only explain part of what power and its exercise consists in. On the one hand, if political power can be exercised only as a right over those with rights (or at least the capacity for rights), then that means other kinds of power can be and will be exercised over those who lack the requisite qualities or capacities to have rights. At the very least, focusing on consent and law – what, after Foucault, we shall call "juridical power" – leaves a whole range of other kinds of power relations unaddressed.[6] Focusing exclusively on the idea of a social contract enables the founding contract "to function as a sort of theoretical matrix for deriving the general principles of an art of government" (Foucault 2000c: 214). But that matrix is incomplete. Consent might provide one answer as to the question of the *legitimacy* of the exercise of power, but it provides only a very limited answer to questions about the exercise of power more generally. Foucault is less interested in legitimacy questions then he is in the analysis of power more generally. But his analysis has implications for thinking about the nature of legitimacy, and indeed about the role that rights play in justifying political power.

Thus Foucault offers us a much broader conceptualization of power. Power is the total structure of actions bearing on the actions of those who are free (2000e: 341–2). Note two aspects of this formulation. First, it suggests that power is everywhere, and that might not sound very promising as a starting-point either for a conceptual analysis of power or a normative argument concerning its exercise. But what Foucault is really suggesting is that we find it not only with regard to those institutions most explicitly associated with rule-giving and enforcement – such as the state and other important social and political actors – but also as helping to *constitute* and organize subjects in a range of different domains. "Power" is much more anonymous and dispersed on his reading; it "circulates … [it] is exercised through networks, and individuals do not simply circulate in those networks; they are in a position to both submit to and exercise this power" (2003: 29). One aspect Foucault was particularly interested in was the way we act on *ourselves* in various ways, including as "subjects acting on others" (see e.g. Foucault 1997d). Power is productive and not merely "repressive"; it does not only act on us as passive recipients, but passes through individuals and allows "bodies, gestures, discourses, and desires to be identified and constituted as something individual". In other words, the individual is not power's "opposite number" but rather, and to varying extents, a "power-effect" (which in itself is no bad thing) (2003: 30). We are always in a position to both submit to and exercise this power.

Foucault also made some interesting suggestions about how we should understand the idea of "government", which are relevant for our consideration of rights. Once again he is interested in broadening the scope of the concept and, at the same time, focusing closely on the changes in usage over time. In fact, "government" becomes another way that he conceptualizes power more generally.[7] Political scientists and political theorists are obviously interested in *the* government. But Foucault points to the wider sense of the term: for example, the way we talk about the "government" of children, souls, communities, families and the sick. In the broadest sense, government just is "action on the action of others", and is "to structure the possible field of action of others" (2000e: 341). Another way to think of it, he suggests, is to say that government aims to regulate the *conduct* of others (as well as oneself), both directly and indirectly. It can do so directly but also indirectly, when it acts on the ways in which people regulate their own behaviour.

Now Foucault has a particular historical story about the emergence of various discourses of government from around the sixteenth century onwards (see esp. Foucault 1979; 2000c,e), the details of which we cannot pursue here. One important form of power that emerges around the seventeenth century, he argues, is "discipline", which developed in the context of a particular set of institutions (schools, armies, manufacturing, etc.), but which then is generalized as a form of government. This is a power exercised over individuals that not only regulates and constrains their behaviour, but also acts on and seeks to develop their capacities for self-control in particular ways and makes them amenable to being shaped by norms. The spread of discipline argues Foucault (along with other forms of power, such as "pastoral power"), is masked by the prominence of the language of sovereignty and rights during this time. It is not that the language of rights did not offer genuine resources for criticizing monarchical power in the seventeenth and eighteenth centuries, as well as in helping to democratize sovereignty in the nineteenth and twentieth centuries; it is just that it also obscured the way new forms of power were also emerging, often directly as a result of the changes inaugurated by the critique of state power from the perspective of individual and collective rights (2003: 36–7).

Stemming from this work is what Foucault came to call, in an important lecture, "governmentality", a neologism combining government and rationality (2000c).[8] By this he means, roughly, a mode of power that is addressed to regulating and governing the *populations* of states, animated by a particular rationality. Conceiving of the members of a state as a "population" is itself something Foucault thinks needs to be explained, and that story forms an important part of the development of governmentality. The key idea is that the state and its agencies becomes increasingly focused on government – understood now as "the conduct of conduct" – as opposed to dominating or intervening directly in people's behaviour. This links governance to all manner of different discourses and "knowledges" – such as criminology, psychology, and economics – as well as dispersing it across a wide range of domains. At the same time, however, the state is itself increasingly "governmentalized"; that is, subsumed into a wider array of programmes of government that stretch beyond the formal relations between state and citizens. Thinking of political power exclusively in terms of sovereignty, argues Foucault, means we miss the generally extra-legal sphere in which governmentality operates. For example, we usually explain sovereignty with reference to the legitimacy and capacity of the state to exercise power (including a monopoly on the use of violence). But as "government" becomes more closely associated with the challenges and problems of enhancing and regulating the well-being of populations, he argues, the state and its agencies is increasingly only one among a range of different instruments and rationalities of government that do so. For many people in the workplace, for example, their daily working lives are shaped not only by the rights and obligations they have *vis-à-vis* their employers and customers, but also the vast array of health and safety regulations, "professional management and development" schemes and various modes of direct and indirect surveillance.

It is the different "rationalities" of government, claims Foucault – the different discourses and conceptual assemblages deployed in particular circumstances – that end up determining what is within the competence of the state to regulate or intervene in, and what is not. These rationalities might include but are not reducible to a theory of sovereignty. In fact, even sovereignty itself can become "governmentalized" in some contexts; that is, deployed as a tactic or instrument as opposed to representing the legitimate exercise of power (democratic or otherwise). Judith Butler, for example, has argued that the American government's suspension of *habeas corpus* and other basic human rights for detainees in Guantanamo Bay is just such an instance: "Sovereignty becomes the instrument of power by which the law is either used tactically or suspended, populations are monitored, detained, regulated, inspected [and] interrogated" (2004: 97). In other words, an assortment of techniques – indefinite detention, "extraordinary rendition", along with the establishment of a kind of secondary judicial system – are used to produce an extra-legal sphere aimed at combating terrorism, a term defined so broadly as to offer almost no limits to the potential scope of this domain.

So we have a distinction, then, between governmentality and sovereignty, and (in many cases) a radical decentring of the state. Foucault actually suggests that this sphere of governmentality only emerges once it has been separated from the "rights of sovereignty" (200b: 214–16). Once we see how the business of managing populations extends beyond the formal instruments of the state and is dispersed across a wide array of instruments, processes and techniques, it becomes increasingly difficult to see how the discourse of sovereignty can capture either what is occurring or provide a justification for these diverse "arts of government". In a striking passage, Foucault summarized his attempt to grasp the "material agency of subjugation" in so far as it helps constitute subjects as doing "precisely the opposite of what Hobbes was trying to do in *Leviathan*" (2003: 28). That is, not to show how a "multitude" can constitute themselves as a people through the institution of *a* sovereign, but rather to show how the subjects are themselves constituted – as subjects of rights – in the first place in a multitude of ways. This is part of what it means to get "around the problem of sovereignty". The question is not only how subjects become subjugated or obliged to the sovereign, but also how the "multiple subjugations" that take place function in the wider social body (*ibid.*: 27).[9]

Now, one of the rationalities of government that Foucault was interested in was liberalism and, in particular, German and American "neo-liberalism" (see 2000c, and esp. 1997b). Liberalism provides, on the one hand, a set of arguments and practices that are aimed at criticizing and containing state power. These obviously include the language of subjective rights. But liberalism also, argues Foucault, offers a particular rationality of government, one in which liberty itself becomes a technique of government, along with law (this has been discussed by Ivison 1997; Rose 1999). Here is a clear example of how the state can itself become "governmentalized". Reducing state interference does not reduce "government"; it merely displaces it into other domains. States are now supposed to allow the "natural systems" of the market and civil society to proceed unhampered by interference, save the protection of a basic framework of rights and the rule of law that enable diverse individuals and groups to act "at liberty". But for those individuals unable or unwilling to act in the appropriately autonomous and rational way required by these systems – migrants, welfare recipients, prisoners and so on – different forms of "government" are justified and required. Foucault's point is that rights discourse, understood exclusively in terms of the idea of the social contract, or the normative problem of sovereignty more generally, misses these complex relations of power and rationalities of government that operate beyond the rule of law. There is the problem of the rightless and the forms of government they are subject to. But there is also the problem of how even those with rights are subject to an extensive array of modes of government that rights discourse struggles to capture. Normative theories of legitimization have been and remain an important force in politics. But they do not capture or cover all that is crucial to understanding power and government in modern liberal democratic societies.

The second aspect of Foucault's account of power that we should notice is the claim that power is exercised over individuals and groups who are *free* (Foucault 2000e: 341–2). This might seem confusing: are freedom and power not fundamentally opposed? For Foucault they are not, and this is one of his most striking claims for our analysis of rights. Power involves the total structure of actions – and here Foucault includes all manner of techniques, systems and processes – on the actions of individuals; and that means there must be freedom to act in order for there to be relations of power. Where there is no room to manoeuvre at all in a relation of power you have *domination*, not power. Relations of power are also, therefore, reversible. But it also means that in reacting against actions on their actions, individuals and groups are not only responding to power, but in turn acting on the actions of others; that is, exercising power over themselves and others. Foucault refers to this as "strategic games between liberties" (1997e: 299).

Liberty is thus an action concept for Foucault, and it locates his argument somewhere between Berlin's (1969) famous distinction between "negative" and "positive" liberty. Foucault's account of freedom clearly is not a purely negative conception of freedom (in which I am free to the extent that I am not interfered with), but nor is it strictly speaking a positive conception of freedom. Unlike other theories of positive liberty (such as Rousseau's, Hegel's or Arendt's), Foucault denies that a necessary condition of a genuinely free action involves the realization of our true nature or essence. As Foucault put it:

> I do not think that there is anything that is functionally – by its very nature – absolutely liberating. Liberty is a *practice*. So there may ... always be a certain number of projects whose aim is to modify some constraints, to loosen, or even break them, but none of these projects can, simply by its nature, assure that people will have liberty automatically, that it will be established by the project itself. The liberty of men is never assured by the institutions and laws that are intended to guarantee them. This is why almost all these laws and institutions are quite capable of being turned around. Not because they are ambiguous, but simply because "liberty" is what must be exercised.
>
> (2000f: 354)

Recall that I distinguished relations of power and domination. Relations of domination are a particular kind of power relation, where there is almost no room for manoeuvre on the part of the person or group that is acted on: in other words, where the possibility of liberty is absent. Slaves are dominated by their masters. Prisoners held indefinitely and confined to their cells for twenty-three hours a day are dominated by their warders. Now sometimes Foucault gave the impression that relations of domination are pervasive and inescapable, and that the history of human societies just is a "repeated play of domination", where "humanity installs each of its violences in a system of rules and thus proceeds from domination to domination" (Foucault 1998: 378). But this is not quite right. Relations of domination could, and certainly do, exist that could be masked by the discourse of rights and sovereignty. But not all modern institutions are dominating in the specific sense of the term. Moreover, it is not helpful to begin with a claim about the ubiquity of domination and then work backwards from there in order to try to confirm it. Instead, as Foucault suggests in various places, we should seek an "ascending analysis of power" and look for its "infinitesimal mechanisms", each with its own history, trajectory and context, and make sense of those first, only then determining how they are extended, modified and generalized (2003: 30). So relations of *power* are ubiquitous, but not necessarily relations of domination. Hence the challenge becomes not avoiding power altogether, but establishing those conditions that would "allow these games of power to be played with a minimum of domination" (1997e: 292). Or, as he put it in his short essay on Kant's "What is Enlightenment?", how it might be that the "growth of capabilities be disconnected from the intensification of power relations" (1997f: 317).

What are the implications of this argument for an understanding of rights? Can they play a role in helping to minimize domination? At first, Foucault's analysis seems close to the Marxist one. But, as I have tried to show, it is significantly different. Foucault's conception of the self as a "power-effect" as opposed to possessing a fundamental essence, or as analysable in terms of certain basic universal features, also sets him at odds with many of the theories of rights we have explored until now. But as we have seen, for Foucault, power and freedom are not conceptually opposed. His conception of power (and government) presupposes selves who are at least free to respond and act on those actions and forces acting on them. And it is important to notice that the forces that act on the self include our acting on ourselves. So there is, at the very least, a minimal, corporeal self made up of shifting assemblages of belief and desire, capable of acting in various ways. But the ethically significant features of the self picked out by these practices are always internal to them, and thus "the subject" is always a particular, historical and contingent kind of subject (see Patton 1998).

Nevertheless, Foucault continued to refer to rights and suggest new ways of thinking about them, even in the midst of this general critique of "juridical political thought". Consider three such examples, which it is hoped will bring out his distinctive approach to rights. First, in a 1976 lecture, Foucault suggested that we are in a sort of "bottleneck" when it comes to rights. We are subject to new forms of disciplinary power and yet we invoke the "famous, old bourgeois right". However it is not capable of limiting the effects of these disciplinary forces. So what should we do? "We should be looking for a new right", argued Foucault, one "that is both antidisciplinary and emancipated from the principles of sovereignty" (2003: 39–40). He also spoke generally about the "right of the governed" as the rights of those who "no longer want to be governed like that, by that, in the name of those principles … and by means of such procedures (1997g: 24). But unlike natural rights in the Lockean tradition, this right is "more precise, more historically determined than the rights of man, while it is wider than the right prescribed in administrative law and the right of the citizen" (*ibid.*).[10] Here Foucault is attempting to locate rights, including human rights, in a space between positive and natural law. We shall return to this point in a moment.

A second sense of rights was invoked in an interview with Paul Rabinow and others. In it, Foucault discussed the idea of dialogical or relational rights in the context of distinguishing between dialogue and polemic. The "serious play" of questions and answers involves a dialogic mode in which each party has rights that are "immanent in the discussion", according to which "each of the two partners takes pains to use only the rights given to him by the other and by the accepted form of the dialogue" (1997c: 111–12; for discussion see Falzon 1998; Tully 1999). On the one hand, the partner asking questions has what we might call the right to justification: that is, to remain to be convinced of the other's claim, or to have that claim justified in a way that is followable by them, or at least in principle acceptable. They have the obligation, however, to listen in good faith and seek common ground where it can be found; or to put it in terms Foucault suggested, to minimize nonconsensuality (see Foucault 1984: 378–9). On the other hand, the partner answering the questions is exercising their right (as granted in the dialogue) to justify themselves, but has the correlative obligation to be consistent, and to justify themselves in a way that respects the reciprocal rights of the other. A polemicist recognizes none of these rights or obligations. The same applies even to the human rights activist engaged in an argument or dialogue: "One must guard against reintroducing a hegemonic thought on the pretext of presenting a human rights theory or policy" (2000h: 472).

The third example is taken from a short speech by Foucault published in the *Liberation* newspaper in 1984, on the occasion of an international conference addressing the situation of the Vietnamese boat people in Thailand (2000i). In a speech entitled "Confronting Governments: Human Rights", Foucault proclaims three basic principles in the course of suggesting that in so far as we are all governed, we are all "obliged to show mutual solidarity". The first principle is that there is an "international citizenship that has its rights and its duties, and that obliges one to speak out against every abuse of power, whoever its author, whoever its victims". The second is that it is the duty of this international citizenship to "bring the testimony of people's sufferings" to bear on governments that claim to have no responsibility for them. In fact, such suffering grounds an "absolute right" (and duty) to speak to those who hold power. The third principle is related to this idea of universal citizenship. Why is it that groups such Amnesty International or Médecins Sans Frontières can and ought to speak up on behalf of those who are suffering, as opposed to waiting for them or their governments to do so? First, because they are independent of governments and so can and ought to do so. Secondly, because it signals a crucial shift in the relation between national governments and the concept of citizenship rights. Stateless people, such as refugees, have no state to speak for them, or against whom to claim their rights. The concept of natural rights, or the Rights of Man, as Foucault has tried to show, is inadequate. So we need a new concept (or at least conception) of human rights: something between the Rights of Man and the extant positive law of a state. And it might well emerge from the increasing role that this international citizenry plays in global politics (*ibid*.: 475).[11]

Recall one of Foucault's key points about power and government: wherever we find power we find freedom. You do not get one without the other. This applies in the case of our practices of rights as well. For example, as certain prerogatives of states come increasingly under question – such as the right to non-interference accompanying the recognition of sovereignty – the kinds of rights the governed can claim will also change. But similarly, as globalization and trade liberalization spread and increase the flow of goods and people across borders, new forms of exclusion and "enclavement" develop alongside it (both internal and external) (see e.g. Turner 2006). The age of globalization is also the age of restricted rights for asylum seekers, refugees and certain suspect minorities, especially in the midst of a "war on terror". Labour mobility is crucial for successful capitalist economies but some workers are more welcome than others, and the diversity it can bring can also generate social tensions and conflict that states must then manage.

Changes occur along other dimensions as well. In another late interview, in the midst of a discussion about how "real autonomy" can be reconciled with the delivery of social security, Foucault again pointed to how changing relations of power can generate new conceptions and practices of rights. In the process of bringing individuals and decision centres closer together in relation to social security, for example, Foucault argued that given the changes to our conception of what a good life now consists in, as well as advances in medical technology, we should think seriously about recognizing a right to suicide or euthanasia (2000g: 380–81). This has become, of course, an issue of major public contention in many liberal democracies. But Foucault's main point is that as institutions, social practices, beliefs and moral sensibilities change, so too does our understanding of the nature of rights, including about their subject, substance, basis and purpose (see Introduction).

Conclusion

All of this adds up to a specific instance of what in Chapter 1 I called a *naturalistic* conception of rights: rights as historically contingent (but not arbitrary), dynamic, within as opposed to outside power, and located in conceptual space between the moral, legal and political, or at least where the lines between these domains are blurred. Foucault's is not the only way of making sense of this idea, but a provocative one and well worth considering. But how is a naturalistic approach compatible with the way in which we talk about *basic* rights, including human rights? Foucault appealed to human rights as something that could be used to confront all governments, in the name of all of those who are governed. But he did not appeal to the inherent dignity of individuals, or to a principle of self-ownership, or even to the idea of autonomy to ground these rights. And he worried about rights "hegemony". So where does this leave human rights? They are increasingly the *lingua franca* of global politics. But a cynic might say that this is because they have relatively weak means of enforcement and thus are a form of "cheap talk". Is there a way of appealing to and justifying human rights that lies between the unwieldy metaphysics of natural law theory and the conventionalism of legal positivism? We need to strike the right balance between cynicism and hope. To that task we now turn.

8 Human rights

Yes we agree about these rights, provided we are not asked
why.   (Jacques Maritain, quoted in An-Na'im 1992: 195)

Introduction
The simplest way to define human rights is to say that they are those
rights that all human beings have just by virtue of being human.
They are rights that individuals have, in other words, not because
of any special relations with others, or through membership of a
particular society, but simply by being human. But it then becomes
apparent that we need to say more about exactly what those rights
are, and to what and to whom the corresponding duties refer. And
to do that we have to show how those rights derive from the relevant sense of our humanity. But what is the relevant sense?

Putting the question in this way can lead us to something like an
argument for natural rights. Or it may lead to something like the
appeal to dignity, as in Kant's moral theory. More generally, in his
influential paper (Hart 1984), Hart distinguished between "general
rights" and "special rights", and many contemporary philosophers
have seen this as offering a way of making sense of human rights
(see the discussion in Beitz 2001; 2003). "General rights" are rights
that belong to all men "capable of choice", in the absence of any
special conditions or relations that give rise to "special rights". The
one general right he identifies is the "equal right of all men to be
free", although there may well be others (*ibid.*). Now it is clear that
natural rights are general rights in this sense, and it might seem that

this means that human rights must be too, if we understand them as grounded in our "common humanity". It is often supposed that this is the only way of making sense of the idea that human rights are universal. But it is not impossible to imagine that there could be special rights – those rights that emerge as a result of "special transactions" or "special relationships" – which are in principle claimable by everyone. There might be, for example, practices and relationships that are so wide-ranging that they include basically everyone.

One consequence of seeing human rights as general rights is to narrow considerably the list of possible human rights. It would certainly force us to remove many of the rights we find on the most well-known international human rights documents. Article 23 of the Universal Declaration of Human Rights, for example, declares that everyone has the right to the free choice of employment, as well as to "just and favourable conditions of work and to protection against unemployment". This presupposes a whole range of social, economic and legal relationships. Work is undoubtedly an important facet of human well-being, the equal access to which we may well want to protect in various ways. But we will not be able to justify a *right* to "just and favourable conditions" without appealing to people's social relations in order to make sense of to whom the duties for enabling the right apply, and from where the resources required to fulfil it are to be found. However, this way of understanding the nature of human rights – as both general and special rights – raises the problem of potential incoherence and rights inflation. James Griffin has put this challenge very clearly:

> It is not that the term "human rights" has no content; it just has far too little for it to be playing the central role that it now does in our moral and political life. There are scarcely any accepted criteria, even among philosophers, for when the term is used correctly and when incorrectly. The language of human rights has become seriously debased. (2001a: 306)[1]

So what kind of content can we give them? If we can imagine certain kinds of special rights that are also universal, why not think of them in these terms? One way of making sense of this idea is to see human rights as emerging out of people's participation in what we might call the "global political structure", or (after Rawls) the "global basic structure" (O'Neill 1996; Beitz 1999, 2001; Pogge 2002; Buchanan 2004). By this I mean that there is a set of economic and political institutions – including norms, rules, practices and processes (World Trade Organization, North American Free Trade Agreement, the World Bank, the International Monetary Fund, the United Nations, etc.) – that have a profound effect on the quality of life of individuals and peoples around the world. It follows that it has a profound effect on the capacity of states and peoples to exercise forms of political agency in ordering their lives as they see fit, according to their own conceptions of the right and the good. Moreover, as Onora O'Neill (1994) has argued, we need to see our actions, including our participation in and support of our domestic political arrangements, as having causal and institutional consequences for others beyond our borders in numerous ways. And thus we have a collective responsibility for these consequences, in the sense that since none of us could individually act effectively to address the inequalities that are generated by the global political structure we participate in, we have to work together to reform the structure to lessen the harms it causes.

One hard question is whether it is the existence of this global political structure that entails our having obligations of global justice, or whether we have such obligations regardless of these particular relations (see Caney 2005). I will not address that question in any detail here. What I do want to say, borrowing from something Foucault suggested and that we discussed in Chapter 7, is that the global political structure represents a complex of relations of power, but it also generates various responses, one of which has been the discourse and practice of human rights.[2] Modern human rights thus have a particular role in international political life, albeit one that is constantly evolving (Beitz 2001: 277; Buchanan 2004). In addition to listing basic rights to do with liberty and the rule of law (e.g. Universal Declaration of Human Rights, Articles 1–14, 18–19), there are provisions associated with the right to "nationality" (Article 15), the right to "take part in the government" of their country (Article 21), and social and economic rights (e.g. Articles 22–6). So as I see them, human rights are meant to provide certain shared standards – or at least a shared framework – for evaluating and criticizing various practices of political societies in relation to their members. They do not necessarily resolve disagreement in themselves, but they discipline the discussion about global standards for the conduct for states and other significant political actors in relation to the individuals and groups subject to their power.[3]

Understood in this way, human rights also do not necessarily share the timelessness often associated with the idea of natural rights. As we have already seen in relation to Article 23, the most prominent declarations and charters of human rights today all contain clauses and articles that presuppose all manner of social institutions and processes that have not existed in all places at all times. They presuppose the existence of separate legal systems, developed economies and the capacity of states (and the various agencies associated with them) to do all kinds of things, such as raise revenue, enforce the rule of law and other norms, as well as provide collective goods (Beitz 2003: 43). In earlier chapters I emphasized the extent to which our understanding of rights is connected to the kinds of threats we face, given the kinds of creatures we are and the kinds of societies we live in. This is no less true of human rights. As our natural, social and technological environment changes, so too will the kinds of threat we face, and therefore so too will the list of human rights (*ibid.*: 44; see also Hart 1972: 189–95; and Introduction and Chapter 1).

However, although Griffin's (2001b) desire to reduce human rights claims to as narrow a range as possible is open to challenge, his general question is surely a good one. What if we cannot find enough settled use, or paradigm cases, on which to build up at least a minimally coherent whole? How can an incoherent and indeterminate set of principles or norms guide anything? The other problem is this: if we intend to rely on the way people have been and currently use the language of human rights, as well as extant international law and custom, how can it become a genuinely critical resource for the dispossessed and poor of the world? Is the problem not precisely that we need to stand back from our current practices and criticize them and seek out new ways of thinking about our rights, as well as our obligations to each other? What about the long history of colonialism and imperialism that has accompanied the development of natural rights theory? What about the problem of how rights discourse can mask, or at least divert our attention from, a whole range of other relations of power that affect us in significant ways? To what extent do human rights presuppose a particular kind of society or level of social development, and what about the capacity of states or "peoples" to govern themselves and make choices about their own social and political development?

In Chapter 7 we saw that one of Foucault's key claims was that there was no institution or set of principles that were, in themselves, liberating. The most well intentioned theory, institution or set of norms can be turned around and used in new ways to act on the actions of individuals that we could not have anticipated. Human rights theory and practice is no different. But it is a mistake to think that one cannot think *both* that human rights are a product of a distinctively European historical tradition and yet also are a genuine critical resource for people everywhere against oppression; nor that they can be deployed to justify imperial aggression, and yet also turned around and used to criticize the consequences of such action. The mistake is to think *a priori* that human rights do either of these things in themselves.

So here is the challenge. If human rights are too vague, they are unenforceable, and subject to manipulation. If there is confusion about their intellectual coherence then it is not clear how they can attract the reasoned loyalty of people around the world. But the more determinate we make them, the more we risk drawing on premises or claims that cannot be justified in conditions of deep social and cultural pluralism. If the justification of human rights depends on sorting out large meta-ethical questions first, then the people who need them most will be waiting for a very long time. If they depend, ultimately, on accepting a particular creed of liberalism, then they risk becoming too sectarian. The point is not that we need to avoid offending non-liberal societies, but that we need to make sense of the different ways and contexts in which liberal values can be realized. Saudi Arabia is not a liberal society, but there are reformers and activists there who look to human rights law and practice for support and inspiration. Iran is a theocracy, but it has a long tradition of social criticism that draws on liberal ideas, including about human rights. The experience of the poor and the oppressed in Sri Lanka or Burma will invariably shape the way activists and reformers there internalize and make use of the idea of human rights. Human rights practice, and human rights theory, needs to remain open to the contexts and ways in which people customize and shape human rights, all the while trying to identify and clarify the central moral and political issues at stake. Human rights aspire to set out the entitlements and duties that apply to all men and women everywhere. But that does not mean they should be conceived as completely indifferent to local circumstances.

Justifying human rights

At their most basic level, human rights are moral claims relating to a particularly important set of human interests. They also refer to interests that are under particular threat from the exercise of arbitrary power, especially by the state and its agencies. And they usually presuppose various kinds of institutional arrangements for both their conceptualization and realization.

If I am bashed in a pub, no doubt my right not to be assaulted has been violated, but we do not describe it as a violation of my human rights. However, if it is the Australian Security Agency that is responsible, then well we might. We may describe the abominable state of the health of Aboriginal people in Australia as a violation of their human rights because we feel the harm they suffer from is, in many ways, officially sanctioned, including not only by the state but by each citizen's indifference to it. If one looks at the rights enumerated in the standard international human rights instruments, for example, they refer frequently to rights delivered by institutional arrangements (e.g. equality before the law [Article 7]; a nationality [Article 15.1]; an education [Article 26.1] or equal pay for equal work [Article 22.2]) that are clearly tied to living in a state, or in an international order (Article 28), in which these basic interests are protected and realized. However, human rights refer not only to governments and their agencies, as if *only* government officials have weighty duties not to interfere or undermine the basic interests of their citizens and others. Many of the duties to which basic human rights refer impose duties on all of us (e.g. especially Articles 1–4). And if we accept something along the lines of the existence of a global political structure as suggested above, each of us has a duty not to cooperate (in so far as we can) with the imposition of an institutional order that does not provide secure access to the basic interests referred to by human rights, as well as a duty to help to promote and secure those interests.[4]

Is there something more that can be said about the nature of human rights? Many of the preambles of the most prominent human rights documents include reference to the "inherent dignity ... of all members of the human family" (Universal Declaration of Human Rights), and that all members of this family are "born free and equal in dignity and rights" (Article 1). The International Covenant on Civil and Political Rights and the International Covenant on Economic, Social and Cultural Rights refer to the "inherent dignity" of human persons, from which "the equal and inalienable rights of all members of the human family ... derive" (Preamble to the Covenants). But as we have seen from earlier chapters, dignity is an elusive concept. A fully satisfactory conception of what dignity entails would come close to a complete conception of morality; but that is not what human rights morality aspires to. Rather, human rights are supposed to pick out a particularly important set of claims that relate to a particularly important set of human interests. They are not meant to provide exhaustive set of criteria for the ethical assessment of every situation and specify every entitlement or duty an individual might have, all things considered. And yet we must be able to say *something* about what lies behind the concept of human rights: something about the basic structure of what is being appealed to.

There are two broad strategies. First, one can try to appeal to as parsimonious a set of norms or values as the subject allows, in order to maximize the opportunity for the kind of convergence on standards that can do real work in politics. Or, one can try to find a more comprehensive justification that, although potentially more controversial, has the merit of offering a richer set of critical standards. The first strategy harks back to Grotius, the second to Kant.

Grotius's strategy, recall, was to try to find a minimal set of propositions that, whatever else one believed, you must accept if any kind of human society was to be possible: a form of ethical minimalism, in Tuck's (1994) phrase (see also Tuck 1999). The belief in the right to self-preservation (and correlative to that, the right to defend oneself), was supposed to be universal in just this sense. The natural ethics of Grotius then, according to Tuck, was not intended to be a comprehensive account of man's moral life, but rather – especially in the international context – to be the basis for "inter-national or inter-cultural negotiation, by providing the common ground upon which the rival and conflicting cultures could meet" (1994: 167).[5] The thought was that the law of nature and the law of nations could be bridged on the basis of a minimalist core of morality observable by all rational creatures, whatever their cultural or religious beliefs. But this in itself said nothing about the conduct of such negotiations, or whether or not others would be accorded the appropriate standing such that they could be said to possess any fundamental rights in the first place. The famous Spanish debates over the status of aboriginal peoples in the sixteenth century made that very clear, as we have seen (see § "Naturalism and rationalism"). Thus, deriving the law of nations from the law of nature certainly did not minimize mutual aggression or war, as subsequent history amply showed. Fairly specific cultural claims – about land use and "improvement", for example – seemed to fall out of what were supposed to be ethically minimalist ones.[6]

The elision of nature and culture in the rights discourse of the early enlightenment is also exemplified by the French Declaration of the Rights of Man and of the Citizen (see Pagden 2003). The "rights of man" still *sound* like natural rights – that is, "natural inalienable and sacred to man" – and yet are also declared in the name of a sovereign people, "constituted in a national assembly". Moreover, the most basic rights are civil and political rights, and as Anthony Pagden points out, seem to "derive from the status of their holders as citizens … and can only have any meaning, within the context not merely of civil society but of a society constituted as a nation" (*ibid.*: 189). The conclusion to be drawn from this genealogy, concludes Pagden, echoing many others, is very clear: rights are "cultural artefacts masquerading as universal, immutable values". It follows that if "we wish to assert any belief in the universal we have to begin by declaring our willingness to assume, and to defend, at least some of the values of a highly specific way of life" (*ibid.*: 172–3): basically, one found in a liberal democratic state. And this has consequences for thinking about contemporary justifications of human rights. "A liberal democratic Islamic state is an oxymoron", argues Pagden, and the changes required to enable religious freedom and equality for women can only come about from outside Islam (*ibid.*: 199 n.68). Although I do not intend to question Pagden's historical thesis here, the moral conclusions he draws are deeply problematic. He offers, I think, a very static and schematic account of the relation between the language of rights and social and cultural norms in general, and of the best way of thinking about the justification of human rights. But he deftly dramatizes the tension between what we might call minimalist and comprehensive justifications of human rights, and the relation between human rights and liberalism more generally. How minimalist can the justification of human rights be without undermining the critical role many see as their *raison d'être* in global politics?

The best justification of human rights is as a *common* standard, but where "common" falls somewhere between comprehensive and minimalist.[7] In his recent Tanner Lectures, Michael Ignatieff argues that human rights have gone global not because they serve the interests of the powerful, but because they managed to "go local": embedding themselves in the "soil of cultures and worldviews independent of the West, in order to sustain ordinary people's struggles against unjust states and oppressive social practices" (2001: 7). Elsewhere (Hesse & Post 1999: 320) he has referred to the emerging language of international human rights as a kind of political "hybridized vernacular", not necessarily cut loose from liberalism, but not dependent on it in the ways critics often suppose. Ignatieff seems to intend this as a descriptive claim – and a hopeful one at that – but I think it provides a helpful normative vision too. What are the conditions required for human rights to go local? One thing it suggests is a form of *justificatory minimalism*. But we need to get clear what this means.[8] Although Ignatieff claims that the best conception of human rights is "minimalist, negative, prudential and historical" (see also Lukes 1993: 36–9), he seems to accept the scope of contemporary human rights norms, which are anything but. It is hard to justify rights without saying non-trivial things about substantive, and thus contestable, conceptions of the person, of justice and political legitimacy.

Human rights and human agency

Let us begin with the relation between human rights and human agency.[9] Human rights aim to protect certain crucial aspects of human agency. But what are these? Let me say immediately that we should not reach for, at this stage, a rich conception of liberal autonomy. As valuable as liberal autonomy is, it is neither necessary nor desirable as a starting-point for thinking about human rights. Very generally, to be an agent means being capable of *having* a life, one that you can call your own in some way; at the very least, it means not to be dominated to such an extent that my life feels as if it just is not mine, and perhaps could not ever be. It also means that the choices I have are real, or at least feasible, which entails that I have the capacities to reflect on them. Having these capacities and being able to pursue your own direction in life also means having the basic material resources required to do so: security from harm, sufficient shelter, health, food, education, property of some kind and access to some kind of cultural structure and the public goods it brings (language, institutions, norms, etc.). So a *degree* of autonomy, liberty and adequate material provision are crucial for agency. These bare notions can be filled out in many different ways. The self-fashioning, Lockean liberal is only one of a family of possible conceptions. Another is Nussbaum's (2000: 78–80) list of basic capabilities, which includes not only these basic elements, but also the capabilities for emotion, "affiliation", enjoyment of nature and play (see also Sen 2004).

Note that all of this is consistent with an emphasis on the fundamentally *relational* nature of agency. It is also consistent with an emphasis on obligations as much as rights. We are dependent beings; dependent on other human beings for our development, security and well-being, as well as on the environment in which we live: on not only the natural environment, but social and cultural ones too. We have obligations in light of these dependencies. However, in order for us to be capable of forming meaningful relationships, and fulfilling our obligations in the first place, certain conditions are required, including achieving certain basic capabilities and thus being protected from harms that prevent us from doing so. Not all of these harms are best addressed through human rights, but they remain one way of marking out and identifying these capabilities and the harms that can befall them. In other words, fulfilling our obligations requires that certain basic rights be respected. This is an old idea, and one we explored in relation to Lockean natural rights. But it has also been used by Joshua Cohen to try to show how human rights can be put to work in societies where there is a strong emphasis on duties derived from ascribed roles, as opposed to individual rights. Human rights can provide the space in which people can fulfil their duties (see Cohen 2004; Bell 2000: 23–105).

Much more could be said, obviously, about the nature of agency appealed to in this understanding of human rights.[10] We need a conception of agency for this purpose that is neither too thick nor too thin; parsimonious, but not empty. The scope for reasonable pluralism expands as we think about the global public sphere, and borderline cases complicate things, as always. Infants and the severely physically or mentally disabled might lack the ability to fully exercise their capacities, but that does not place them outside the circle. Children are usually in the process of *developing* these capabilities, accepting that there are hard questions about *when* we think of children as becoming fully developed agents. And the severely disabled can exercise them to different degrees, the success of which is often less to do with their inherent ability then it is with the unwillingness of others to help them to do so (Stainton 1994; Nussbaum 2006). We need to remain open-minded about exactly who is in or out in relation to the category of "human" in human rights. Great apes, who share many capabilities with us, are clearly candidates for human rights too, as our views change about the margins of our species (see Cavalieri & Singer 1995).[11] It was not that long ago, after all, that many people struggled with the idea that Africans, or indigenous peoples, or even women, had the moral standing that entitled them to claim basic rights. Perhaps "human rights", then, should go the way of the "rights of man" and we should instead simply talk about "basic rights" (Edmundson 2004: 191).

The right to have rights

Another way to think of the connection between human agency and human rights is in terms of what Arendt (1966) called the "right to have rights". The right to have rights is that basic right – that basic claim – on which more specific conceptions of rights can be constructed. So the right to have rights is something like a right to *participation* in the sense that to treat me as someone capable of holding rights in the first place is to see me as entitled to be part of the process of determining the meaning and articulation of the rights in question. This is not only because these determinations will have a clear impact on my well-being. It also involves according to individuals the moral standing and capacity to participate in deliberating over and settling these questions in a responsible manner (Waldron 1998: 238–9). The right to have rights forms the threshold – the condition of possibility – against which to test the construction of various particular rights, and also our judgements about the limits of those rights. Two candidates for making further sense of this idea are what Rainer Forst (1999) has called the "right to justification", and what Bernard Williams (2005b) has called the "basic legitimation demand" or "BLD".[12] Both are linked to the notion that what it means to be treated as a human agent involves being treated in a manner for which adequate reasons can be provided. The crucial question then is the nature of those reasons, and Forst and Williams offer two interesting ways to think about it.

Forst (1999) offers an essentially Kantian argument, albeit modified through an adaptation of certain key themes from Habermas; there is no question of deriving human rights from a formal principle of the moral law, or the Kantian conception of the moral person. For him, the adequacy of reasons will be determined through processes of reciprocal justification involving actual dialogue between culturally and historically situated individuals. The validity of any proposed universal norm or rule, however – including about human rights – does not depend on literal acceptability, but instead is determined in relation to the outcome of a suitably designed communicative procedure (the discourse principle); one in which everyone is, ideally at least, able to deliberate over those rules and norms that affect their most important interests. The right to have rights just is this "right to justification". Forst is attempting to save a Kantian idea of reasonableness poised between a positivist story about the validity of human rights (they exist only where they are actually enforceable through law) and a purely rationalist one (human rights as moral rights disclosed through universal reason).

Williams (2005b), on the other hand, offers an even less Kantian and more historicist account of a roughly similar idea. Legitimate rule will be that which would be acceptable to individuals thinking reflectively about their situation, albeit from the vantage point of an avowedly "internalist" as opposed to "externalist" meta-ethical stance.[13] The less legitimate the system of political rule, the more likely the violation of human rights. But we still need to know whether what is acceptable to individuals is a product of the very relations of power we want the BLD to address. Hence what Williams (2005b: 6, 14, 71–2) calls the "critical theory principle": "the acceptance of a justification does not count if the acceptance itself is produced by the coercive power which is supposedly being justified" (*ibid.*: 6). The paradigm case of failing to meet the BLD is unmediated coercion; might makes right.[14] This, at least, is a human universal: that some human beings coerce others, or try to, and that most human societies need some form of political order and thus some form of political authority distinguishable from mere coercion.

But the particular answers as to what is acceptable with regard to legitimization can vary.[15] Liberals set much higher standards as to what counts as the kind of disadvantages we should care about, and which cannot be rationalized by the obvious need for some kind of political order. And this is precisely one role that human rights play in liberal discourse, in terms of providing such basic standards. The state itself cannot become part of the problem for which it provides an answer (i.e. the need for political order). Nor can hierarchical structures be legitimized, for example, simply by reference to their continuing existence; once their legitimacy is questioned, some kind of justification must be forthcoming, and it must be acceptable to those who are subject to it. If not, then we are back in the domain of might makes right, and thus the potential violation of human rights. This gives us a clear line to the most basic of human rights, against torture, arbitrary detention, denial of religious freedom and so on. But the further we move away from the paradigmatic cases, the more difficult the judgements become. It is one thing to say that people are owed certain things as a *right* – that someone would be wronged in being denied it – and another to say it would be a very good thing indeed if they had a particular good, or achieved some level of capability. But there is no hard line between these points and as social, political and historical circumstances change, so too might our judgements about where to draw such a line.

Williams's conception of the BLD provides an attractive way of thinking about the kind of justification we need to underpin a self-consciously political theory of human rights. The justification, and thus the rights themselves, need to be conceived of in close relation to politics, and especially the experience of injustice, as opposed to being something imposed from the outside. People demand reasons as to why they are being treated in certain ways; they demand justifications for the rules, laws and norms to which they are subject. The adequacy of the reasons proffered has to be determined reciprocally, but always in relation to the forms of power and structures of interdependency that individuals are struggling with and against, and at the same time trying to reshape. The right to have rights, then, is something like the right to contest those relations of power acting on you and your most vital interests. The BLD can thus be conceived also as a kind of democratic norm, just in so far as it is a right of participation. However, there are stronger and weaker ways of interpreting this connection. Habermas, and many influenced by his work, tie legitimacy tightly to an ideal of deliberative democracy. (Recall his argument about the internal relation between the rule of law and democracy, discussed above at § "Habermas: discursive rights"). But we need not go that far. The benefits of some form of democratic participation (realizable in modern conditions) can also be cashed out in terms of the protection it offers against arbitrary exercises of power, independent of any particular theory of liberal autonomy, or a Rousseauean ideal of self-government.

Human rights as enforceable claims

To the extent that human rights gain internal sources of support within a society, they gain legitimacy.[16] Of course, intervention is sometimes unavoidable, especially in the most egregious circumstances of gross violations of basic human rights. If we can prevent an atrocity, or at least limit its effects, then we have an obligation to do so. But it is one thing to criticize a state or a set of practices and another to decide to intervene. In each case separate considerations apply and good political judgement must be exercised, particularly in relation to interventions. Note also that "intervention" can manifest itself in different ways. You can support, by proxy, different sides fighting a civil war or an insurgent campaign (as was common during the Cold War, and still goes on today). Upholding human rights standards can be written into regional and international trade agreements, or made a condition for membership in major international institutions (Beitz 2001). Military intervention, however, even low-intensity peacekeeping, is costly and, especially in the current geopolitical climate, often arbitrary. On what grounds do we distinguish between intervening in Iraq or Bosnia, but not Darfur? Or in Darfur, but not the Congo (see e.g. Mamdami 2007)? Human rights considerations have been invoked in each case. Moreover, such intervention can have unintended consequences that can undermine the very goals invoked to justify it. Context is everything; humanitarian intervention implies that there are clear lines to be drawn between the perpetrators and the victims, and clearly sometimes there are, but not always. It is one thing to make a moral case for intervention, another to understand and take responsibility for the long-term consequences of doing so, especially given existing complex political circumstances. If there is one thing we can learn from the history of colonialism it is that just about every intervention by European powers was justified on the basis of something like "humanitarian intervention". That does not mean it never is justified or indeed required. But it does mean we should tread cautiously and with a cool-headed appreciation of the potential costs and risks involved.

So human rights cannot become real unless there is an effective political and legal authority in place whose institutions have some kind of legitimacy. Sometimes this can be provided in the short term by an occupying army or international agencies, but not for long. Recall Habermas's claim about the co-dependence between public and private autonomy, and of the functional role that positive law places in modern societies (see § "Habermas: discursive rights"). It is importantly true that states violate human rights regularly, and this is a key motivation for having transnational standards and institutions that can enforce human rights in the first place. Moreover, an effective legal and political order is not by definition a *national* political order, although states are still a crucial provider of security for their citizens. I take it that one of the great projects of twenty-first-century political thought is to develop new models of transnational and global political order that can provide not only effective security and welfare provision for citizens, but that can also become the object of people's reasoned loyalty; to construct, in other words, new forms of transnational democracy (see Held 1995; Habermas 2001a; 2005). But however we define their ultimate shape and scope, effective local political institutions and norms are still crucial for protecting the interests to which human rights refer. The absence of an effective political and legal authority creates the conditions in which others – the military, multinational corporations, insurgent movements – can do serious harm.

One problem is how human rights can be effectively "localized" in particular cultures and societies. Sometimes this problem is described as a choice between affirming a religion (or tradition) and claiming human rights (see Okin 1999; Shachar 2001). And at first glance, the extant human rights instruments do not seem to offer much guidance. For example, the United Nations Declaration of Human Rights protects religious freedom (Article 18) – including the freedom to manifest one's religion in "teaching, practice, worship and observance" – as well as providing protection against interference with one's "privacy, family, home or correspondence" (Article 12), and yet also protects "equal rights as to marriage, during marriage and at its dissolution" (Article 16). But we know that religious practices often reinforce, in combination with other social norms, discriminatory treatment against women. And yet women, just like men, seek religious freedom *and* freedom from discrimination in marriage, as well as in society more generally. So in order to realize women's freedom from discrimination, it will require not simply positing human rights "against religion" (or "against culture"), but adapting and shaping the human rights standard to local contexts and circumstances, including in societies where religious beliefs and norms play a substantial role in the public culture. As Moira Gatens has put it, "if we are to see a normative shift in relations between the sexes, such rights will need to resonate with at least some aspects of the particular imaginaries from which the norms of male domination derive their legitimation" (2004: 288).

There are at least three levels at which variation around the justification of human rights can occur: in their legal form, in their interpretation or background justification, and in the actual substance of the list of rights or norms themselves (Donnelly 1989: 110–24; Taylor 1999: 136–40, 143). Although analytically distinct, these levels can become blurred in various ways. Different background justifications might lead to different lists, just as they may entail different legal forms. In fact, variation is inevitable and unavoidable. There can be variation and thus conflict between different instances of different rights. And there can be variation and thus conflict between different instances of the same right, due to the different kinds of duties a single right can generate (Waldron 1989: 514–15). Within each of these possible variations, cultural and social norms also play a role. These cultural views, of course, are complex and not homogeneous. Lee Kwan Yew might think that security and community should take priority over civil and political liberties in Asian societies, but it does not follow that all of his fellow citizens do (see Donnelly 1989: ch. 10; Bell 2000: 175–275). And some Muslims (along with many non-Muslim commentators) might associate Islam with a rejection of a right to religious liberty, but that does not constitute the final word in Islam about religious freedom (see the discussion in Little *et al.* 1988; An-Na'im 1990; Abou El Fadl 2003).

This scope for variation and customization, however, is interpreted by some philosophers as deeply problematic. O'Neill (1996: 131–6), for example, argues that the difference between liberty rights, on the one hand, and social and welfare rights, on the other, points to a deeper problem with the morality of human rights in general. When a liberty right is violated, she argues, whether or not there are specific institutions established, there are determinate others to whom the violation can (in principle, at least) be imputed. If I break your arm, or lock you in your house against your will, then I have failed in my duty to abstain from violating your personal liberty. It might be easier for you to enforce your claim if there are police nearby and an effective court system is in place, both of which require resources (Shue 1996). But there is no doubt about who is responsible for discharging the duty, and no doubt that your right is directly claimable (or waivable) in relation to *me*. In the case of social and welfare rights, however, the same is not true, claims O'Neill. Rights to goods and services can only be claimable, she argues, "if a system of assigning agents to recipients has already been established, by which the counterpart obligations are 'distributed'" (1996: 131). For example, if I have a universal right to welfare and yet no institutions have been established for distributing or allocating the obligations for providing it, then there is "systematic unclarity" – and not just contingent uncertainty – about identifying the violators of such a right and thus whether or not it was claimable in the first place. These rights can only be provided through the establishment of some kind of institutional scheme, she argues, unlike in the case of liberty rights. O'Neill is not denying that there might well be good reasons to establish such universal rights, but believes that we are in danger of undermining the critical force of human rights talk in general if we do not pay attention to the need for institutional enforcement:

> Proclamations of universal "rights" to goods or services without attention to the need to justify and establish institutions that identify corresponding obligation bearers may seem bitter mockery to the poor and needy, for whom these rights matter most. When advocates of Human Rights proclaim universal rights to food or to work or to welfare, yet fail to show who has corresponding obligations, or where claims of right or redress may be lodged, they hurl a weapon that may become a boomerang. *At best* a premature rhetoric of rights *may* have political point and impact ... *At worst* a premature rhetoric of rights can inflate expectations while masking a lack of claimable entitlements.   (*Ibid.*: 133)

This is a powerful criticism, and the importance of institutionalizing our duties of justice so as to make them more specific, concrete and enforceable is undeniable. It clearly applies to the point made earlier that once we move away from the paradigmatic cases of rights violations – torture, indefinite detention, denial of religious freedom and so on – the job of extending the standards becomes more complex, and difficult (see § "The right to have rights"). But as Kok Chor Tan (2004: 51) has put it, we should not confuse a conceptual claim with a strategic one. There is no conceptual reason why social and economic rights could not become human rights, however distant that prospect now seems.

Put more positively, looseness can be a valuable property for practical reasoning about human rights, just as it can be for practical reasoning more generally. As Sen has argued, "loosely specified obligations must not be confused with no obligations at all" (2004: 341). If we had a duty for every good reason we have to do something, we would be tied up in moral knots. Human rights already mark out a certain set of moral and political considerations for particular urgency. But even within these considerations, the question of how different rights should be balanced, or which deserve more urgent attention than another, will entail acting on the basis of some reasons rather than others. The underlying "right to have rights" implies that we are obliged to take seriously the effective conditions required for agency. This inaugurates a chain of moral and political reasoning, but it does not conclude it. Given the limits of our capacities, competing priorities and deep disagreement, some obligations will emerge as more important than others. In fact, borrowing a distinction from Kant (who in turn took it from Grotius), we can say that there are "perfect" and "imperfect" obligations even within human rights, the exact configuration of which changes over time and in relation to different historical circumstances and demands (see § "Right and justice"; O'Neill 1996: 145–7; Sen 2004: 338–42; Kok 2004). Human rights always correspond with duties. But the nature and force of those obligations can vary, and unavoidably so.

Pluralizing human rights

So human rights are universal (or, at least, they can be), but they also need to be embodied in legitimate, concrete legal and political orders in order to have a better chance of becoming real. But how should this occur? Ideally, states should incorporate human rights norms democratically, embedding them in their domestic constitutions, legal processes, and broader political culture (since human rights can be promoted by more than just legal means). But this returns us to the problems we discussed in the previous section. How far can the process of customization go, and to what extent does the value of self-determination conflict with the demands of human rights norms? Some theorists have turned to the idea of the gradual constitutionalization of international law; that is, the gradual development of a "higher" law, through treaties and the foundation of international organizations that can take priority over national- and transnational-level decisions (see e.g. Fassbender 1998; Cottier & Hertig 2003). But there are worries here too. Does such a view depend on a particularly European narrative of social and cultural development, as well as a particular European conception of the appropriate form of legal and political order (cf. Pagden 2003; Muthu 2004; Tully 2005)? Can such a model generate the kind of legitimacy it requires not only to be effective, but to meet the standard of justification required by liberalism? By and large, these models seem to move decision-making and enforcement further away from democratic decision-making bodies, and even from the more indirect forms of democratic control exercised through civil society: those networks of communication that are plugged into the processes of the formation of a public political will. As a result, some theorists have sought very different models, more pluralistic and less uniform in approach and design (Taylor 2004; Connolly 2005; Tully 2005).

One general step towards doing so is to take *toleration* seriously as a principle of international law, but at the same time to reconceptualize its meaning in a way conducive to the demands of global politics. But this only serves to dramatize what is a fundamental tension when thinking about the foundations of international law today; between a principled respect for, and recognition of, on the one hand, the collective agency or self-determination of peoples and states, and on the other, of human rights. This tension is, in fact, written into the various international treaties, declarations and norms that make up modern human rights (e.g. Article 1 of the United Nations Charter, compared to Article 27 of the Optional Protocol of the Convention on International Civil and Political Rights). These treaties and norms emerged out of inter-*state* negotiations, after all. But the issues at stake are fundamentally normative as well. How can a principle of toleration be reconciled with a commitment to human rights? How can we both accept the idea of the existence of a global basic structure, and yet not simply put up with but value pluralism, including the collective agency and autonomy of states and "peoples"? Moreover, is toleration even the right concept to appeal to in these circumstances? Too often it can take the form of a hierarchical "permission concept". Since I am only tolerant when I put up with something I disapprove of (and could suppress if I wanted), it can seem like a grudging as opposed to a genuine manifestation of equal respect (see helpful discussion in McKinnon 2005; and esp. Forst 2003).

An important strand of recent work on global justice denies that there is any tension between human rights and the value of self-determination since, according to this account, the moral significance of states or peoples is entirely derivative from their contribution to securing justice.[17] Although the details of the theory of justice to which these arguments appeal varies, they all place a significant emphasis on individual autonomy. Thus self-determination, and any accompanying right to non-intervention are owed to states or peoples only on the grounds that observing them contributes to the realization of individual autonomy. It might be that there are pragmatic or prudential reasons to adhere loosely to principles of non-intervention and self-determination, but no principled ones. The best understanding of our commitment to human rights dissolves any principled tension between toleration and human rights. When states violate justice, toleration must yield to remediation and rectification.

The danger of this approach – admittedly, for some, its primary virtue – is that it assumes there is basically no difference between a liberal theory of justice for a particular society, and a global theory of justice. But toleration matters in the international sphere, and for the following reasons. A theory or rights cannot just ignore social and cultural difference, as if it were a regrettable feature of the world, but rather tries to make sense of it and tell us something about how we should relate to each other given this diversity (Jones 2001).[18] The point is not, then, that toleration itself is a foundational value for the justification of human rights, but that it is an appropriate response to the diversity of views about the good and the right that characterize both domestic and international political life. Grounding the justification of human rights in a comprehensive theory of liberalism, especially on a particularly rich conception of liberal personhood, sets human rights on a collision course with diversity. And it can promote a sense in which human rights are indeed fundamentally at odds with "Islam", "Confucianism" or "indigenous peoples", and that what we are really calling for, as Pagden puts it, is the imposition of a distinct way of life ("regime change") on non-liberal political societies. (It does not help that the history of many liberal-democratic states, as I have already pointed out, is entwined in complex ways with the history of empire; see Ivison 2002; Muthu 2004; Pitts 2005.)

But then what are the limits of toleration in the international sphere, and how are they to be established? The limits are given in part by the common standard of human rights. But then how can we ensure that recognizing the value of different forms of collective self-determination will not involve accommodating deeply unequal and unjust social and political relations?

Rawls has come under sustained attack recently for doing precisely this, in so far as he allows for the toleration of "decent" non-liberal peoples, even when they deny their members significant basic liberal rights (for Rawls [1999a: 71–8, 78–82], "human rights" refer to a set of basic rights considerably narrower than the extant major documents concerning human rights provide for) (for criticism see Kok 2000; Beitz 2001: 276–7; Caney 2002; Buchanan 2004: 159–76). As long as a society provides the basic means to subsistence, bodily security and liberty (understood in a relatively narrow sense), and possesses a "common good idea of justice" that takes into account the fundamental interests of all and is manifested in some kind of consultative political system, it should be tolerated.[19] "Decent societies", Rawls argues – including "decent hierarchical societies" – "should have the opportunity to decide their future for themselves" (1999a: 85). "Outlaw states", on the other hand, violate the human rights of their citizens, are not "well-ordered" (i.e. lack even a shared "common good" conception of justice) and are aggressive and present a regular threat to their neighbours and the "law of peoples" in general. They lack, therefore, any right against the imposition of sanctions or to non-intervention. This still seems to mean, however, that a society that systematically excluded women or religious minorities from political office, or denied them an adequate education, could be tolerated.

As many critics have argued, at least in terms of ideal theory, the list of "human rights proper" seems far too lean, as much as it represents an independent argument for human rights and is not simply an intercultural *modus vivendi*. One can accept that the content of a common standard of human rights applicable in the international sphere will be different from liberal constitutional rights and liberal citizenship rights, without necessarily accepting Rawls's particular list. One major problem with his approach is the inference he draws from accepting what he calls the "burdens of judgment" – giving proper weight to the fact that reasonable people will draw very different conclusions over fundamental normative matters to do with justice and the good (see Rawls 1993: 54–8) – to the toleration of non-liberal societies and practices. Although I shall not go into the details of this complex debate here, the main point is that

Rawls does not really provide an argument for why, even accepting something like the burdens of judgement, we should limit the list of human rights in the way that he does.

Central to Rawls's definition of a decent society is that it is organized around a "common good conception of justice" that, although perhaps grounded in a comprehensive moral or religious doctrine, recognizes some minimal commitment to the equality of persons, in so far as everyone's "fundamental interests" are taken into account (Rawls 1999a: 67). But, as we have seen, this seems to be compatible with not treating everyone's good *equally*.[20] But how to do this without simply imposing liberal-democratic institutions and a liberal theory of justice on non-liberal societies? Recall that I noted a fundamental ambiguity about modern human rights, in that given their scope and their presumption about the existence of certain institutions and so on, they often resemble citizenship rights (an ambiguity that goes back to the Declaration of the Rights of Man and of the Citizen).[21] But no global state or society exists in which one could think of oneself as a global citizen. And the diversity of moral and religious comprehensive views means that it would be hard to settle independently on a comprehensive list anyway.[22]

And so one way of thinking about the common standard of human rights that would address the shortcomings of Rawls's approach, but accept his emphasis on toleration, is to think of human rights as providing cross-cultural norms for evaluating what is required for effective agency – conceived in the parsimonious way suggested above (§ "Human rights and human agency") – among which is included the value of membership in a self-determining political society.[23] In other words, we would see human rights as standards for those capacities required for a society to be seen as a fair scheme of cooperation in the first place, accepting that there will be different forms and understandings of what counts as a fair cooperative scheme. The task of the common standard of human rights is to set limits to such reasonable diversity. Note that this should also give us a sense of the costs of being *excluded* from these goods, and thus guidance as to what our attitudes should be towards those "in-between" or without political membership, such as refugees or displaced persons.[24] This gives us, I think, a far richer set of transnational standards for evaluating how political societies treat individuals and groups, and yet also acknowledges the force of pluralism.

But there is another important amendment to Rawls's argument that is required, and it has to do with the nature of self-determination. I argued above that there exists something like a global political structure; namely, "a set of economic and political institutions that has profound and enduring effects on the distribution of the burdens and benefits among peoples and individuals around the world" (O'Neill 1996; Beitz 1999; Pogge 2002; Buchanan 2004: 213). So any principled respect for self-determination will have to acknowledge not only the practical constraints this involves, but also the moral ones. No state or people can be assumed to be either economically self-sufficient or distributively autonomous. Rawls, surprisingly, rejects this, and insists that it is mainly good government and political culture that determines the basic quality of life for citizens (1999a: 106, 108). It follows that since inequalities between societies are mainly the result of domestic choices, and the principle of toleration precludes imposing a liberal theory of justice on them (or even criticizing their choices in the name of liberal justice), better-off societies have a duty only to help "burdened societies" to become more decently self-governing. These are societies that lack the "political and cultural traditions, the human capital and know-how, and, often, the material and technological resources needed to be well-ordered" (*ibid.*: 106).

Once again we can reject some of Rawls's assumptions and yet still acknowledge the importance of toleration in the international sphere. Self-determination and collective governance are valuable because they enable individuals and groups to live decent lives and to contest those relations of power acting on them. And respecting collective self-governance involves respecting the members of that society and their identification with that way of life. But we need to specify the nature of self-determination more clearly, and this is no easy task. Because we always stand in varying relations of interdependence with others both within and beyond our borders, and our actions can affect their basic interests, any claim to self-determination will be limited. Thus we need to conceive of collective self-determination and self-governance in less absolute and more relational terms (see e.g. Young 2002: 252–5; Buchanan 2004: 331–424). Moreover, there are different ways of exercising self-determination, ranging from localized modes of self-government and forms of intra-state autonomy, to secession and independent statehood, some of which may be better or worse at realizing the goods noted above.[25] This means unbundling the attributes of sovereignty usually associated exclusively with states, and pluralizing the "selves" eligible for the attribution of the legal powers associated with the exercise of sovereignty. Although there are complex questions of transnational institutional design here, especially with regard to embedding different kinds of self-determining units (national, federal, regional, intra-state, etc.) in various kinds of interlocking networks, the common standard of human rights has an important role to play. To realize the goods of self-determination, collective decisions must be based on processes that actually represent the interests and views of all those who are subject to that society's laws and regulations, especially the most vulnerable. In global politics, the role of a common standard of human rights should be to help guide judgements about the extent to which a society can plausibly claim to be genuinely protecting or advancing the good of all those subject to its laws and regulations. And this means going beyond the substantive minimalism that Rawls endorses.

It is probable, however, that a society that passed this test, and certainly did not violate its citizens' human rights, might still be considered unjust according to a liberal theory of justice. This returns us to the problems associated with the value of toleration. A very difficult question here is whether or not realizing the good of self-determination as I have described it requires a fairly specific form of democratic self-government. One can be discriminated against short of persecution, for example, and not necessarily be unable to live a decent life. I think this thought lies behind Rawls's insistence that equal political rights not be a condition for recognizing a non-liberal society as decent. But then the crucial question is: what is required to think that any such inequalities in treatment – for example, differences in the treatment of men and women – would be justified from the perspective of the common standard of human rights? Gross discrimination and persecution on the basis of gender or religion would be ruled out, but what about the unequal distribution of legal rights shaped by local understandings and attitudes about, say, family law?

One short answer is that it is not the task of human rights to encompass every kind of social and political injustice. Human rights do not, and should not, express all the goods we value, so much as point to conditions or constraints that apply in the pursuit of them. In addition to human rights we have other concepts and theories to draw on to help us make sense of disadvantage and injustice. But in terms of evaluating the background conditions against which these more localized practices are carried out, we can appeal to the structure of the BLD outlined above. If we are concerned with the need to create space for local interpretations and applications of human rights norms – of enabling them to "go local" in other words – is it a necessary condition that political societies be organized along democratic lines? It all depends on what we mean by invoking democracy here. The justification of democracy rests in part on the claim of respecting the equal moral worth of individuals. But what does this actually entail? It can be interpreted to mean that everyone has an equal say in the most important political decisions that affect them, and that there exists an equal distribution of political power and influence between citizens (see e.g. Bohman 1998; Beitz 1989). Would insisting on this ideal as a component of the common standard of human rights – insisting that basic human rights include a right to democracy in this specific sense – not involve imposing much more than a common standard? Would accepting anything less undermine the critical role that human rights are supposed to play in international politics (see Sen 1999: esp. 147–8, 154–5, 178–84, 227–48)? This is a dilemma for anyone who values human rights as a common standard, and yet also takes cultural and social difference seriously.

One option would be to deny that the richer account of democracy is a necessary condition for adequate self-determination, and opt instead for minimal standards of "consultation" or accountability. This is Rawls's strategy (Habermas, on the other hand, seems to go in the other direction). Another option would be to argue for something like a democratic minimum as the appropriate constraint on collective self-governance, taking advantage of the great variety of ways of interpreting (and institutionalizing) the idea of political equality. The choice is not between Rousseau and Schumpeter. The aim should be to promote the conditions in which members of the society are freely able to express their views about those norms and rules that affect their most urgent interests, as well as what counts as a basic interest in the first place. This will require that they enjoy certain amounts of bodily security and liberty, as well as secure access to sufficient resources to engage in some form of political participation and reflection (the demands of citizenship are unwieldily if you do not have enough to eat). Human rights standards should be aimed at evaluating these conditions, above all, which it is hoped will also help initiate – over time – new modes of collective self-questioning and critical scrutiny.[26]

Indigenous peoples and the future of human rights

Our discussion of human rights has until now been fairly abstract, and yet I have been emphasizing the importance of history and context. To conclude, I want to provide an example of the kinds of challenges and possibilities that the language and practice of human rights face, conceived as a common standard. I want to return to the case of indigenous peoples, to whom I have referred at various points in this book. Turning to non-state actors in the global sphere provides us with a glimpse of a future trajectory for one dimension of our practices of rights. As I emphasized in the Introduction, our most influential theories of rights emerged out of the consolidation of states such as the USA, France, the United Kingdom and Germany. But today, and for the forseeable future, our rights practices will be faced by challenges found in countries more like Nigeria and Indonesia on the one hand, and Iraq and the Congo on the other. They will also be faced by the changes occurring in Europe and elsewhere, given the current vast movement of peoples across borders, and the evolution of the economic and political structures of the European Union. These will generate new pressures on the promotion and enforcement of traditional liberal democratic rights, as well as demands for new configurations and interpretations of those rights. The situation of Muslim minorities in European countries today presents a particularly complex set of problems in this regard, in which the question of rights – especially in relation to official discourses of multiculturalism and social integration – plays an important part.

It might seem strange to associate the situation of indigenous peoples with these developments, but they have been part of the process of extending limited multicultural rights to groups within liberal states as a way of promoting fairer terms of association between national groups and the state (Kymlicka 1989, 1995; Ivison *et al.*

2000). Their situation is importantly distinct from migrant groups, as well as other national groups, but their struggle for political recognition has formed an important part of the multicultural turn in political theory. Also, their conceptual location between states, their "internal exclusion" from equal citizenship, and their legal and political struggles drawing on a range of domestic and international instruments make them, I believe, an interesting case to ponder when thinking about the future of human rights.

Non-state actors have tended to frame their claims in the international sphere in at least five ways: through self-determination, minority rights, human rights, historic sovereignty and prior occupation (see Kingsbury 1992: 482; 2001). Despite the fact that each can be justified along separate lines, the arguments are often mixed and overlapping, as well as unsettled. Two of the most prominent lines of argument pursued in recent years have involved the language of self-determination and human rights. The most explicit manifestation of these overlapping discourses in the international sphere has been the proposed Declaration on the Rights of Indigenous Peoples.[27] There have been (at least) three stumbling blocks faced by indigenous peoples, and they are uneasily addressed in the Draft Declaration. The first is whether they are indeed a "people" – at least for the purposes of international law – and, relatedly, who counts as "indigenous" in the first place.[28] The second is whether the principle of self-determination actually applies to them, given that they reside within states whose borders are, for the most part, recognized as legitimate by the international community. The final stumbling block is the extent to which demands for self-determination on the basis of prior sovereignty or cultural difference are compatible with the general thrust of human rights. Is there a human right to self-determination? Can a collective "person" be the subject of human rights?

Unfortunately, this lands indigenous peoples into a "conceptual morass" in international law more generally (see Kingsbury 2001: 217; Buchanan 2004: pt III; see also Anaya 1996; Tully 2000a; Keal 2003). The categories or units to which a right of self-determination applies have never been clearly defined, in theory or in practice. And, historically at least, indigenous peoples have been explicitly excluded from even those vague categories and principles that have emerged. They were excluded from participating equally in the establishment of the international state system from the sixteenth century onwards because of European expropriation and conquest of their territories (for a survey of this history see Pagden 1995). And although various domestic courts in Canada, Australia, New Zealand and elsewhere (along with the International Court of Justice) have begun – albeit slowly and often inconsistently – to dismantle the legal consequences of these assumptions, indigenous peoples have still tended to be defined not as "peoples" with legal standing for potential self-determination, but rather as "populations" or "minorities" existing within the extant (and supposed) boundaries of legitimate states (see ICJ Reports 1975).

One major reason for this has to do with international norms concerning territorial integrity, which are heavily weighted against upsetting the status quo in order to minimize the opportunity for conflict within the international system as a whole (see Crawford 1979). Where self-determination has been allowed or recognized, the principle of *uti possidetis juris* (literally, "as you possess") has applied, either to the pre-existing external boundaries (as was the case in South America and Africa in the 1960s and 1970s) or to various extant internal boundaries (e.g. the former Soviet Union and Yugoslavia in the 1990s) (see the UN Declaration on the Granting of Independence to Colonial Countries and Peoples [1960] and the Declaration on Principles of International Law Concerning Friendly Relations and Co-operation among States in Accordance with the Charter of the United Nations [1965]). But in the former case, this meant that only *overseas* colonial possessions were entitled to self-determination (the famous "saltwater thesis"). And in the latter case, it was clear that the application of the principle was being driven by the facts and existing geopolitical forces, as opposed to any coherent practice or doctrine established in international law. In either case, indigenous peoples were deemed ineligible for similar treatment. The realist justification, such that it is, is that they are simply too small and powerless to constitute a genuine threat in the international order so as to motivate states to recognize and negotiate with them. The alternative justification is that, in so far as the state within which they currently reside is not violating their human rights, and offers the possibility for various modes of "internal" self-determination, the claim to self-determination has been met.

Thus indigenous peoples have found themselves between a rock and a hard place. There is no clear agreement on who counts as indigenous in the first place. There is no clear agreement on whether they even are a "people" entitled to self-determination in international law. There is acceptance of the legitimacy of the territorial boundaries and exclusive jurisdiction of states against whom indigenous peoples' claims are directed. Indigenous peoples are granted status as a minority group, entitled under Article 27 of the International Covenant on Civil and Political Rights (1966, in force 1976) to "enjoy their own culture", which is, however, compatible with policies that deny them any effective means to do so. Lastly, there is ambiguity about whether the increasingly prominent discourse and practice of human rights can accommodate both individual and collective rights, the latter of which are taken to be central to indigenous peoples' arguments. On top of this, indigenous peoples have had to deal with the forces of economic globalization, in which, among other things, neo-liberal economic policies, reinforced through the discipline imposed by global trade and currency markets, along with international economic bodies and institutions, have constrained the capacity for effective democratic control over valuable resources, including natural resources, which are often of crucial importance to the economic well-being of indigenous peoples. There could not be a better example, in the right to self-determination, of how rights can often be invoked, simultaneously, as statuses, instruments and conduits.

We should expect as much. Once international law began to be conceived more positivistically from the nineteenth century onwards (and especially in civilizational terms), non-state actors such as indigenous peoples lost whatever meagre international status they might once have had (for more background see Anaya 1996; Keene 2002; Keal 2003). Still, our purpose is not merely to describe what happened, but to ask normative questions about what ought to happen now, given this history, or at least to sketch out various possibilities. Adopting a purely positivist or natural law approach will not do, since the two perspectives are difficult to separate when thinking about the law in general. For example, there were hundreds of treaties signed between indigenous peoples and European powers between 1600 and 1800, which arguably remain a source of international law and intersocietal custom governing relations between them (Slattery 1991: 685–91, 700–703; Williams 1997a). But many of these treaties were unfair, many were honoured only in the breach and many indigenous peoples did not sign treaties at all. So we need to combine a concern for the practice of intersocietal engagement and negotiation with some broad principles and norms that might emerge from such practices.

Consider, for example, the way self-determination has been conceived both in terms of intra-state and "external" forms of autonomy, and yet also in relation to the language of human rights. It might seem to follow, given the history recounted above, that indigenous peoples deserve to be accorded the same right to self-determination that was accorded to other groups during the previous decolonization era. But, as we saw, since there is no settled principle of self-determination in international law, it is not clear what that would mean. If it means necessarily independent statehood, then this is problematic for both moral and pragmatic reasons. Secondly, it is not clear that this is what indigenous peoples want, at least as I understand it from how self-determination has been discussed by indigenous representatives in debates over the Draft Declaration, and by many indigenous political theorists. As they tend to point out, European notions of sovereignty and statehood are not necessarily the best match for indigenous understandings of government and political community (see e.g. Boldt & Long 1984; Venne 1998; Alfred 1999). This does not mean that the existing restrictions on the application of the principle of self-determination, or the way human rights norms concerning minority rights have been interpreted, are any less objectionable (see e.g. Turpel 1992; Barsh 1994a). But it does suggest a more thoroughgoing rethinking of these norms in international law and practice more generally.

As I argued above, there is a pressing need to detach self-determination from any necessary relation to statehood and, at the same time, to embed the discourse in broader theories of transnational justice and democracy (see Kingsbury 2001; Buchanan 2004). This is part of a general shift away from thinking of state sovereignty as absolute and indivisible, to thinking of it as a bundle of rights and privileges that can be unbundled and reassembled in various ways.[29] But there is a prior question of the extent to which self-determination is a claim demanded by justice, and then what follows from this in terms of the specific form and scope of such a right.

As I understand it, self-determination enables a group not only to be self-governing, but to ensure that its members enjoy something like freedom as non-domination: that is, the freedom not to be interfered with arbitrarily, to be able to contest those relations of power acting on you, and to have your views and interests taken into account equally. But since we are always enmeshed in a series of involuntary and overlapping forms of interdependency – personal and collective, national and international – self-determination cannot mean primarily freedom from interference *tout court*. The problem is *arbitrary* interference, not interference *per se* (see Pettit 2000). Once again, answers to the question of what constitutes arbitrary interference will vary according to time and circumstances. And once again, the conception of human rights conceived as a common standard can help us evaluate these different responses, without assuming they will take or require a single, universal form.

So if we justify the value of self-determination along these lines, where does this leave the principle as applied to indigenous peoples? It generates a principle that says indigenous people are owed some degree of political control over important aspects of their common life, but shaped also by unavoidable moral and practical interdependency. And as Allen Buchanan has pointed out, given the wide range of possible ways of interpreting what self-determination means and what is required to achieve it, it is actually a mistake to talk about *the* right to self-determination: there are different possibilities and variations. If the language of self-determination is used too narrowly without sensitivity to context, history and appropriateness of fit, it can end up telescoping demands and deepening conflict where flexibility and accommodation are required (see the extensive discussion in Buchanan 2004: pt III). Recall the emphasis on the relational character of rights, as well as conceptions of autonomy more generally (Nedelsky 1993; Kingsbury 2001: 225–6; Young 2002). Political self-determination is as much about the structure of one's relationships with others as about acting apart from them. And so, for example, the Draft Declaration insists on a right to self-determination for indigenous peoples, including the right to determine their own membership and the structure of their own institutions, but also states that individual members have the right to obtain other citizenship (Article 32). Indigenous institutions are also subject to internationally recognized human rights standards (Article 33), which are meant to apply equally to male and female "indigenous individuals" (Article 43). The Draft Declaration seeks to constrain states from encroaching on the right of indigenous communities to "maintain and strengthen" their distinct political, economic, social and cultural characteristics, and legal systems (Article 4), but the "specific form" of this capacity is left ambiguous between "self-determination", "autonomy" and "self-government" (Article 31).

The danger with the discourse of self-determination is the extent to which it encourages political mobilization that fixes rather than pluralizes political identities, a process that we know can go terribly wrong. Exclusion, xenophobia, maltreatment of minorities and "internal" dissenters and, at worst, ethnic cleansing and murder have all been justified in the name of self-determination (see Eisenberg & Spinner-Halev 2005). Hence the emphasis on relational self-determination and the attempt to disaggregate self-determination from any necessary connection with separate statehood. But again we face conceptual and practical challenges. Given their long exclusion from the global public sphere, indigenous peoples had little opportunity to contribute to or shape the major human rights instruments drafted in the immediate aftermath of the Second World War (see esp. Barsh 1994a; Anaya 1996: esp. 19–23). The activism surrounding the Draft Declaration is undoubtedly an attempt to redress that deficit. But the language of the Draft Declaration also presents a challenge to human rights discourse, for it talks not only about respecting the rights of "indigenous individuals" (see above) but also the rights of *peoples*, a group right. (Note that the right to self-determination proclaimed in the United Nations Charter, as well as in the International Covenant on Civil and Political Rights and the International Covenant on Economic, Social and Cultural Rights, also conflicts with the Universal Declaration of Human Rights, so the problem is not unique to the situation of indigenous peoples, but is endemic to the state system as a whole.) If modern human rights entails moral individualism all the way down, does this mean that any normative framework based on them cannot accommodate indigenous peoples' claims? The short answer is no. But a more interesting answer must pursue the possibilities and tensions raised in the process of customizing human rights norms to indigenous peoples' circumstances.

First, we need to know what kind of group right we are talking about. A group right usually means a right that can be exercised (or waived or alienated) by a group, and not an individual. (There can also be individual rights that are only exercisable by members of a group, but not by the collective entity as such; i.e. "personal" collective rights.) Thus, the right to self-determination or to self-government is a group right in the sense that it is exercised by the group, or the members of the group acting collectively. The crucial issue is the standing accorded to the group along these lines; it is to the *group* to whom duties are owed, and only to individuals derivatively as members of that group. And so a right of self-government is justified with reference to the interests jointly held of each member of the group to live in a self-governing community, a right that can only be realized jointly and not individually. Or a right to cultural integrity is a right that appeals to the interest jointly held by members of a group to practice their culture free from arbitrary interference, and can only be realized jointly and not individually. What is doing the deep justificatory work here? I think at this point we reach a kind of discursive *modus vivendi* between different justifications of indigenous rights. People can agree on the legitimacy of some forms of collective rights, but not necessarily on the appropriate justificatory structure (for the idea of a "discursive *modus vivendi*" see Ivison 2002). For defenders of indigenous rights within the extant human rights framework, group rights are ultimately only justifiable with reference to the basic interests of individuals. Thus, although there can be no group *human* rights, there can be collective legal rights – to self-government or to forms of cultural integrity – that help realize or protect more basic human rights, or individual autonomy more generally (see Jones 1999; Buchanan 2004). According to this view, rights to self-government, cultural integrity and the recognition of customary law are essentially remedial rights; they could equally well apply to other groups, but the circumstances of indigenous peoples are such that they most often obtain in relation to them (see Levy 2000: 161–96; Buchanan 2004: 415–24).

On the other hand, there are those who argue that some indigenous peoples' rights must be understood as corporate rights, in the sense that the moral standing is ultimately possessed by the group, and not merely derivatively from the interests of the individual members of that group. Sometimes this view is ascribed to indigenous peoples on the grounds that their understanding of the kinds of liberties and obligations referred to in European political thought is very different from within indigenous political theories (see e.g. Barsh 1994b).[30] There are deep differences, to be sure, and these differences will mean conflicts between different understandings of rights held by different groups. But it is not clear that they are ultimately incommensurable. Indigenous people themselves have certainly made use of the language of rights, as we have seen (see § "Conclusion: two problems"). And I have previously emphasized how the meaning and force of a concept or language can change when put to work in new contexts, and especially by those who were originally excluded from its initial formulation. In particular, the *modus vivendi* between collective and corporate justifications of indigenous rights might well encourage various institutional experiments for working out the appropriate fit between abstract principles of human rights and the particular histories, cultures and circumstances in which they are applied. The diversity of approaches to indigenous rights, often taken as incoherence, might in fact offer greater possibilities given the range of contextual and historic differences faced by different peoples in different parts of the world. One need only think of the situation of indigenous groups in North America and Australasia, compared with those in Asia and Africa, to appreciate the need for such an approach (see Kingsbury 1998).

Conclusion: emergent universalism

To conclude, let me highlight one broad way in which these disagreements and struggles over theorizing indigenous peoples' rights might provide intimations of what we might call an *emergent* universalism (or cosmopolitanism). A property is emergent in so far as it arises out of some lower-level properties in place, but is not merely those lower-level properties differently described. What I want to suggest is that the struggle to accommodate and shape international norms and laws to meet indigenous peoples' demands provides intimations of transnational modes of political community that go beyond "explanatory nationalism" and "explanatory cosmopolitanism" (and explanatory realism, for that matter).[31] They point beyond the nation-state- and exclusively inter-state-made law, but not necessarily to the structure of a global political community derived from freestanding universal moral principles. Instead, their demand for justification of their exclusion from existing international norms and principles points to the way historical injustice and difference can structure our moral concepts, and presents deep challenges to the justificatory ambitions of liberal theories of global justice. And yet their demand for justification in itself, combined with their re-interpretation and application of these norms in new ways, points to a practice of seeking more just relations between them and existing states and international institutions that is pluralist but not state-centric, immanent but also universalist.

For all of the work currently underway in demonstrating the emergence of supranational and global forms of "governance" and so on, we still lack plausible models of political membership to accompany these new modes of global political authority. We have emerging notions of "post-sovereign citizenship" and the like, but they remain underdeveloped. The concept of global citizenship on its own is too vague and too weak. How can the basic goods of citizenship – of self-protection and self-government – be realized beyond territorially bound political communities? Appealing to international human rights standards and non-elected human rights commissions, important as this activity can be, is a thin approximation of the already attenuated forms of rights-based self-government and self-protection within liberal democratic states. Still, it seems clear that in order to secure the conditions in which self-rule and self-protection can be realized, various transnational and global processes have to be taken into account when theorizing about the value of political membership. And although these developments and interdependencies themselves do not add up to the outline of a transnational polity, they do suggest certain possibilities.

One of these possibilities is the increasing relevance of overlapping forms of political membership, not merely as a consequence of interdependency, but as required by or relevant to considerations of justice. In other words, in order to secure the goods of political membership, including protection and promotion of our basic rights, we need effective forms of multiple political membership, and these need to be *constructed* politically and not merely postulated (see Williams 2007). The situation of indigenous peoples is interesting in this regard, and should be theorized in relation to emerging conceptions of "de-centered democracy" and "multi-level governance" (see e.g. Young 2002; Bohman 2004; Tully 2000b). They have sought to negotiate the terms of their membership within the states in which they currently reside, and yet also secure international standing as members of particular "peoples", and at the same time re-theorize what a "people" refers to. They are territorially rooted, and yet also cosmopolitan in orientation, just in so far as they see the protection and promotion of their fundamental interests in various forms of shared jurisdiction and overlapping political membership across and within borders. Of course, their experience of existing between national citizenship and international standing has more often than not been one of frustration and disadvantage, as opposed to one of possibility. And their push for recognition of overlapping political membership is still viewed sceptically, and often resentfully, by some of their fellow citizens. But notice the conceptual space opened up between nationalism and cosmopolitanism. Most significantly, in appealing to liberal norms of legitimacy that derive their moral force from ideals of mutual justification and equality, the claims of indigenous peoples link history and prudence with justice, and thus normativity with politics.

Notes

Introduction

1. Here I have been influenced by Stuart Hampshire, *Justice is Conflict* (London: Duckworth, 1990) and Bernard Williams, *In the Beginning Was the Deed* (Princeton, NJ: Princeton University Press, 2005).
2. For further discussion, to which I am indebted, see Paul Patton, "Nietzsche and Hobbes", *International Studies in Philosophy* 33(3) (2001), 99–116, and Brian Leiter, *Nietzsche: On Morality* (London: Routledge, 2002).
3. See also Nietzsche, *Human, All Too Human*, D. Fuss (ed.) (London: Routledge, 1996), 93. Note that this cuts both ways. Since there is an intimate connection between power and beliefs about power, rights extend just as far as one "appears valuable, essential, unlosable, unconquerable and the like to the other" (*ibid.*). The weak may very well have rights too in this sense, but they will always be more limited than those of the strong.
4. I have drawn on the discussion in Ian Shapiro, *The Evolution of Rights in Liberal Theory* (Cambridge: Cambridge University Press, 1986).
5. Hohfeld's analysis is discussed extensively in the secondary literature and in just about every book written in the twentieth century about rights. Two very helpful and clear discussions can be found in Wayne Sumner, *The Moral Foundation of Rights* (Oxford: Clarendon Press, 1987), ch. 2, and William Edmundson, *An Introduction to Rights* (Cambridge: Cambridge University Press, 2004), ch. 5.
6. The language of core and periphery is from W. Sumner, "Rights", in *The Blackwell Guide to Ethical Theory*, H. Lafollette (ed.), 288–305 (Oxford: Blackwell, 2000), 291.
7. For an interesting attempt to elaborate the distinctive nature of Canadian constitutionalism, see Jeremy Webber, *Reimagining Canada: Language, Culture and the Canadian Constitution* (Montreal: McGill-Queen's University Press, 1994). For a broader discussion of multinational constitutionalism see James Tully, *Strange Multiplicity: Constitutionalism in an Age of Diversity* (Cambridge: Cambridge University Press, 1995) and Alaig G. Gagnon & James Tully (eds), *Multinational Democracies* (Cambridge: Cambridge University Press, 2001) esp. 1–33. The distinctiveness of Canadian rights culture is also discussed by Michael Ignatieff, *The Rights Revolution* (Toronto: Anansi Press, 2000), 9–15.
8. See the Canadian Charter of Rights and Freedoms (1982), § 33(1).

1. A naturalistic approach

1. To borrow the terms introduced by Wesley Hohfeld and discussed in the Intro-duction above. See Walter Wheeler Cook (ed.), *Fundamental Legal Conceptions as Applied to Judicial Reasoning* (Westport, CT: Greenwood Press, 1978).

2. The example is from Robert Post, "Democratic Constitutionalism and Cultural Heterogeneity", *Australian Journal of Legal Philosophy* 25(2) (2000), 65–84.

3. For more general remarks on realism in political theory see Williams, *In the Beginning Was the Deed*, 1–17.

4. Recall Baier's genealogy of rights discussed above, in the Introduction.

5. The phrase is Knud Haakonssen's (*The Science of a Legislator: The Natural Juris-prudence of David Hume and Adam Smith* [Cambridge: Cambridge University Press, 1981], 43). For David Hume, history provides the material through which to identify and fix the "principles of [the moral philosopher's] science", just as the "natural philosopher becomes acquainted with the nature of plants ... by the experiments which he forms concerning them"; see *A Treatise of Human Nature*, L. A. Selby-Bigge (ed.) (Oxford: Clarendon Press, [1739–40] 1978), 84. Ambition, avarice, self-love, vanity, friendship, generosity and public spirit operate in just about every society.

6. The idea of a "second nature" is from Moira Gatens and Genevieve Lloyd, *Collective Imaginings: Spinoza, Past and Present* (London, Routledge, 1999) pp. 118, 136.

7. Note that the claim is evaluative: all human beings have the innate equipment required for practical reasoning, and so on, but Nussbaum presupposes a nor-mative premise that these capabilities are ones we actually do value, or at least should value, given the opportunity to think through the consequences of deny-ing their centrality to our lives. For Nussbaum the political goal is capability, not functioning.

8. I am indebted here to Leif Wenar's discussion in "Rights", *Stanford Encyclo-paedia of Philosophy*, http://plato.stanford.edu/ (accessed October 2007), esp. §6.2.

9. "We say that black South Africans have the moral right to full representation even though this right has not been accorded legal recognition, and in saying this we mean to point to the right as a moral reason for changing the legal system so as to accord it recognition" (Sumner, *The Moral Foundation of Rights*, 13). But cf. Derrick Darby, "Blacks and Rights: A Bittersweet Legacy", *Law, Culture and Humanities* 2(3) (2006), 420–39.

10. For example, John Chesterman and Brian Galligan refer to native title rights as evidence of "the acknowledgment that Aborigines possess certain rights that do not pertain to other Australians" (*Citizens Without Rights: Aborigines and Australian Citizenship* [Cambridge: Cambridge University Press, 1997], 193). Similarly, they suggest that, with the legal recognition of native title, "Aborigi-nes, for the first time, have been recognised by the law to possess certain rights that cannot be possessed by non-Aborigines" (*ibid.*, 199). In other contexts they speak as though these rights themselves, and not simply their recognition or institutionalization, develop and change over time. They therefore appear to accept both that Aboriginal rights are not reducible to legal rights and that these rights are evolving over time. I am grateful to Paul Patton for discussion on this point.

11. I am indebted in the paragraphs that follow to discussion with and forthcom-ing work by Paul Patton.

12. The control refers to three powers: to waive the duty; to enforce the duty; or to waive *Y*'s duty to compensate me for his original breach.

13. See the discussion of Locke in Chapter 3. It was precisely the logical possibil-
    ity of alienation that Grotius and Hobbes took advantage of in linking natural
    rights to the justification of authoritarian rule. In fact, the denial of inalienability
    has often been linked to a denial of those aspects of human agency that warrant
    ascribing rights to particular individuals in the first place, as in the case of slaves,
    indigenous peoples and women (although with reference to different properties
    or capacities in each case).
14. The most important contemporary defence of the interest theory of rights
    is Joseph Raz, *The Morality of Freedom* (Oxford: Oxford University Press,
    1986).
15. Note that this puts a brake on third-party beneficiaries, which is a problem
    for other kinds of interest theories, since third-party beneficiaries do not have
    interests sufficiently strong to warrant having a right in the way Raz sets the
    condition (my interest has to be such that it justifies X's duty to me). How-
    ever, it is not clear that Raz has fully escaped the problem of third-party ben-
    eficiaries here; see the discussion by Gopal Sreenivasan, "A Hybrid Theory of
    Claim-Rights", *Oxford Journal of Legal Studies* 25(2) (2005), 257–74, esp.
    265–7.
16. For Raz, only those things that have ultimate, non-derivative value can have
    rights, hence not plants; this raises various complications, but still leaves a
    fairly wide array of possible rights-holders. See the discussion in *The Morality
    of Freedom*, 175–80.

2. Natural law and natural rights

1. For a penetrating critique of the distinction between negative and positive rights
   along these lines see Stephen Holmes and Cass Sunstein, *The Cost of Rights:
   Why Liberty Depends on Taxes* (New York: Norton, 1999).
2. For a very interesting discussion of the "work" of politics in this sense see Jill
   Frank, *A Democracy of Distinction: Aristotle and the Work of Politics* (Chicago,
   IL: University of Chicago Press, 2005).
3. The emergence of this idea of natural rights can be traced back at least to
   the first part of the fourteenth century and the English Franciscan William of
   Ockham, and his redefinition of *dominium* as a power of action. See Brian
   Tierney, *The Idea of Natural Rights: Studies on Natural Rights, Natural Law
   and Church Law 1150–1625* (Atlanta, GA: Scholars Press, 1997); cf. Quentin
   Skinner, *The Foundations of Modern Political Thought Volume Two: The Age of
   Reformation* (Cambridge: Cambridge University Press, 1978), 176–70.
4. Vitoria himself did not think the Indians had done any such thing with regard
   to the Spanish. On this conception of "commerce" and the "right of hospitality"
   see Anthony Pagden, "Stoicism, Cosmopolitanism and the Legacy of European
   Imperialism", *Constellations* 7(1) (2000), 3–22; see also his *Lords of All the
   World: Ideologies of Empire in Spain, Britain and France c. 1500–c.1800* (New
   Haven, CT: Yale University Press, 1995), 51–62. Cf. Sankar Muthu, *Enlightenment Against Empire* (Princeton, NJ: Princeton University Press, 2004).
5. On the emergence of Catholic and Protestant resistance theory see Quentin
   Skinner's now classic *Foundations of Modern Political Thought, Volume One:
   The Renaissance* (Cambridge: Cambridge University Press, 1978) and *Volume
   Two: The Age of Reformation*.
6. This concern with unity, and the relation between the unity of the city and
   nature, is a central issue for what historians of this period refer to as "civil
   philosophy" or *scientia civilis*; see Quentin Skinner, "Hobbes's Changing

Conception of Civil Science", in his *Visions of Politics Volume III: Hobbes and Civil Science*, 66–86 (Cambridge: Cambridge University Press, 2001).

7. This is one of the key themes in Richard Tuck's groundbreaking *Natural Rights Theories: Their Origin and Development* (Cambridge: Cambridge University Press, 1981).

8. See A. Brett, "Natural Right and Civil Community: The Civil Philosophy of Hugo Grotius", *Historical Journal* 43(1) (2002), 31–51, esp. 48–9.

9. Scholars disagree about the extent to which scepticism is the central philosophical problem for Hobbes. See Richard Tuck, *Philosophy and Government 1572–1651* (Cambridge: Cambridge University Press, 1993), and Quentin Skinner, *Reason and Rhetoric in the Philosophy of Hobbes* (Cambridge: Cambridge University Press, 1996), who emphasizes the role played by rhetoric and its effect on the stability of moral concepts.

10. On the centrality of rhetoric to his philosophical project in *Leviathan*, see Skinner, *Reason and Rhetoric*.

11. Laws are not laws unless God commands them (Thomas Hobbes, *Leviathan*, E. Curley [ed.] [Indianapolis, IN: Hackett, 1994], xv.41). God's right to reign over us derives not from the fact that he created us, but rather from his "irresistible power", which also makes it difficult for us to understand many of his actions (*ibid.*, xxxi.5). But as Edwin Curley notes (*ibid.*, 100–101, n.17), the passage in *Leviathan* where Hobbes writes that God's command transforms prudential theorems into laws is dropped in the later Latin *Leviathan*, published in 1668.

12. On the difference between consent as legal agreement versus a coincidence of judgement, see the helpful discussion in Ross Harrison, *Hobbes, Locke and Confusion's Masterpiece: An Examination of Seventeenth-Century Political Philosophy* (Cambridge: Cambridge University Press, 2002), 188–9.

13. Hobbes also thinks, like Grotius, that in order to preserve my life I can contract with someone to exercise almost total control over it (Hobbes, *Leviathan*, xx.10–12).

14. Conscience, for Hobbes, is simply the individual's judgement, not some special source of knowledge or revelation linked directly to God (*Leviathan*, xxix.6–7). It cannot be our ultimate guide to action since we give it up when we lay down our right in forming the commonwealth. People often say that they have conflicting commands from God and their sovereign, but it is one thing to believe that you do and another to know that you do (*ibid.*, xliii.1). Hobbes expresses deep scepticism about our ability to know whether or not someone really has had a genuine revelation, and therefore counsels caution about listening to those – other than the sovereign – who claim to know what God's will actually is (see e.g. *ibid.*, xxxvi.19).

15. In fact, there are two agreements made in the course of establishing a state: first, agreement to constitute an association or union, followed by a decree (by majority) to establish the particular form of government capable of providing for their security; and secondly, a reciprocal agreement between the members of the association (citizens) and the sovereign, the former to obey and carry out their civic duties, and the latter to protect and care for the state. See Samuel Pufendorf, *On the Duty of Man and Citizen According to Natural Law*, James Tully and Michael Silverthorne (eds) (Cambridge: Cambridge University Press, 1991), II.6.9–10.

3. Rights as property

1. I have argued this at much greater length in *The Self at Liberty: Political Argument and the Arts of Government* (Ithaca, NY: Cornell University Press, 1997);

see also Knud Haakonssen, "From Natural Law to the Rights of Man: A European Perspective on American Debates", in *A Culture of Rights: The Bill of Rights in Philosophy, Politics and Law 1791 and 1991*, M. Lacey & J. Haakonssen (eds), 19–61 (Cambridge: Cambridge University Press, 1991), 46ff.; James Tully, "Governing Conduct", in his *An Approach to Political Philosophy: Locke in Context*, Q. Skinner (ed.), 179–241 (Cambridge: Cambridge University Press, 1993).

2. For a radical challenge to these assumptions see some of the work of Peter Singer, collected in his *Unsanctifying Human Life: Essays on Ethics*, Helga Kuhse (ed.) (Oxford: Blackwell, 2002).

3. In addition to the work of Singer, see Tom Regan, *The Case for Animal Rights* (Berkeley, CA: University of California Press, 2004).

4. He is not alone in thinking this in relation to the foundations of rights: see also Michael Perry, *The Idea of Human Rights: Four Enquiries* (Oxford: Oxford University Press, 1998), 11–42, and John Finnis, *Natural Law and Natural Rights* (Oxford: Clarendon Press, 1980).

5. Hobbes defines a person as "he, whose words or actions are considered, either as his own, or as representing the words or actions of an other man, or of any other thing to whom they are attributed, whether Truly or by Fiction" (*Leviathan*, xvi.1).

6. If, as Hobbes argues, the father is taken to represent the family (*Leviathan* xxii.162–3) and exercises its rights on the behalf of its members, then servants and women cannot be counted as natural persons "since they lack the required capacity to speak and act on their own behalf" (Quentin Skinner, "Hobbes and the Purely Artificial Person of the State", in his *Visions of Politics Volume III*, 177–208, esp. 192).

7. See his extraordinary discussion of the case of the "strange and deformed birth" in *The Elements of Law: Natural and Politic*, F. Tonnies (ed.), M. Goldsmith (intro.) (London: Cass, 1969), 189, and *On the Citizen*, R. Tuck & M. Silverthorne (eds and trans.) (Cambridge: Cambridge University Press, 1998), XVII, xii.

8. However note that they have not forfeited all of their rights, despite potentially being lawfully killed to protect others. They have been given the law of nature but have chosen to disregard it. They remain bound by it but can be legitimately treated differently than other rights-bearing and duty-bound moral agents.

9. There is an excellent discussion of Locke on the family and the rights of children in A. John Simmons, *The Lockean Theory of Rights* (Princeton, NJ: Princeton University Press, 1992), 167–221.

10. This is why, for Locke, atheists could not be tolerated; they lacked the capacity for the right kind of moral agency and were basically untrustworthy, however much they might be sensitive to the "law of opinion and reputation" (see John Locke, *A Letter Concerning Toleration*, J. Tully [ed.] [Indianapolis, IN: Hackett, 1983], 51). Of course, we might well want to ask about the force of the argument underlying this view (for a spirited, albeit carefully couched and limited defence of aspects of it, see Jeremy Waldron, *God, Locke and Equality: Christian Foundations in Locke's Political Thought* [Cambridge: Cambridge University Press, 2002], ch. 8). The crucial issue is the relation between the capacity for abstraction and our conception of ourselves as moral beings. Locke assumes that the capacity for abstraction is from God and that through it we are able to conceive of ourselves as moral agents bound by his laws. But we might start from the capacity for abstraction and move directly to moral agency independently of God; Locke might reject this move, but we might not.

11. Locke is often read as denying tolerance to Catholics, and there are points in *A Letter Concerning Toleration* where this seems clear (esp. p. 50). But his main problem is with the political consequences of various Catholic principles, especially as they affected political obligation and rights of resistance, as opposed to Catholic worship itself, which many of his contemporaries claimed was idolatrous. That means that at least some Catholics might be tolerable, at least if they renounced certain political principles, as much as others were not. See the very interesting discussion in John Marshall, *John Locke, Toleration and Early Enlightenment Culture* (Cambridge: Cambridge University Press, 2006), 682–94; cf. interpretations of Waldron, *God, Locke and Equality*, 219–23, and Richard Ashcraft, *Revolutionary Politics and Locke's Two Treatises of Government* (Princeton, NJ: Princeton University Press, 1986), 501–4.

12. However, this is a claim based on *charity*, not justice (see *Two Treatises*, I.42). Locke also clearly endorses fairly substantial material inequalities between property owners and the landless, since once money is introduced (via consent) some can accumulate considerably more wealth than others without violating the provisos. For more discussion see John Tully, *A Discourse on Property: John Locke and his Adversaries* (Cambridge: Cambridge University Press, 1980); Jeremy Waldron, *The Right to Private Property* (Oxford: Oxford University Press, 1991); and Gopal Sreenivasan, *The Limits of Lockean Rights in Property* (Oxford: Oxford University Press, 1995).

13. Taylor considers Locke's argument to be one of the prime examples of an atomist political theory.

14. There are other Hofheldian rights too. See the excellent discussion in Simmons, *The Lockean Theory of Rights*, ch. 2 *passim*; cf. Ashcraft, *Revolutionary Politics and Locke's Two Treatises*; Tully, *A Discourse on Property*; John Dunn, *The Political Thought of John Locke: An Historical Account of the Argument of the "Two Treatises of Government"* (Cambridge: Cambridge University Press, 1983).

15. See, for example, *Two Treatises*, II.22, where Locke talks of a liberty to "follow my own Will in all things, where the Rule prescribes not; and not to be subject to the inconstant, uncertain, unknown, Arbitrary Will of another Man".

16. See for example the way Section 2(b) of the Canadian Charter of Rights (protecting freedom of expression, among other things) has been interpreted in relation to Section 15 (guaranteeing members of minority groups the right to equal protection and equal benefit of the law) in the Supreme Court of Canada decision *R. v. Keegstra* (1990). For a clear and rigorous analysis of this whole issue see L. W. Sumner, *The Hateful and the Obscene: Studies in the Limits of Free Expression* (Toronto: University of Toronto Press, 2004).

17. Note that a right to freedom of speech is a liberty: it involves my being free to express (or not express) my views. The right to the equal protection of the laws is a claim-right: that is, it imposes duties on others (in this example) to not express certain opinions (i.e. views that promote hatred against others).

18. Pocock does not deny the importance of Lockean arguments to the American revolutionary literature. His point is that Locke cannot be taken as the exclusive source for their arguments, nor should he be seen as representing the core of American political ideology from the eighteenth century onwards.

19. The phrase is Tully's: see his "Placing the Two Treatises", in *Political Discourse in Early Modern Britain*, Nicholas Phillipson and Quentin Skinner (eds), 253–80 (Cambridge: Cambridge University Press, 1993), 254.

20. This is shown brilliantly by Tully, "Placing the Two Treatises". See also Steve Pincus, "Neither Machiavellian Moment nor Possessive Individualism: Commercial Society and the Defenders of the English Commonwealth", *American*

Historical Review **103**(3) (1998), 705–36. Both Pocock and Skinner acknowledge how, at times, Locke sits between these two languages of political thought: see for example, J. G. A. Pocock, "A Discourse on Sovereignty", in *Political Discourse*, Phillipson and Skinner (eds), 416–17, and Quentin Skinner, "The State", in *Political Innovation and Conceptual Change*, Terence Ball, James Farr and Russell L. Hanson (eds), 90–131 (Cambridge: Cambridge University Press, 1989), 114–16.

21. For an interesting development of this theme, albeit along different lines than pursued here, see Thomas Pangle, *The Spirit of Modern Republicanism: The Moral Vision of the American Founders and the Philosophy of Locke* (Chicago, IL: University of Chicago Press, 1988).

22. Locke's most extensive discussion of virtue is probably in *Some Thoughts Concerning Education*, R. H. Quick (ed.) (Cambridge: Cambridge University Press, 1902).

23. As Locke wrote: "the great principle and foundation of all virtue and worth is plac'd in this: That a man is able to deny himself his own desires, cross his own inclinations, and purely follow what Reason directs as best, tho' the Appetite lean the other Way" (*Some Thoughts Concerning Education*, §33).

24. For Locke, slaves are essentially rightless human beings who have "quit" the law of nature or reason (see *Two Treatises*, II.16, II.24, II.85, II.172–3). Interestingly, he thinks it possible that people can be taken lawfully as slaves in a just war; see (*ibid.*, II.16, II.24, II.85).

25. For criticism of the distinction between civic and ethnic nationalism see Bernard Yack, "The Myth of the Civic Nation", in *Theorizing Nationalism*, Ronald Beiner (ed.), 103–18 (New York: SUNY Press, 1999).

26. Of course the other great scourge of natural rights was Edmund Burke, who in his *Reflections on the Revolution in France* (1790) argued against the idea of abstract natural rights (in the context of a general critique of abstraction and rationalism in politics) and claimed that rights only made sense in light of the particular history, traditions, customs and institutions of the country in which they were claimed.

27. "All governments that we have any account of have been gradually established by habit, after having been formed by force … Contracts come from governments, not governments from contracts" (Jeremy Bentham, "Anarchical Fallacies", in *Nonsense Upon Stilts: Bentham, Burke and Marx on the Rights of Man*, J. Waldron [ed.] [London: Methuen, 1987], 55).

28. As has been pointed out, this means that Bentham accepts that we *can* have non-convential moral duties that are not, in every instance, analysable in terms of concrete legal sanctions or social recognition.

29. Of course, a consequentialist might include the protection of moral rights as among the things to be promoted since doing so promotes utility or well-being overall. This is John Stuart Mill's argument; see Chapter 6 below.

30. Ronald Dworkin is clearly one philosopher who takes moral rights to be fundamental in some sense. But even he claims that although the most important moral rights are "natural" – in the sense of not being the product of any legislation or convention or hypothetical contract – this does not mean they are akin to "spectral attributes worn by primitive men like amulets … to ward off tyranny" (*Taking Rights Seriously* [Cambridge, MA: Harvard University Press, 1977], 176). Instead, on the "constructive model", what is required is that the best political programme will be one that takes the protection of *certain* important individual choices to be fundamental and not subordinate to just any social goal or duty.

4. Dignity

1. Here, as in many places, Kant is deeply indebted to Rousseau: first, for Rousseau's critique (in the *Discourse on the Origins of Inequality*) of our increasing need for relative esteem as we learn to compare ourselves with others and thus come to depend on others (unfortunately, at least for Rousseau, for all the wrong reasons); and secondly, for his republican vision in the *Social Contract* in which genuinely reciprocal relations cancel out the bad effects of unequal dependence, and thus dignity is attributed to all as members of the common will. For a nice genealogy of this notion of dignity see Charles Taylor, "The Politics of Recognition", in his *Multiculturalism and the Politics of Recognition*, A. Gutman (ed.), 44–51 (Princeton, NJ: Princeton University Press, 1991).

2. The section numbers in references to Kant's work refer to the standard Berlin Academy Edition unless indicated otherwise.

3. Another way to express this idea is to say that Kant conceives of human beings as reason-responsive beings; we bind ourselves to norms and act on the basis of reasons, and think of ourselves as free just in so far as we do. It follows that we ought to treat others as reason-responsive too, and thus capable of binding themselves according to norms that they legislate for themselves. For a systematic contemporary elaboration of this theme see Robert Brandom, *Making it Explicit: Reasoning, Representing and Discursive Commitment* (Cambridge, MA: Harvard University Press, 1994); see also his historical reconstruction of the idealist tradition in *Tales of the Mighty Dead* (Cambridge, MA: Harvard University Press, 2002).

4. On the historical background and emergence of Kant's moral philosophy see Jerome Schneewind, *The Invention of Autonomy: A History of Modern Moral Philosophy* (Cambridge: Cambridge University Press, 1998).

5. On Kant's reading of Hobbes see especially Richard Tuck, *Rights of War and Peace: Political Thought and the International Order from Grotius to Kant* (Oxford: Oxford University Press, 1999), 207–25.

6. Whether or not Kant can actually keep his anthropology apart from his metaphysics is a topic of considerable dispute. See for example Ian Hunter, *Rival Enlightenments: Civil and Metaphysical Philosophy in Early Modern Germany* (Cambridge: Cambridge University Press, 2001).

7. Of course, there might be cases where an exception to this rule is justified, despite what Kant suggests in some places. For a helpful discussion see Allen W. Wood, *Kant* (Oxford: Blackwell, 2005), 136–7.

8. This point is well emphasized by a number of commentators, including Schneewind, *The Invention of Autonomy*, and Wood, *Kant*, ch. 7.

9. "*Recht*" or right refers to "right" but also to the legal system in its entirety, as well as its rational foundation. Kant uses it in all these senses.

10. Virtue is "the moral strength of a human being's will in fulfilling his duty, a moral constraint through his own lawgiving reason, insofar as this constitutes itself an authority executing the law" (6:405). For more discussion of this important aspect of Kant's moral and political theory, see Patrick Riley, *Kant's Political Philosophy* (Totowa, NJ: Rowman & Littlefield, 1983); Jerome Schneewind, "Autonomy, Obligation and Virtue: An Overview of Kant's Ethics", in *The Cambridge Companion to Kant*, Paul Guyer (ed.), 309–41 (Cambridge: Cambridge University Press, 1992); Robert B. Louden, *Kant's Impure Ethics: From Rational Beings to Human Beings* (Oxford: Oxford University Press, 2000).

11. The problem is this. Politics cannot be said to provide *incentives* for us to act morally, since our duty to be moral derives from reason, and not from any desire to avoid punishment or from prudential considerations more generally. Right

might be said to create the conditions in which *others* cannot interfere with our acting morally, but Kant is clear that whatever physical constraints we face, our *willing* cannot be obstructed from the outside: "Even if, by a special disfavour of fortune or by the niggardly provision of a stepmotherly nature, this will should wholly lack the capacity to carry out its purpose ... then like a jewel, it would still shine by itself, as something that has its full worth in itself" (4:394). So right concerns only our *external* actions. But how then is it ultimately related to morality?

12. One of Kant's most important contributions to moral philosophy is to have begun to detach the normativity of moral and legal norms from any necessary relation to religion. Having said that, his own views on religion have a complex relation to his overall moral theory. For two very interesting but very different interpretations of this relation see Onora O'Neill, "Kant on Reason and Religion", in *The Tanner Lectures on Human Values, 18*, G. Peterson (ed.), 267–308 (Salt Lake City, UT: University of Utah Press, 1997); and Frederick Beiser, "Moral Faith and the Highest Good", in *The Cambridge Companion to Kant and Modern Philosophy*, Paul Guyer (ed.), 588–629 (Cambridge: Cambridge University Press, 2006).

13. Interestingly, on this interpretation, Kant has a legitimate claim to be included in the history of the development of the concept of "freedom as non-domination" that Phillip Pettit claims was eclipsed by the Hobbesian analysis of liberty as non-interference from the seventeenth century onwards. See above, § "Rights republicanism", and Pettit, *Republicanism: A Theory of Freedom and Government* (Oxford: Oxford University Press, 1997), esp. 41–5. Arthur Ripstein also makes the connection in "Beyond the Harm Principle", *Philosophy and Public Affairs* **34**(3) (2006), 215–45.

14. Also, "a public can achieve enlightenment only slowly. A revolution may well bring about a falling off of personal despotism and of avaricious or tyrannical oppression, but never a true reform in one's way of thinking" ("An Answer to the Question: What is Enlightenment?", in Kant, *Practical Philosophy*, 8:36). On the the nature of Kantian teleology see Riley, *Kant's Political Philosophy*, 172–7, cf. Elisabeth Ellis, *Kant's Politics: Provisional Theory for an Uncertain World* (New Haven, CT: Yale University Press, 2005), 62–9.

15. For two excellent discussions of this aspect of Kant's political theory, to which I am indebted, see Muthu, *Enlightenment Against Empire*, and Ellis, *Kant's Politics*.

16. Kant goes so far as to describe right as "that which is not mingled with anything ethical" (6:232). See also Robert Pippin, "Mine and Thine? The Kantian State", in *The Cambridge Companion to Kant and Modern Philosophy*, Guyer (ed.), 416–46, esp. 434.

17. Hence the otherwise puzzling claim by Kant, that "the problem of establishing a state is soluble, even for a nation of devils (if only they have understanding) ... For the problem is not the moral improvement of human beings but only the mechanism of nature, and what the task requires one to know is how this can be put to use in human beings in order so to arrange the conflict of their unpeaceable dispositions within a people that they themselves have to constrain one another and submit to coercive law and so bring about a condition of peace in which laws have force' (*Perpetual Peace*, 8:366).

18. This has very interesting implications for Kant's analysis of the property claims of colonial powers in the "new world", since he thinks it is perfectly possible for a group to claim ownership of a territory without having cultivated it or used it in some particularly productive way. For more discussion see Muthu,

Enlightenment Against Empire, and Ivison, "The Nature of Rights and the History of Empire", in *British Political Thought in History, Literature and Theory, 1500–1800*, David Armitage (ed.), 191–211 (Cambridge: Cambridge University Press, 2006). But cf. James Tully, "The Kantian Idea of Europe: Critical and Cosmopolitan Perspectives", in *The Idea of Europe: From Antiquity to European Union*, Anthony Pagden (ed.), 331–58 (Cambridge: Cambridge University Press, 2002).

19. I am indebted here and in the following paragraph to Arthur Ripstein, "Private Order and Public Justice: Kant and Rawls", *Virginia Law Review* **92** (2006), 1391–438, and "Beyond the Harm Principle".

20. If I use your property without your permission, or I damage it and thus disable you from using it for your purposes, I have coerced you. If I violate the terms of our contract then I coerce you in the sense of depriving you of the means you were entitled to under the terms of our agreement. If I take advantage of you as your teacher or parent then I also coerce you by using you for my purposes, as opposed to respecting you as an end in yourself. All of these are instances of coercion that are inconsistent with any kind of reciprocal limits on freedom. Coercion that hinders these forms of coercion is consistent with freedom as non-dependence.

21. This obviously bears a striking resemblance to familiar modes of Christian thought. For an interesting attempt to make provisional right much more central to Kant's political theory, see Ellis, *Kant's Politics*, esp. ch. 4.

22. I am indebted here to Pippin, "Mine and Thine?", 438–9. I am also grateful to Sankar Muthu for many helpful conversations about these issues in Kant's work more generally.

23. In fact, Kant thinks democracy is *necessarily* a despotism (see 8:352–3).

24. Ideal rational beings – independent of being determined by any kind of sensible impulse – in willing the law obey it, and would obey the laws of a just state as naturally as the laws of gravity. But human beings are not those kinds of agents. For a provocative discussion of what he calls "the metaphysical anthropology of *homo duplex*" in Kant's *Metaphysics of Morals*, see Hunter, *Rival Enlightenments*, 320–37.

25. We have a duty of *charity* towards the poor, but it is an *imperfect* duty, one with a wide degree of latitude as to how we are supposed to discharge it. Recall also that to be dependent on the charity or generosity of another is to lack autonomy in the strong sense that Kant associates with our being free moral agents. Of course, many of us might come to lack enough resources to pursue our own ends through no fault of our own because of the consequences of a series of otherwise rightful private transactions. For this reason Kant thinks the state *does* have the right to tax the rich to support the poor, but only as a means of protecting them against falling into this kind of "no-fault" dependence (see 6:233). This kind of dependency is inconsistent with the idea of people sharing a genuinely united will, which is supposed to make the exercise of political and legal power consistent with our fundamental freedom and equality.

26. This is, of course, precisely the kind of argument that Locke uses to justify revolution in various circumstances; see for example his *Second Treatise*, §222.

27. This is yet another example, as we saw in our discussion of Locke, and as I emphasized in the Introduction, of how taking the picture of *boundaries* as central to the language of rights can mask the ways in which rights also enable and reify forms of dependence or "interference".

28. The basic problem for women, labourers and workers is that they are dependent on others for their "existence" *in the wrong way*: they lack the independence

required for civil personality (they are mere "underlings of the commonwealth" 6:314–15). The problem for women is more serious; they seem to be unfit "by nature" for active citizenship, even though Kant says that in principle "anyone" can work his way up from the passive condition to the active one (6:315). For more discussion of the status of women in Kant, see Susan Mendus, "Kant: An Honest but Narrow-Minded Bourgeois?", in *Women in Western Political Philosophy: Kant to Nietzsche*, Ellen Kennedy and Susan Mendus (eds), 21–43 (Brighton: Harvester, 1987).

29. The idea of the reasonable and the rational are present in John Rawls, *A Theory of Justice*, 2nd rev. edn (Cambridge, MA: Harvard University Press, 1999), but play a much bigger role in his later *Political Liberalism* (New York: Columbia University Press, 1993). Very generally, the rational refers to the pursuit of my own particular good or advantage, and the reasonable to a willingness to moderate one's claims out of a respect for others and their legitimate claims. One way he elaborates the idea of the reasonable is to describe "reasonable persons". Reasonable persons accept the fact of "reasonable pluralism" (the inevitability of disagreement over fundamental worldviews due to the free exercise of reason) and the "burdens of judgement" (the unavoidability of ambiguity, indeterminacy and complexity in relation to judgements about different moral views. But they also wish to cooperate with other reasonable persons, holding different moral views than their own, on terms they all can accept. This is a central theme of *Political Liberalism* (see e.g. 61ff.).

30. For an excellent discussion of constructivism in Rawls and Kant, to which I am indebted, see Onora O'Neill, "Constructivism in Rawls and Kant", in *The Cambridge Companion to Rawls*, Samuel Freeman (ed.), 347–67 (Cambridge: Cambridge University Press, 2003), and *Toward Justice and Virtue: A Constructive Account of Practical Reasoning* (Cambridge: Cambridge University Press, 1996).

31. On the "fact of reasonable pluralism" see Rawls, *Political Liberalism*, xvi; on the reasonable, *ibid.*, 81–2.

32. Recall, from above, how Kant sees the legislator as bound by the thought experiment of asking whether every citizen could subscribe to the law in question: "he must give his law as if it could have risen from the united will of an entire people" (8:297). If laws are not compatible with the equal freedom of all, or if they undermine the conditions constitutive of the state of right in general, then they are invalid. Of course for Kant this is an entirely abstract process. The actual consent of citizens is not required in any way. Nor must the process through which laws are developed be democratic. Non-democratic as much as democratic legislators are equally capable of providing just laws (and unjust ones).

33. Primary goods are those goods all of us need given our two moral powers and our capacity to be "fully cooperating"; see John Rawls, *Justice as Fairness: A Restatement*, E. Kelly (ed.) (Cambridge, MA: Harvard University Press, 2001), 57–8. They also provide a way for us to see who is worse off relative to others: those lacking adequate income and wealth (after the basic liberties are secured), or those lacking the social bases of "self-respect", are said to be worse off than others lacking other kinds of goods.

34. This means, interestingly enough, that he is wiling to tolerate trade-offs within the general scheme of liberties, if interfering with some liberties increases the security or enjoyment of the scheme of basic liberties overall for citizens. See the discussion in *A Theory of Justice*, §38, 212–13, 266.

35. Recall that the principles of justice are supposed to apply to the basic structure as a whole, not just to one part of it. So Rawls thinks that the inequalities generated

by both *laissez faire* capitalism and welfare state capitalism are problematic. He offers the idea of a "property-owning democracy" as an alternative, in which ownership of productive property is widespread and concentrations of wealth minimized. But the details are sketchy; see Rawls, *Justice as Fairness*, 135.

36. He also suggests that adjusting the basic liberties in this way will be required to help create the conditions for realizing deliberative democracy and the exercise of public reason, an aim shared with "civic republicanism" (see *ibid.*, 145–6).

37. This interpretation has been developed in some detail by Arthur Ripstein, "Private Order and Public Justice: Kant and Rawls", *Virginia Law Review* 92 (2006), 1391–438; cf. Thomas Pogge, "Three Problems with Contractarian-Consequentialist Ways of Assessing Social Institutions", in *The Just Society*, Ellen Frankel Paul, F. D. Miller, Jr, and Jeffrey Paul (eds), 241–66 (Cambridge: Cambridge University Press, 1995).

38. For an illuminating discussion of these aspects of justice see Jiwei Ci, *The Two Faces of Justice* (Cambridge, MA: Harvard University Press, 2006).

39. "Reciprocity", as Rawls calls it, is required to ensure a stable system of mutual cooperation across time, and is a realistic assumption about human moral psychology (note that it implies a much richer moral psychology than rational egoism; it marks a reciprocal commitment to justice, not just a strategic move to get what I want). The Humean idea of the "circumstances of justice" is an important background condition for Rawls, and one aspect of those conditions is an assumption about the limited role of altruistic feelings. See Rawls, *A Theory of Justice*, 109–12. On the difference between reciprocity, mutual advantage and impartiality see Rawls, *Political Liberalism*, 16–17. For more general discussion see Brian Barry, *Theories of Justice: A Treatise on Social Justice, Vol. 1* (Berkeley, CA: University of California Press, 1989), and Jiwei Ci, *The Two Faces of Justice*.

40. As Bernard Yack points out, it cannot be an empirical claim, since it is hard to imagine how to confirm it, and Rawls offers no systematic empirical or historical evidence on which to ground it. See Bernard Yack, "The Problem with Kantian Liberalism", in *Kant and Political Philosophy: The Contemporary Legacy*, Ronald Beiner and William Booth (eds), 224–44 (New Haven, CT: Yale University Press, 1993), 233–4; see also Simone Chambers, "The Politics of Equality: Rawls on the Barricades", *Perspectives on Politics* 4(1) (2006), 81–90, esp. 86–8.

41. For the extension of Rawls's theory to the international sphere, see his *The Law of Peoples* (Cambridge, MA: Harvard University Press, 1999).

42. There are important differences between Rawls and Habermas; see Habermas, "Reconciliation through the Public Use of Reason: Remarks on John Rawls's Political Liberalism", *Journal of Philosophy* 92(3) (1995), 109–31, and Rawls's response in the same issue (also published in the paperback edition of *Political Liberalism*, 372–434).

43. Indeed, Habermas is careful to note that discourse ethics is distinct from Kantian ethics in various ways, however much it is also deeply indebted to it; see his *Moral Consciousness and Communicative Action*, Christian Lenhart and Shierry Weber Nicholsen (trans.) (Cambridge, MA: MIT Press, 1990), 195–211. This issue is very well discussed by Thomas A. McCarthy, *The Critical Theory of Jürgen Habermas* (Cambridge, MA: MIT Press, 1979), 325–33.

44. For the full elaboration of his account of "communicative rationality", see Jürgen Habermas, *The Theory of Communicative Action, Volume 1: Reason and the Rationalization of Society*, Thomas McCarthy (trans.) (Cambridge: Polity, 1984). The secondary literatures is vast, but for three excellent discus-

sions to which I am indebted see McCarthy, *The Critical Theory of Jürgen Habermas*; Stephen White, *The Recent Work of Jürgen Habermas: Reason, Justice and Modernity* (Cambridge: Cambridge University Press, 1988); and Simone Chambers, *Reasonable Democracy: Jürgen Habermas and the Politics of Discourse* (Ithaca, NY: Cornell University Press, 1996).

45. Habermas limits moral discourse to the discussion of norms or rules we have a duty to observe, as opposed to the values or ends we ought to pursue (the domain of "ethics"). The former concerns justice, the latter reflect questions about the nature of the good life, and so on, that are rooted in more particular conceptions of ourselves and the societies we are socialized into.

46. I am also presupposing things such as: that competency to speak entitles participation in a discourse; that any assertion can be questioned by any participant; that assertions can be introduced by anyone into the discourse; and that everyone is allowed to express their attitudes, desires and needs (Habermas, *Moral Consciousness and Communicative Action*, 89).

47. See also Jürgen Habermas, "Remarks on Legitimation through Human Rights", in *The Postnational Constellation: Political Essays*, Max Pensky (ed.), 113–29 (Cambridge, MA: MIT Press, 2001). I have emphasized above how Kant understands rights to be "relational" as well. We shall explore the relation between mutual recognition and rights in more detail in Chapter 5.

48. I am indebted here to the very lucid discussion in Kenneth Baynes, "Democracy and the Rechstat: Habermas's Faktizitat und Geltung", in *The Cambridge Companion to Habermas*, Stephen K. White (ed.), 201–32 (Cambridge: Cambridge University Press, 1995), 209–10.

49. Recall our characterization (§ "Property, contract and status") of Kant's justification of taxation in order to support provision for the poor: people should not be subject to the choices of others in ways that are inconsistent with their status as free and equal. People cannot genuinely act together as authors of the laws to which they are subject if some of them exist in relations of unwarranted dependency on others.

50. Taylor is careful to limit his discussion to someone like Nozick, as opposed to Rawls or Habermas.

51. The example is discussed in Barry, *Theories of Justice*, 161–3.

52. For a systematic treatment of the challenge mental impairment and physical disability present for liberal assumptions about autonomy, justice and rights see Tim Stainton, *Autonomy and Social Policy: Rights, Mental Handicap and Community Care* (Aldershot: Avebury, 1994); T. M. Scanlon, *What We Owe to Each Other* (Cambridge, MA: Belknap, 1998), 177–87; and Martha Nussbaum, *Frontiers of Justice: Disability, Nationality, Species Membership* (Cambridge, MA: Harvard University Press, 2006).

53. Rawls, to his credit, is aware of the problem; see *Political Liberalism*, 20; *Justice as Fairness*, 168–76.

54. I have discussed some of the advantages of the justice as capabilities approach in more detail in Duncan Ivison, *Postcolonial Liberalism* (Cambridge: Cambridge University Press, 2002), ch. 5.

55. This criticism is most commonly associated with Iris Marion Young; see her "Difference as a Resource for Democratic Communication", in *Deliberative Democracy: Essays on Reason and Politics*, James Bohman and William Rehg (eds), 383–406 (Cambridge, MA: MIT Press, 1997); and *Inclusion and Democracy* (Oxford: Oxford University Press, 2002).

56. To be fair, Habermas explicitly addresses this criticism; see especially *Between Facts and Norms*, 418–27.

57. I am grateful to Glen Coulthard and Alex Livingston for helpful discussions on these issues.

58. The idea, roughly speaking, is that Aboriginal self-government also means bringing to bear Aboriginal political philosophies and values on the wider community and its decision-making processes. Without the recognition of both separateness and interdependency, Aboriginal people lack the means to effectively contest those norms and institutions acting on their most important interests.

5. Recognition

1. "R" and "A" in references to the *Philosophy of Right* refer to the remarks and additions in Hegel's text.

2. Hegel's analysis and diagnosis of this problem, and its continuing relevance for us today, is central to Charles Taylor's influential writings on Hegel; see especially *Hegel and Modern Society* (Cambridge: Cambridge University Press, 1979).

3. He also thinks their conception of the self is fundamentally incoherent. Identifying ourselves too closely with whatever impulses or desires we have leads to much instability and arbitrariness in our personality (G. W. F. Hegel, *Elements of the Philosophy of Right*, Allen Wood [ed.], H. B. Nisbet [trans.] [Cambridge: Cambridge University Press, 1991], §§11–12; 16–17). Rational behaviour is not fundamentally instrumental but guided by norms I give myself, although they are not, as in Kant, exclusive products of my autonomous will but rather intersubjectively constituted norms. For three very clear discussions of Hegel's critique of social contract theory in the context of his wider political thought, see Steven B. Smith, *Hegel's Critique of Liberalism: Rights in Context* (Chicago, IL: University of Chicago Press, 1989); Allen Patten, *Hegel's Idea of Freedom* (Oxford: Oxford University Press, 1999); and Frederick Neuthouser, *Foundations of Hegel's Social Theory* (Cambridge, MA: Harvard University Press, 2000).

4. Spirit (*Geist*) can be interpreted in more and less "substantial" ways. Some see it as the idea of an intersubjectively constituted "self" that emerges through its relations with others over time. Others attribute to it an independent reality or substantiality that manifests itself over time through individuals. Hegel also uses it to refer to the characteristics of a nation or culture as a whole. On this enormously important and complex aspect of Hegel's philosophical system see Charles Taylor, *Hegel* (Cambridge: Cambridge University Press, 1977), 90–94; but cf. Paul Redding, *Hegel's Hermeneutics* (Ithaca, NY: Cornell University Press, 1997) esp. 97–122.

5. And here, needless to say, Hegel means by "men", *men*: Hegel makes it clear that he associates the "actual substantial" life of men ("powerful and active") in the state, in learning, in work and in struggle with himself and the external world (*Philosophy of Right*, §166). Women, on the other hand, are "passive and subjective", have their substantial vocation only in the family, where their fundamental ethical disposition consists in "piety". Nor are women made for the higher sciences, including philosophy, or for political office, "for their actions are based not on the demands of universality but on contingent inclination and opinion" (§166A).

6. Technically, right for Hegel is an existence of any sort "which is the existence of the free will. Right is therefore in general freedom, as Idea" (§29). Or, as he puts it later: "Right is primarily that immediate existence which freedom gives itself in an immediate way" (§40).

7. Also: "a religious feeling which is partly in control of someone else is no religious feeling at all" (§66A). Note that Hegel was, in fact, not opposed to an established church, as existed in Prussia in his day. But he thought the different sects should be free, in a limited sense, to practise their faith.

8. A key question here is whether or not Hegel has shown that *private* property is what is required to achieve personality (as he says it is at §46), or whether it could be done on the basis of a system of common property.

9. This is well emphasized by Waldron, *The Right to Private Property*, 302. Waldron's general discussion of property is one to which I am indebted.

10. See also Hegel's *Encyclopaedia of the Philosophical Sciences* (1817), §§430–37. On Hegel's different uses of recognition see the excellent discussion by Redding, *Hegel's Hermeneutics*, 99–181, 219–37, and Robert Pippin, "What is the Question for which Hegel's Theory of Recognition is the Answer?", *European Journal of Philosophy* 8(2) (2000), 155–72.

11. On the bracing role of the fear of death more generally see G. W. F. Hegel, *Hegel's Phenomenology of Spirit*, A. V. Miller (trans.), J. N. Findlay (ed.) (Oxford: Oxford University Press, 1977), ¶194.

12. Hegel's views on the relation between religion and the state are interesting. In the *Philosophy of Right* (§270R) he alludes to the fundamental divinity of the state, and he criticizes social contract theory, in part, for failing to grasp this aspect of it (see esp. §258R). But he also criticizes those forms of religious belief that counsel indifference to worldly interests, and those that offer consolation to the oppressed but are themselves oppressive in their form. Religions that set themselves up as final arbiters of the legitimacy of state laws and institutions are also deeply problematic, since they can destabilize political relations and foment fanaticism. But in the same long remark, he points out that the state should protect at least *genuine* religion, and help in the realization of its ends, since religion is an "integrating factor in the state". In fact, a state "should even require all its citizens to belong to a church – but only *a* church, since the content of a man's faith depends on his private ideas, which the state can't interfere with" (§270R).

13. "When a father asked him for advice about the best way of educating his son in ethical matters, a Pythagorean replied: 'Make him the citizen of a state with good laws'" (§153).

14. But equally, nor should the state ever ask me to sacrifice for it my basic interests understood merely in terms of providing security for my property and rights, as "civil society" in other words (§324). For more on Hegel's critique of this conception of political society, see below.

15. This problem is very well summarized in Taylor, *Hegel*, 373.

16. Marx, of course, thought Hegel had no means to criticize the poverty and economic inequality that arose as a result of bourgeois civil society; see Karl Marx, "Critique of Hegel's Doctrine of the State", in his *Early Writings,* Rodney Livingstone & Gregor Benton (trans.), 57–198 (Harmondsworth: Penguin, 1992).

17. This is especially true of Locke, in so far as he thought that people had a discretionary domain of freedom of action protected by their natural rights. See the discussion above in Chapter 2. This point is well-made by Patten, *Hegel's Idea of Freedom*, 116–17, and Smith, *Hegel's Critique of Liberalism*.

18. Note that it is the failure of recognition in being excluded from a guild or "estate" and the loss of self-respect that for Hegel explains what is wrong with unemployment and poverty.

19. Someone who did not reflect on themselves in this way, who engaged in a constant cost–benefit analysis of which desire he could realize best out of the extant set he has, engages only in "weak evaluation" or is a "simple weigher of

alternatives" (Charles Taylor, "What is Human Agency?", in his *Human Agency and Language: Philosophical Papers 1*, 14–44 [Cambridge: Cambridge University Press, 1985], 23).

20. Taylor actually recognizes this aspect of Rawls's argument; see *Sources of the Self: The Making of the Modern Identity* (Cambridge, MA: Harvard University Press, 1989), 87 n.60. For a very helpful discussion of Taylor and Rawls see Stephen Mulhall and Adam Swift, *Liberals and Communitarians*, 2nd edn (Oxford: Blackwell, 1996), ch. 3, esp. 123–5.

21. Taylor has expressed dissatisfaction with the label of "communitarianism" being applied to his work; see "Reply and Re-articulation", in *Philosophy in an Age of Pluralism: The Philosophy of Charles Taylor in Question*, James Tully (ed.), 213–57 (Cambridge: Cambridge University Press, 1994), 250. In fact, this is true of most of the prominent communitarians!

22. Indeed, Rawls has been vociferously criticized for being insufficiently individualist in his writings on international law and global justice, where he takes "peoples" to be the primary unit of moral analysis, as opposed to individuals; see the *Law of Peoples*.

23. Each one of the elements mentioned here is controversial: what do we mean by a cultural structure? Which national groups? And what kind of rights? We shall explore some of these questions in Chapter 8. They have been the subject of much recent scholarly attention. For two very fine discussions, from very different viewpoints, see Joseph Carens, *Culture, Citizenship and Community* (Oxford: Oxford University Press, 2000); and Chandran Kukathas, *The Liberal Archipelago: A Theory of Diversity and Freedom* (Oxford: Oxford University Press, 2003).

24. For a recent attempt to apply the recognition thesis to the justification of rights see Rex Martin, *A System of Rights* (Oxford: Oxford University Press, 1993). See also the interesting discussion in Derrick Darby, "Unnatural Rights", *Canadian Journal of Philosophy* 33(1) (2003), 49–82; and "Blacks and Rights".

25. See also: "A right is a power of which the exercise by the individual or by some body of men is recognised by a society either as itself directly essential to a common good or as conferred by an authority of which the maintenance is recognised as so essential" (T. H. Green, *T. H. Green: Lectures on the Principles of Political Obligation and Other Writings*, P. Harris and J. Morrow [eds] [Cambridge: Cambridge University Press, 1986], §103).

26. This is what Hohfeld called a "claim-right"; see the discussion in the Introduction.

27. For a comprehensive discussion of the political thought of British idealism see Peter Nicholson, *The Political Philosophy of the British Idealists* (Cambridge: Cambridge University Press, 1990); also M. Dimova-Cookson, *T. H. Green's Moral and Political Philosophy* (Basingstoke: Palgrave, 2001).

28. This was the example used by W. D. Ross against Green; see *The Right and the Good* (Oxford: Oxford University Press, 1930), 51; cf. Green, *T. H. Green: Lectures*, 103ff. Green suggests that until he sees himself in a certain way (as a goal-determined, rationally ordered agent) and lives in a certain kind of society, the slave's rights are "in suspense". For more discussion of Ross's objection see Gerald F. Gaus, "Green's Rights Recognition Thesis and Moral Internalism", *British Journal of Politics and International Relations* 7(1) (2005), 5–17.

6. Rights, consequences and terrorism

1. As Waldron puts it, "An individual has a right to G when the importance of his interests in G, considered on its own, is sufficient to justify holding others

to be under a duty to promote G" (*Liberal Rights: Collected Papers 1981–91* [Cambridge: Cambridge University Press, 1993], 359).

2. I am indebted here to T. M. Scanlon, *The Difficulty of Tolerance: Essays in Political Philosophy* (Cambridge: Cambridge University Press, 2003), 116; see also Jack Donnelly, *Universal Human Rights in Theory and Practice* (Ithaca, NY: Cornell University Press, 1989).

3. Recall that consequentialism, in general, involves identifying the right option or action as that which promotes the best objectively probable consequences; see Philip Pettit, "Consequentialism", in *A Companion to Ethics*, Peter Singer (ed.), 230–40 (Oxford: Blackwell, 1991).

4. For a classic defence of utilitarianism against these kinds of worries see David Lyons, "Human Rights and the General Welfare", *Philosophy and Public Affairs* 6(2) (1977), 113–29.

5. We should also be concerned about "adaptive preferences", in which people's perception of their well-being is swayed by manipulation or adaptive attitudes, given their circumstances and the context in which their choices are made. For the general problem see Jon Elster, *Sour Grapes: Studies in the Subversion of Rationality* (Cambridge: Cambridge University Press, 1983), 109–40; see also Amartya Sen, *Inequality Reexamined* (Cambridge, MA: Harvard University Press, 1995); and Martha Nussbaum, *Women and Human Development: The Capabilities Approach to Justice* (Cambridge: Cambridge University Press, 2000), 111–66.

6. A mental or social state that is a by-product is one that has the property of having come about from actions undertaken for other ends; that is, it can only be brought about by my (or our) not intentionally willing it. See Elster, *Sour Grapes*, 43–108.

7. For my purposes, terrorism standardly involves the use of violence to generate fear with the aim of degrading or destabilizing an existing social order or, in some cases, the use of the threat of violence and fear to stabilize an existing social order. The first is generally associated with non-state actors, the second with state terror, but conceivably can be practised by either. For more discussion, to which I am indebted, see Samuel Scheffler, "Is Terrorism Morally Distinctive?", *Journal of Political Philosophy* 14(1) (2006), 1–17, and Jeremy Waldron, "Terrorism and the Uses of Terror", *Journal of Ethics* 8(1) (2004), 5–35.

8. For an intriguing analysis of the relation between constitutionalism and war, and the changes that 11 September 2001 might herald for the international order, see Philip Bobbitt, *The Shield of Achilles: War, Peace and the Course of History* (New York: Knopf, 2002).

9. The government argued (in a memo written by a young Berkeley law professor on secondment to the Justice Department) that because the kind of armed conflict in which members of Al-Qaeda and the Taliban were involved was not explicitly mentioned in the Conventions, the prohibitions on torture or "cruel interrogation" did not apply (Karen J. Greenberg and Joshua L. Dratel [eds], *The Torture Papers: The Road to Abu Ghraib*, 38–79 [Cambridge: Cambridge University Press, 2005], 38–79).

10. Office of Legal Counsel memo, 1 August 2002, known as the "Bybee memo", reprinted in Greenberg and Dratel (eds), *The Torture Papers*, 172–217. The memo argued that the definition of torture should be narrowed so as to cover only (basically) the kind of pain that could cause massive organ failure or death.

11. For a critical discussion of the use of this metaphor see Jeremy Waldron, "Security and Liberty: The Image of Balance", *Journal of Political Philosophy* 11(2) (2003), 191–210.

12. Nozick, for example, admits that in the face of "catastrophe and moral horror", moral absolutes, including individual rights, may have to give way; see *Anarchy, State and Utopia* (Oxford: Blackwell, 1974), 30n.

13. But note that the Vienna Declaration (1993) of states that signed the main international human rights instruments declared that "all human rights are universal, indivisible and interdependent and interrelated".

14. Here he is apparently drawing on the work of the former Canadian Attorney General and prominent legal scholar Irwin Cotler, "Thinking Outside the Box: Foundational Principles for a Counter-terrorism Law and Policy", in *The Security of Freedom: Essays on Canada's Anti-Terrorism Bill*, Ronald Daniels, Patrick Macklem and Kent Roach (eds), 111–30 (Toronto: University of Toronto Press, 2001).

15. For a defence of torture as a means of extracting vital intelligence when doing so may lead directly to saving lives, see Alan Dershowitz, *Why Terrorism Works: Understanding the Threat, Responding to the Challenge* (New Haven, CT: Yale University Press, 2002). For forceful responses to Dershowitz's argument, see David Luban, "Liberalism, Torture and the Ticking Time Bomb", *Virginia Law Review* 91(6) (2005), 1425–61, and Jeremy Waldron, "Torture and Positive Law: Jurisprudence for the White House", *Columbia Law Review* 105(6) (2005), 1681–750, esp. 1713–18. See also the classic article by Henry Shue, "Torture", *Philosophy and Public Affairs* 7(2) (1978), 124–43.

16. Walrdon discusses the ban on torture and the *habeas corpus* statutes as legal "archetypes": "a rule or positive law provision that operates not just on its own account ... but operates also in a way that expresses or epitomises the spirit of the whole structural area of doctrine" ("Torture and Positive Law", 1723).

17. See, for example, Article 11 of the Convention for the Protection of Human Rights and Fundamental Freedoms (the European Convention on Human Rights), which allows for restrictions on freedom of assembly and association "necessary in a democratic society in the interests of national security or public safety, for the prevention of disorder or crime, for the protection of health or morals or for the protection of the rights and freedoms of others". The convention makes clear, however, that there is no derogation permitted in any circumstances with regard to certain other basic rights, including being subject to "torture or to inhuman or degrading treatment or punishment" (Article 3).

18. Cf. "It is a paradoxical articulation, for what must be inscribed within the law is something that is essentially exterior to it, that is, nothing less than the suspension of the juridical order itself" (Giorgio Agamben, *State of Exception*, Kevin Attell [trans.] [Chicago, IL: University of Chicago Press, 2005], 33).

19. Also: "It is almost as if, starting from a certain point, every decisive political event were double-sided: the spaces, the liberties, and the rights won by individuals in their conflicts with central powers always simultaneously prepared a tacit but increasing inscription of individuals' lives with the state order" (Giorgio Agamben, *Homo Sacer: Sovereign Power and Bare Life*, D. Heller-Roazen [trans.] [Palo Alto, CA: Stanford University Press, 1998], 121). We shall explore this idea in more detail in Chapter 7.

20. It is interesting to note that in 2006 President Bush issued an executive order *limiting* the use of the taking of private property for public use. This concern with restricting state interference with property rights is striking when compared with the measures taken in relation to civil liberties in the "war on terror".

21. Similarly, although international law allows that there can be different categories of prisoners – prisoner of war, spies, unlawful combatants, and so on – it also

provides procedures for determining whether such reclassification is appropriate (procedures that, until recently, the US Government has simply ignored).
22. Remarkably, the self-defence and necessity arguments were appealed to in the notorious "torture memo" issued by the US Office of Legal Counsel referred to above. That memo sought to limit the scope of the implementing legislation of the Convention against Torture and Cruel, Inhuman and Degrading Treatment. It attempted to defend torture against detainees, as well as the constitutional authority of the president to use extra-legal means to defend the nation, on the basis of both self-defence and necessity.
23. On the deeply problematic analogy between the "war on terror" and the fight against Hitler and Soviet Communism during the Cold War, see Stephen Holmes, "Neo-Con Futurology", *London Review of Books* 28(19) (5 October 2006) (www.lrb.co.uk/v28/n19/holm01_.html).
24. I am referring to the *Habeas Corpus Act* (1679). Justice Stevens reaffirmed this principle in the recent case of *Rasul v. Bush* 542 US 466 (2004).
25. See *Hamdan v. Rumsfield* (2006). The Bush administration passed a new Bill in light of this decision, taking up the court's offer that it ask Congress for specific permission to set up the commissions. However, the new Bill retains many controversial aspects of the original Military Order issued in 2001, including denying *habeas* rights.
26. Rogers M. Smith, "Arraigning Terror", *Dissent* (Spring 2004), 39–44, argues that criminal processes are not as incapable of dealing with terrorism as critics suppose. He also points out that the main problem before 9/11 was not so much the delays caused by having to adhere to ordinary standards of "probable cause" and "reasonable doubt" standards for conviction, or even the inability to gather intelligence, as it was the ineptness of key governmental agencies to share and analyse the information they had. See also Ian Shapiro, *Containment: Rebuilding a Strategy Against Global Terror* (Princeton, NJ: Princeton University Press, 2007).

7. Rights as conduits

1. Joshua Cohen has argued that human rights can be thought of as providing a protected space within which people can act on their particular moral duties (see above, pp. 207–8). But he accepts moral pluralism, and thus the nature of those duties will vary between societies and traditions. See his "Minimalism About Human Rights: The Most We can Hope for?", *Journal of Political Philosophy* 12(2) (2004), 190–213.
2. What is distinctive about human beings is not only our socially productive activity, but also our essentially cooperative nature: the enormous complex of social relations we engage in. See Karl Marx, "Theses on Feuerbach", in *The Marx–Engels Reader*, R. Tucker (ed.), 143–5 (New York: Norton, 1978): "But the human essence is no abstraction inherent in each single individual. In its reality it is in the ensemble of the social relations" (Thesis VI, 145).
3. See also Marx's critique of distributive justice in his "Critique of the Gotha Program", in *The Marx–Engels Reader*, Tucker (ed.), 525–41, esp. 531–2.
4. We shall return to this idea of "contingent universals" in our discussion of human rights in Chapter 8.
5. The right to exercise power is usually accompanied, as it is in Locke, by assumptions about the capacity to do so as well. For a subtle and illuminating discussion of how these two ideas structure much discussion of power in Western political thought see Barry Hindess, *Discourses of Power: From Hobbes to Foucault*

(Oxford: Blackwell, 1996), and Peter Morriss, *Power: A Philosophical Analysis*, 2nd edn (Manchester: Manchester University Press, 2002).

6. "When I say right, I am not thinking just of the law, but of all the apparatuses, institutions, and rules that apply it" (Michel Foucault, "14 January 1976", in *Society Must be Defended: Lectures at the College de France 1975–1976*, Mauro Bertani and Alessandro Fontana [eds], David Macey [trans.], 23–41 [New York: Picador, 2003], 27).

7. Especially after the publication of *The History of Sexuality, Vol I*, Robert Hurley (trans.) (Harmondsworth: Penguin, 1978) and *Discipline and Punish*, Alan Sheridan (trans.) (New York: Vintage, 1979).

8. This lecture has proved remarkably fruitful for researchers in a wide range of disciplines. For two very helpful surveys see Hindess, *Discourses of Power*, and Nikolas Rose, *Powers of Freedom* (Cambridge: Cambridge University Press, 1999).

9. "We have to study power outside the model of Leviathan, outside the field delineated by juridical sovereignty and the institution of the State" (Foucault, *Society Must be Defended*, 34).

10. This general view of the nature of rights is elaborated repeatedly throughout the lectures gathered together in *Society Must be Defended*.

11. At one point Foucault claimed that the idea of human rights was inherently negative, in so far as they are "above all ... the limits that one places on all possible governments" ("The Moral and Social Experience of the Poles", in his *Power: The Essential Works of Foucault 1954–1984, vol. 3*, J. D. Faubion [ed.], 465–73 [Harmondsworth: Penguin, 2000], 471). Also: "a new internationalism must ... strive for the rights of the stateless, and for forms of self-determination that do not resolve into capricious and cynical forms of state sovereignty" (Judith Butler, *Precarious Life: The Powers of Mourning and Violence* [London: Verso, 2004], 99). We address the question of human rights in greater detail in Chapter 8.

8. Human rights

1. For a similar worry see Anthony Langlois, "Human Rights and Modern Liberalism: a Critique", *Political Studies* 51(3) (2003), 509–23. Langlois draws the opposite conclusion from these same concerns than Griffin does.

2. For an intriguing discussion of how the global political structure – or what they call "empire" – generates distinctive forms of resistance, see Michael Hardt and Antonio Negri, *Empire* (Cambridge, MA: Harvard University Press, 2000).

3. This idea of human rights providing a shared framework is emphasized by Charles Beitz, "Human Rights as a Common Concern", *American Political Science Review* 95(2) (2001), 269–82, and Cohen, "Minimalism About Human Rights".

4. Here I am indebted to Thomas Pogge, "The International Significance of Human Rights", *Journal of Ethics* 4(1–2) (2000), 45–69.

5. It is important to distinguish this from what we might call the "actual overlapping consensus" argument. The claim here is that human rights should be the product of an *actual* overlapping agreement between the existing conventional moralities in the world today. The main problem with this approach is that actual agreement is far too strong a condition to impose on the justification of critical standards. It ties the standards too closely to the extant content of people's moral beliefs and practices. We need to build in at least some kind of reflective principle to our notion of "equal acceptability". We shall discuss this

in more detail. For Walzer's discussion of a "thin", cross-cultural moral minimum see *Thick and Thin: Moral Argument at Home and Abroad* (Notre Dame, IN: University of Notre Dame Press, 1994), 9–10. For further critical discussion see Simon Caney, "Human Rights, Compatibility and Diverse Cultures", in *Human Rights and Global Diversity*, Simon Caney and Peter Jones (eds), 51–72 (London: Frank Cass, 2001), 56–7; and Beitz, "Human Rights as a Common Concern", 273–4.

6. See also Hart, *The Concept of Law* (Oxford: Oxford University Press, 1972), 189–95, who tries to specify what he calls the "minimum content of natural law" by appealing to as minimalist a story about human nature as possible – one that is universal, but only contingently so – in contrast with the teleological approaches of traditional natural law theory, including Grotius's.

7. The idea of a "common standard" can be found in the important papers Beitz, "Human Rights as a Common Standard" and Cohen, "Minimalism about Human Rights"; there is a slightly different sense in Tully, *Strange Multiplicity*, in so far as he appeals to a certain model of practical reasoning found in the common law. I draw on all of these here.

8. For the phrase see Cohen, "Minimalism About Human Rights, 193. I go on to develop this idea in a slightly different way than he does, although I am indebted to his discussion.

9. This touches on a very large question in political and moral philosophy, but for a clear connection between theories of agency and human rights see James Griffin, "First Steps in an Account of Human Rights", *European Journal of Philosophy* 9(3) (2001): 306–27; Sen, "Elements of a Theory of Human Rights", *Philosophy and Public Affairs* 32(4) (2004), 315–56; and Nussbaum, *Women and Human Development*.

10. For a more elaborate claim about the kind of agency relevant to justifying human rights see Allan Gewirth, "Why There Are Human Rights", *Social Theory and Practice* 11(2) (1985), 235–48. For Gewirth, human rights protect a rich conception of purposive agency, such that lacking the capability to exercise such agency might entail a lesser set of rights (Gewirth distinguishes between basic rights, "nonsubtractive rights" and "additive rights"). Someone who is comatose is entitled to the first, but not necessarily to the other two.

11. We should not infer from the fact that, say, a dog is not capable of being included in the category "human" that we are therefore free to torture it. Rights are not the only way of talking about our moral responsibilities to others, including to non-human animals. Many people do, of course, want to extend the language of rights to non-human animals. Nothing I have said here necessarily counts against that, except to rule out the need to extend "human rights" to them. Whatever rights dogs, cats or fish may have, they do not have human rights.

12. See also Waldron's formulation of the right to have rights in terms of the right to participate in the elaboration and determination of the meaning of the rights that individuals claim for themselves and others, especially in those circumstances where we disagree about those meanings; *Law and Disagreement* (Oxford: Oxford University Press, 1998), ch. 11.

13. On the distinction between "internalism" and "externalism" see Bernard Williams, "Internal and External Reasons", in his *Moral Luck: Philosophical Papers 1973–80*, 101–13 (Cambridge: Cambridge University Press, 1981).

14. Consider this recent description of the situation in Burma: "By one tally ... as juntas go, this one has been remarkably successful: It has kept its grip on power for two decades, despite giving the people of Myanmar little reason to support it. It jails its critics, dragoons townspeople into forced labor and keeps order

through fear while pauperizing a potentially thriving nation through economic incompetence" (Seth Mydans, "From their Nation-Turned-Bunker, Burmese Generals Peer Out, and In", *New York Times*, 26 September [2007] [www. nytimes.com/2007/09/26/world/asia/26myanmar.html]).

15. This is especially true across time. Williams is concerned to distinguish what he calls the "relativism of distance" from standard relativism. The former is entirely plausible, the latter is false. We can ask, if we want, whether Caligula violated the human rights of his subjects, but the universality of human rights does not require that it be correct at all time and in all places in that sense. See Bernard Williams, "Human Rights and Relativism", in his *In the Beginning Was the Deed*, 62–74, esp. 68–9.

16. This is a moral claim about the generalizability of human rights, not a sociological one. The question of the empirical conditions in which human rights norms become internalized in domestic practices informs my discussion, but will not be discussed here in any detail. See T. Risse, S.C. Ropp and K. Sikkink, *The Power of Human Rights: International Norms and Domestic Change* (Cambridge: Cambridge University Press, 1999), esp. Introduction. See also Stephen Krasner, *Sovereignty: Organized Hypocrisy* (Princeton, NJ: Princeton University Press, 1999). For an overview and criticism of these standard accounts see Andrew Moravcsik, "The Origins of Human Rights Regimes: Democratic Delegation in Postwar Europe", *International Organization* 54(2) (2000), 217–52.

17. I am referring here to the important work done by Brian Barry, Charles Beitz, Allen Buchanan, Simon Caney and Thomas Pogge.

18. I take this to be one of the deep, underlying motives of Rawls's project in *Political Liberalism*.

19. See the detailed list of conditions in Rawls, *The Law of Peoples*, 37–43. To be clear, that does not make them as reasonable and just as liberal societies. He separates the question of how peoples treat each other as members of the same society and how peoples treat other peoples (*ibid.*, 83–4).

20. It could be argued that if Rawls is serious that everyone's good is to be taken into account, then it at least places a burden on those who would deny, say, the rights of religious minorities to participate effectively in politics to show how this is compatible with their good being taken seriously.

21. For example, they include, aside from rights to life, security and freedom from torture and so on, rights to education, work, cultural inclusion, expression, participation and an international scheme in which these rights are protected.

22. For a claim that all theories of justice are necessarily tied to thicker and more particular communal and cultural contexts, see David Miller, "National Self-Determination and Global Justice", in his *Citizenship and National Identity*, 161–79 (Cambridge: Polity, 2000), 168–70.

23. For the emphasis on human agency see Griffin, "First Steps in an Account of Human Rights". On the interests shared by all persons as conditions for a decent life, see Allen Buchanan, *Justice, Legitimacy and Self-Determination: Moral Foundations for International Law* (Oxford: Oxford University Press, 2004), 128. On the value of membership see Cohen, "Minimalism About Human Rights", 197–8.

24. Thus the right of states to regulate membership has to be balanced against the need to protect basic personhood, or agency as I have called it here. This tension is very well discussed by Linda Bosniak, *The Citizen and the Alien: Dilemmas of Contemporary Membership* (Princeton, NJ: Princeton University Press, 2006).

25. It is important to note that in existing international law, talk of the *right* to the self-determination of "peoples" tends to refer narrowly to those under colo-

nial domination – and then only overseas domination, otherwise known as the "saltwater thesis" – or military occupation. This is part of what the emerging international law of indigenous peoples is challenging.

26. For an important discussion of this kind of process with regard to the claims of cultural groups within states, see Shachar, *Multicultural Jurisdictions: Cultural Differences and Women's Rights* (Cambridge: Cambridge University Press, 2001); see also Ivison, *Postcolonial Liberalism*.

27. *Draft Declaration on the Rights of Indigenous Peoples*, 44th Sess., Agenda item 14, at 50, Annex I, UN Doc. E/CN.4/Sub.2/1993/29 (1993). Article 3 of the draft declaration states: "Indigenous peoples have the right of self-determination. By virtue of that right they freely determine their political status and freely pursue their economic, social and cultural development".

28. Lack of space prevents consideration of this complicated issue here. For further discussion see especially Benedict Kingsbury, "Indigenous Peoples in International Law: A Constructivist Approach to the Asian Controversy", *American Journal of International Law* 92(3) (1998) 414–57; cf. Jeremy Waldron, "Indigeneity? First Peoples and Last Occupancy", *New Zealand Journal of Public Law* 1(1) (2003), 55–82.

29. There is, however, good reason to think that sovereignty has never been as absolute and indivisible as political theorists often assume; see Krasner, *Sovereignty*.

30. For a sharp critique of the language of rights as applied to the situation of indigenous peoples in Canada, see Taiaiake Alfred, *Peace, Power, Righteousness: An Indigenous Manifesto* (Oxford: Oxford University Press, 1999).

31. The phrase "explanatory nationalism" is from Thomas Pogge, *World Poverty and Human Rights* (Cambridge: Polity, 2002), 15, 110–12, ch. 5.

Bibliography

Abou El Fadl, K. 2003. "Islam and the Challenge of Democracy". *Boston Review* (April–May) (http://bostonreview.net/BR28.2/abou.html).

Ackerman, B. 2006. *Before the Next Attack*. New Haven, CT: Yale University Press.

Agamben, G. 1998. *Homo Sacer: Sovereign Power and Bare Life*, D. Heller-Roazen (trans.). Palo Alto, CA: Stanford University Press.

Agamben, G. 2005. *State of Exception*, K. Attell (trans.). Chicago, IL: University of Chicago Press.

Alfred, T. 1999. *Peace, Power, Righteousness: An Indigenous Manifesto*. Oxford: Oxford University Press.

Anaya, J. 1996. *Indigenous Peoples in International Law*. Oxford: Oxford University Press.

An-Na'im, A. A. 1990. *Toward an Islamic Reformation: Civil Liberties, Human Rights and International Law*. Syracuse, NY: Syracuse University Press.

An-Na'im, A. A. (ed.) 1992. *Human Rights in Cross-Cultural Perspectives*. Philadelphia, PA: University of Pennsylvania Press, 1992.

Appiah, K. A. 2005. *The Ethics of Identity*. Princeton, NJ: Princeton University Press.

Aquinas, T. 2002. *Political Writings: St Thomas Aquinas*, R. W. Dyson (ed.). Cambridge: Cambridge University Press.

Arendt, H. 1966. *Origins of Totalitarianism*. New York: Harcourt.

Aristotle 1998. *Politics*, C. D. C. Reeve (trans.) Indianapolis, IN: Hackett.

Aristotle 1999. *Nicomachean Ethics*, T. Irwin (trans.). Indianapolis, IN: Hackett.

Armitage, D. 2000. *The Ideological Origins of the British Empire*. Cambridge: Cambridge University Press.

Arneson, R. 2001. "Against Rights". *Philosophical Issues* 11: 172–201.

Ashcraft, R. 1986. *Revolutionary Politics and Locke's Two Treatises of Government*. Princeton, NJ: Princeton University Press.

Astell, M. 1996. *Political Writings*, P. Springborg (ed.). Cambridge: Cambridge University Press.

Avineri, S. 1974. *Hegel's Theory of the Modern State*. Cambridge: Cambridge University Press.

Ayers, M. 1991. *Locke: Epistemology and Ontology*, 2 vols. London: Routledge.

Baier, A. 1995. *Moral Prejudices: Essays on Ethics*. Cambridge, MA: Harvard University Press.

Barry, B. 1992 "Ethics". In *Encyclopedia of Ethics*, 2 vols, L. Becker (ed.), 322–9. New York: Garland Press.

Barry, B. 1989. *Theories of Justice: A Treatise on Social Justice, Vol. 1*. Berkeley, CA: University of California Press.

Barsh, R. 1994a. "Indigenous Peoples in the 1990s: From Object to Subject of International Law?". *Harvard Human Rights Journal* 7 (Spring): 33–86.

Barsh, R. 1994b. "Indigenous Peoples and the Idea of Individual Human Rights". *Native Studies Review* 10(2): 35–55.

Baynes, K. 1995. "Democracy and the Rechstat: Habermas's Faktizitat und Geltung". In *The Cambridge Companion to Habermas*, Stephen K. White (ed.), 201–32. Cambridge: Cambridge University Press.

Beiser, F. 2006. "Moral Faith and the Highest Good". In *The Cambridge Companion to Kant and Modern Philosophy*, Paul Guyer (ed.), 588–629. Cambridge: Cambridge University Press.

Beitz, C. 1989. *Political Equality: An Essay in Democratic Theory*. Princeton, NJ: Princeton University Press.

Beitz, C. 1999. *Political Theory and International Relations*, 2nd edn. Princeton, NJ: Princeton University Press.

Beitz, C. 2001. "Human Rights as a Common Concern". *American Political Science Review* 95(2): 269–82.

Beitz, C. 2003. "What Human Rights Mean". *Daedalus* 132(1) (Winter): 36–46.

Bell, D. 2000. *East Meets West: Human Rights and Democracy in East Asia*. Princeton, NJ: Princeton University Press.

Benhabib, S. 1992. *Situating the Self*. London: Routledge.

Benhabib, S. 2002. *The Claims of Culture*. Princeton, NJ: Princeton University Press.

Bentham, J. [1789] 1907. *An Introduction to the Principles of Morals and Legislation*. Oxford: Clarendon Press.

Bentham, J. 1962. *The Works of Jeremy Bentham*, 11 vols, J. Bowring (ed.). New York: Russell & Russell.

Bentham, J. 1987a. "Anarchical Fallacies". In *Nonsense Upon Stilts: Bentham, Burke and Marx on the Rights of Man*, J. Waldron (ed.). London: Methuen.

Bentham, J. 1987b. "Supply Without Burthern". In *Nonsense Upon Stilts: Bentham, Burke and Marx on the Rights of Man*, J. Waldron (ed.). London: Methuen.

Berlin, I. 1969. "Two Concepts of Liberty". In his *Four Essays on Liberty*, 121–54. Oxford: Oxford University Press.

Blackstone, W. [1783] 1978. *Commentaries on the Laws of England*, 4 vols. New York: Garland Press.

Bobbitt, P. 2002. *The Shield of Achilles: War, Peace and the Course of History*. New York: Knopf.

Bohman, J. 1998. "The Coming of Age of Deliberative Democracy". *Journal of Political Philosophy* 6(4): 400–425.

Bohman, J. 2004. "Republican Cosmopolitanism". *Journal of Political Philosophy* 12(1): 336–52.

Bohman, J. 2005. "The Democratic Minimum: Is Democracy a Means to Global Justice?" *Ethics & International Affairs* 19(1): 101–16.

Boldt, M. & J. A. Long 1984. "Tribal Traditions and European-Western Political Ideologies: The Dilemma of Canada's Native Indians". *Canadian Journal of Political Science* 17(3): 537–53.

Borrows, J. 1994 "Contemporary Traditional Equality". *University of New Brunswick Law Journal* 43(1): 19–48.

Borrows, J. 2000a. "Domesticating Doctrines: Aboriginal Peoples after the Royal Commission". *McGill Law Journal* 46(3): 615–61.

Borrows, J. 2000b. "Landed Citizenship". In Citizenship in Diverse Societies, W. Norman & W. Kymlicka (eds), 326–44. Oxford: Oxford University Press.

Bosniak, L. 2006. *The Citizen and the Alien: Dilemmas of Contemporary Membership*. Princeton, NJ: Princeton University Press.

Bracken, H. M. 1984. *Mind and Language: Essays on Descartes and Chomsky*. Dordrecht: Foris.

Brandom, R. 1994. *Making it Explicit: Reasoning, Representing and Discursive Commitment*. Cambridge, MA: Harvard University Press.

Brandom, R. 2002. *Tales of the Mighty Dead*. Cambridge, MA: Harvard University Press.

Brett, A. 1997. *Liberty, Right and Nature: Individual Rights in Later Scholastic Thought*. Cambridge: Cambridge University Press.

Brett, A. 2002. "Natural Right and Civil Community: The Civil Philosophy of Hugo Grotius". *Historical Journal* 43(1): 31–51.

Brett, A. 2003. "The Development of the Idea of Citizens' Rights". In *States & Citizens: History, Theory, Prospects*, Q. Skinner & B. Stråth (eds), 97–114. Cambridge: Cambridge University Press.

Buchanan, A. 2004. *Justice, Legitimacy and Self-Determination: Moral Foundations for International Law*. Oxford: Oxford University Press.

Burnyeat, M. 1984. "The Sceptic in his Time and Place". In *Philosophy and History*, R. Rorty, J. B. Schneewind & Q. Skinner (eds), 225–54. Cambridge: Cambridge University Press.

Butler, J. 2004. *Precarious Life: The Powers of Mourning and Violence*. London: Verso.

Byers, M. 2005. *War Law: Understanding International Law and Armed Conflict*. Vancouver: Douglas & McIntyre.

Callinicos, A. 2000. *Equality*. Cambridge: Polity.

Campbell, T. 1983. *The Left and Rights: A Conceptual Analysis of the Idea of Socialist Rights*. London: Routledge.

Caney, S. 2001. "Human Rights, Compatibility and Diverse Cultures". In *Human Rights and Global Diversity*, S. Caney & P. Jones (eds), 51–72. London: Frank Cass.

Caney, S. 2002. "Cosmopolitanism and the Law of Peoples". *Journal of Political Philosophy* 10(1): 95–123

Caney, S. 2005. *Justice Beyond Borders: A Global Political Theory*. Oxford: Oxford University Press.

Carens, J. 2000. *Culture, Citizenship and Community*. Oxford: Oxford University Press.

Cavalieri, P. & P. Singer (eds) 1995. *The Great Ape Project: Equality Beyond Humanity*. London: Fourth Estate.

Chambers, S. 1996. *Reasonable Democracy: Jürgen Habermas and the Politics of Discourse*. Ithaca, NY: Cornell University Press.

Chambers, S. 2006. "The Politics of Equality: Rawls on the Barricades". *Perspectives on Politics* 4(1): 81–90.

Chesterman, J. & B. Galligan 1997. *Citizens Without Rights: Aborigines and Australian Citizenship*. Cambridge: Cambridge University Press.

Cohen, G. A. 1998. *Self-ownership, Freedom and Equality*. Cambridge: Cambridge University Press.

Cohen, J. 2004. "Minimalism About Human Rights: The Most We can Hope for?" *Journal of Political Philosophy* 12(2): 190–213.

Connolly, W. E. 2005. *Pluralism*. Durham, NC: Duke University Press.

Constant, B. 1988. *Political Writings*, B. Fontana (ed.) Cambridge: Cambridge University Press.

Cook, W. W. 1978. *Fundamental Legal Conceptions as Applied to Judicial Reasoning*. Westport, CT: Greenwood Press.

Cotler, I. 2001. "Thinking Outside the Box: Foundational Principles for a Counter-terrorism Law and Policy". In *The Security of Freedom: Essays on Canada's Anti-Terrorism Bill*, R. Daniels, P. Macklem & K. Roach (eds), 111–30. Toronto: University of Toronto Press.

Cottier, T. & M. Hertig 2003. "The Prospects of 21st Century Constitutionalism". *Max Planck Yearbook of United Nations Law* 7(1): 261–322.

Crawford, J. 1979. *The Creation of States in International Law*. Oxford: Clarendon Press.

Darby, D. 2001. "Two Conceptions of Rights Possession". *Social Theory and Practice* 27: 16–18.

Darby, D. 2003. "Unnatural Rights". *Canadian Journal of Philosophy* 33(1): 49–82.

Darby, D. 2006. "Blacks and Rights: A Bittersweet Legacy". *Law, Culture and Humanities* 2(3): 420–39.

Dershowitz, A. 2002. *Why Terrorism Works: Understanding the Threat, Responding to the Challenge*. New Haven, CT: Yale University Press.

Dimova-Cookson, M. 2001. *T. H. Green's Moral and Political Philosophy*. Basingstoke: Palgrave.

Donnelly, J. 1989. *Universal Human Rights in Theory and Practice*. Ithaca, NY: Cornell University Press.

Dunn, J. 1983. *The Political Thought of John Locke: An Historical Account of the Argument of the "Two Treatises of Government"*. Cambridge: Cambridge University Press.

Dworkin, R. 1977. *Taking Rights Seriously*. Cambridge, MA: Harvard University Press.

Edmundson, W. 2004. *An Introduction to Rights*. Cambridge: Cambridge University Press.

Eisenberg, A. & J. Spinner-Halev (eds) 2005. *Minorities within Minorities: Equality, Rights and Diversity*. Cambridge: Cambridge University Press.

Ellis, E. 2005. *Kant's Politics: Provisional Theory for an Uncertain World*. New Haven, CT: Yale University Press.

Elster, J. 1983. *Sour Grapes: Studies in the Subversion of Rationality*. Cambridge: Cambridge University Press.

Falzon, C. 1998. *Foucault and Social Dialogue*. New York: Routledge.

Fassbender, B. 1998. "The United Nations Charter as Constitution of the International Community". *Columbia Journal of Transnational Law* 36(1): 529–619

Feinberg, J. 1978. "Voluntary Euthanasia and the Inalienable Right to Life". *Philosophy and Public Affairs* 7(2): 93–123.

Feinberg, J. 1980. "The Nature and Value of Rights". In his *Rights, Justice and the Bounds of Liberty*, 143–58. Princeton, NJ: Princeton University Press.

Finnis, J. 1980. *Natural Law and Natural Rights*. Oxford: Clarendon Press.

Flathman, R. 1976. *The Practice of Rights*. Cambridge: Cambridge University Press.

Forst, R. 1999. "The Basic Right to Justification". *Constellations* 6(1): 35–60.

Forst, R. 2003. *Toleranz im Konflict: Geschichte, Gehalt und Gegenwart eines umstrettenen Begriffs*. Frankfurt: Suhrkamp.

Foucault, M. 1978. *The History of Sexuality, Volume 1*, R. Hurley (trans.). Harmondsworth: Penguin.

Foucault, M. 1979. *Discipline and Punish*, A. Sheridan (trans.). New York: Vintage.

Foucault, M. 1984. "Politics and Ethics: An Interview". In *The Foucault Reader*, P. Rabinow (ed.), 373–80. New York: Pantheon.

Foucault, M. 1997a. *Ethics: The Essential Works of Foucault 1954–1984, vol. 1*, P. Rabinow (ed.). Harmondsworth: Penguin.

Foucault, M. 1997b. "The Birth of Biopolitics". See Foucault (1997a), 73–9.

Foucault, M. 1997c. "Polemics, Politics, and Problematizations". See Foucault (1997a), 111–19.

Foucault, M. 1997d. "Technologies of the Self". See Foucault (1997a), 223–51.

Foucault, M. 1997e. "The Ethics of a Concern for Self as a Practice of Freedom". See Foucault (1997a), 281–301.

Foucault, M. 1997f. "What is Enlightenment". See Foucault (1997a), 303–19.

Foucault, M. 1997g. "What is Critique". In *The Politics of Truth*, S. Lotringer & L. Hochroth (eds), 23–87. New York: Semiotexte.

Foucault, M. 1998. "Nietzsche, Genealogy, History". In *Aesthetics, Method and Epistemology: The Essential Works of Foucault 1954–1984, vol. 2*, J. D. Faubion (ed.), 369–91. Harmondsworth: Penguin.

Foucault, M. 2000a. *Power: The Essential Works of Foucault 1954–1984, vol. 3*, J. D. Faubion (ed.). Harmondsworth: Penguin.

Foucault, M. 2000b. "Truth and Power". See Foucault (2000a), 111–33.

Foucault, M. 2000c. "On Governmentality". See Foucault (2000a), 201–22.

Foucault, M. 2000d. "Omnes et Singulatim: Toward a Critique of Political Reason". See Foucault (2000a), 298–325.

Foucault, M. 2000e. "The Subject and Power". See Foucault (2000a), 326–48.

Foucault, M. 2000f. "Space, Knowledge and Power". See Foucault (2000a), 349–64.

Foucault, M. 2000g. "The Risks of Security". See Foucault (2000a), 365–81.

Foucault, M. 2000h. "The Moral and Social Experience of the Poles". See Foucault (2000a), 465–73.

Foucault, M. 2000i. "Confronting Governments: Human Rights". See Foucault (2000a), 474–5.

Foucault, M. 2003. *Society Must be Defended: Lectures at the College de France 1975–1976*, M. Bertani & A. Fontana (eds), D. Macey (trans.). New York: Picador.

Frank, J. 2005. *A Democracy of Distinction: Aristotle and the Work of Politics*. Chicago, IL: University of Chicago Press.

Frost, R. 1999. "The Basic Right to Justification: Towards a Constructivist Conception of Human Rights. *Constellations* 6(1): 35–60.

Gagnon, A. G. & J. Tully (eds) 2001. *Multinational Democracies*. Cambridge: Cambridge University Press.

Gatens, M. & G. Lloyd 1999. *Collective Imaginings: Spinoza, Past and Present*. London: Routledge.

Gatens, M. 2004. "Can Human Rights Accommodate Women's Rights? Towards an Embodied Account of Social Norms, Social Meaning, and Cultural Change". *Contemporary Political Theory* 3(3): 275–99.

Gaus, G. F. 2005. "Green's Rights Recognition Thesis and Moral Internalism". *British Journal of Politics and International Relations* 7(1): 5–17.

Geuss, R. 2001. *History and Illusion in Politics*. Cambridge: Cambridge University Press.

Geuss, R. 2005a. *Outside Ethics*. Princeton, NJ: Princeton University Press.

Geuss, R. 2005b. "Neither History nor Praxis". See Geuss (2005a), 29–39.

Gewirth, A. 1985. "Why There Are Human Rights. *Social Theory and Practice* 11(2): 235–48.

Gewirth, A. 1996. *The Community of Rights*. Chicago, IL: University of Chicago Press.

Glendon, M. A. 1991. *Rights Talk: The Impoverishment of Political Discourse*. New York: Free Press.

Green, T. H. 1986. *T. H. Green: Lectures on the Principles of Political Obligation and Other Writings*, P. Harris and J. Morrow (eds). Cambridge: Cambridge University Press.

Green, T. H. [1883] 1990. *Prolegomena to Ethics*, A. C. Bradley (ed.). Oxford: Clarendon Pres.

Greenberg, K. J. & J. L. Dratel (eds) 2005. *The Torture Papers: The Road to Abu Ghraib*. Cambridge: Cambridge University Press.

Griffin, J. 2001a. "First Steps in an Account of Human Rights". *European Journal of Philosophy* 9(3): 306–27.

Griffin, J. 2001b. "Discrepancies Between the Best Philosophical Account of Human Rights and the International Law of Human Rights". *Proceedings of the Aristotelian Society* 101(1): 1–28.

Grotius, H. [1604] 1950. *De Jure Praedae Commentarius: Commentary on the Law of Prize and Booty*, 2 vols, G. L. Williams (trans.) with W. H. Zeydel. Oxford: Clarendon Press.

Grotius, H. [1609] 2004. *The Free Sea*, R. Hayluyt (trans.), D. Armitage (ed.). Indianapolis, IN: Liberty Fund.

Grotius, H. [1625] 2005. *On the Rights of War and Peace*, 3 vols, R. Tuck (ed.). Indianapolis, IN: Liberty Fund.

Haakonssen, K. 1981. *The Science of a Legislator: The Natural Jurisprudence of David Hume and Adam Smith*. Cambridge: Cambridge University Press.

Haakonssen, K. 1991. "From Natural Law to the Rights of Man: A European Perspective on American Debates". In *A Culture of Rights: The Bill of Rights in Philosophy, Politics and Law 1791 and 1991*, M. Lacey & K. Haakonssen (eds), 19–61. Cambridge: Cambridge University Press

Haakonssen, K. 2002. "The Moral Conservatism of Natural Rights". In *Natural Law and Civil Sovereignty: Moral Right and State Authority in Early Modern Political Thought*, I. Hunter & D. Saunders (eds), 27–42. New York: Palgrave Macmillan.

Haakonssen, K. 2004. "Protestant Natural Law Theory". In *New Essays on the History of Autonomy: A Collection Honouring J. B. Schneewind*, N. Brender (ed.), 109–31. Cambridge: Cambridge University Press.

Habermas, J. 1984. *The Theory of Communicative Action, Volume 1: Reason and the Rationalization of Society*, T. McCarthy (trans.). Cambridge: Polity.

Habermas, J. 1987. *The Theory of Communicative Action, Volume 2: Lifeworld and System: A Critique of Functionalist Reason*, T. McCarthy (trans.). Cambridge: Polity.

Habermas, J. 1990. *Moral Consciousness and Communicative Action*, C. Lenhart & S. W. Nicholsen (trans.). Cambridge, MA: MIT Press.

Habermas, J. 1993. "On the Pragmatic, the Ethical and Moral Employments of Practical Reason". In *Justification and Application: Remarks on Discourse Ethics*, C. Cronin (trans.), 1–18. Cambridge, MA: MIT Press.

Habermas, J. 1995. "Reconciliation through the Public Use of Reason: Remarks on John Rawls's Political Liberalism". *Journal of Philosophy* 92(3) (1995): 109–31.

Habermas, J. 1996. *Between Facts and Norms: Contributions to a Discourse Theory of Law and Democracy*, W. Rehg (trans.). Cambridge, MA: MIT Press.

Habermas, J. 2001a. *The Postnational Constellation: Political Essays*, Max Pensky (ed.). Cambridge, MA: MIT Press.

Habermas, J. 2001b. "Remarks on Legitimation through Human Rights". See Habermas (2001a), 113–29.

Habermas, J. 2005. "Eine politische Verfasung fur die pluraistiche Wletgessellschaft?". In his *Zwischen Naturalism und Religion: Philosophiische Aufsatze*. Frankfurt: Suhrkamp.

Hacking, I. 2002. *Historical Ontology*. Cambridge, MA: Harvard University Press.

Haksar, V. 1979. *Justice, Equality and Perfectionism*. Oxford: Clarendon Press.

Hampshire, S. 1990. *Justice is Conflict*. London, Duckworth.

Hardt, M. & A. Negri 2000. *Empire*. Cambridge, MA: Harvard University Press.

Harrison, R. 2002. *Hobbes, Locke and Confusion's Masterpiece: An Examination of Seventeenth-Century Political Philosophy*. Cambridge: Cambridge University Press.

Hart, H. L. A. 1972. *The Concept of Law*. Oxford: Oxford University Press.

Hart, H. L. A. 1983. "Utilitarianism and Natural Rights". In his *Essays in Jurisprudence and Philosophy*, 181–97. Oxford: Clarendon Press.

Hart, H. L. A. [1955] 1984. "Are There Any Natural Rights?". Reprinted in *Theories of Rights*, J. Waldron (ed.), 77–90. Oxford: Oxford University Press.

Hegel, G. W. F. *Introduction to the Lectures on the History of Philosophy*, T. M. Knox & A. V. Miller (trans.). Oxford: Oxford University Press.

Hegel, G. W. F. 1977. *Hegel's Phenomenology of Spirit*, A. V. Miller (trans.), J. N. Findlay (ed.). Oxford: Oxford University Press.

Hegel, G. W. F. [1821] 1991. *Elements of the Philosophy of Right*, A. Wood (ed.), H. B. Nisbet (trans.). Cambridge: Cambridge University Press.

Held, D. 1995. *Democracy and the Global Order*. Cambridge: Polity.

Hesse, C. & R. Post (eds) 1999. *Human Rights in Transition: Gettysburg to Bosnia*. New York: Zone Books.

Hill, T. Jr. 2000. *Respect, Pluralism and Justice: Kantian Perspectives*. Oxford: Oxford University Press.

Hindess, B. 1996. *Discourses of Power: From Hobbes to Foucault*. Oxford: Blackwell.

Hirschl, R. 2004. *Towards Juristocracy: The Origins and Consequences of the New Constitutionalism*. Cambridge, MA: Harvard University Press.

Hobbes, T. [1650] 1969a. *The Elements of Law: Natural and Politic*, F. Tonnies (ed.), M. Goldsmith (intro.). London: Cass.

Hobbes, T. [1681] 1969b. *Behemoth or The Long Parliament*, 2nd edn, F. Tonnies (ed.), M. Goldsmith (into.). London: Cass.

Hobbes, T. [1651] 1994. *Leviathan*, E. Curley (ed.). Indianapolis, IN: Hackett.

Hobbes, T. [1642] 1998. *On the Citizen*, R. Tuck & M. Silverthorne (eds and trans.). Cambridge: Cambridge University Press.

Hochstrasser, T. J. 2000. *Natural Law Theories in the Early Enlightenment*. Cambridge: Cambridge University Press.

Hohfeld, W. 1978. *Fundamental Legal Conceptions as Applied to Judicial Reasoning*. Westport, CT: Greenwood Press.

Holmes, S. 2006. "Neo-Con Futurology". *London Review of Books* 28(19) (5 October) (www.lrb.co.uk/v28/n19/holm01_.html).

Holmes, S. & C. Sunstein 1999. *The Cost of Rights: Why Liberty Depends on Taxes*. New York: Norton.

Hont, I. & M. Ignatieff. 1983. "Needs and Justice in the *Wealth of Nations*: An Introductory Essay". In *Wealth and Virtue: The Shaping of Political Economy in the Scottish Enlightenment*, I. Hont & M. Ignatieff (eds). Cambridge: Cambridge University Press.

Hornqvist, M. 2001. *Machiavelli and Empire*. Cambridge: Cambridge University Press.

Hume, D. 1973. *Enquiries Concerning Human Understanding and Concerning the Principle of Morals*, P. H. Nidditch (ed.). Oxford: Clarendon Press.

Hume, D. [1739–40] 1978. *A Treatise of Human Nature*, L. A. Selby-Bigge (ed.). Oxford: Clarendon Press.

Hunter, I. 2001. *Rival Enlightenments: Civil and Metaphysical Philosophy in Early Modern Germany*. Cambridge: Cambridge University Press.

Ignatieff, M. 2000. *The Rights Revolution*. Toronto: Anansi Press.

Ignatieff, M. 2001. *Human Rights as Politics and Idolatry*. Princeton, NJ: Princeton University Press.

ICJ Reports 1975. "Western Sahara, Advisory Opinion", *ICJ Reports* 16 October: 12.

Ivison, D. 1997. *The Self at Liberty: Political Argument and the Arts of Government*. Ithaca, NY: Cornell University Press.

Ivison, D. 2002. *Postcolonial Liberalism*. Cambridge: Cambridge University Press.

Ivison, D. 2006. "The Nature of Rights and the History of Empire". In *British Political Thought in History, Literature and Theory, 1500–1800*, David Armitage (ed.), 191–211. Cambridge: Cambridge University Press.

Ivison, D., P. Patton & W. Sanders (eds) 2000. *Political Theory and the Rights of Indigenous Peoples*. Cambridge: Cambridge University Press.

James, S. 2003. "Rights as Enforceable Claims". *Proceedings of the Aristotelian Society* 103: 133–47.

Jiwei Ci 2006. *The Two Faces of Justice*. Cambridge, MA: Harvard University Press.

Jones, P. 1994. *Rights*. Basingstoke: Macmillan.

Jones, P. 1999. "Human Rights, Group Rights and Peoples' Rights". *Human Rights Quarterly* 21(1): 80–107.

Jones, P. 2001. "Human Rights and Diverse Cultures: Continuity or Discontinuity?" In *Human Rights and Global Diversity*, S. Caney & P. Jones (eds), 27–50. London: Frank Cass.

Kant, I. [1784] 1983. "Idea for a Universal History with a Cosmopolitan Intent". In *Immanuel Kant: Perpetual Peace and Other Essays*, T. Humphrey (ed.), 34–9. Indianapolis, IN: Hackett.

Kant, I. 1996. *Immanuel Kant: Practical Philosophy*, M. Gregor (ed.). Cambridge: Cambridge University Press.

Keal, P. 2003. *European Conquest and the Rights of Indigenous Peoples: The Moral Backwardness of International Society*. Cambridge: Cambridge University Press.

Keene, E. 2002. *Beyond the Anarchical Society: Grotius, Colonialism and Order in World Politics*. Cambridge: Cambridge University Press.

Kingsbury, B. 1992. "Claims by Non-State Groups in International Law". *Cornell International Law Journal* 25(3): 481–513.

Kingsbury, B. 1998. "Indigenous Peoples in International Law: A Constructivist Approach to the Asian Controversy". *American Journal of International Law* 92(3): 414–57.

Kingsbury, B. 2001. "Reconciling Five Competing Conceptual Structures of Indigenous Peoples' Claims in International and Comparative Law". *New York University Journal of International and Comparative Law* 34(1): 189–252.

Knowles, D. 1983. "Hegel on Property and Personality". *Philosophical Quarterly* 33: 45–62.

Kok Chor Tan 2000. *Toleration, Diversity and Global Justice*. University Park, PA: Pennsylvania State University Press.

Kok Chor Tan 2004. *Justice without Borders: Cosmopolitanism, Nationalism and Patriotism*. Cambridge: Cambridge University Press.

Korsgaard, C. M. 1985. "Kant's Formula of Universal Law". *Pacific Philosophical Quarterly* 66(1): 24–47.

Kramer, M., N. E. Simmonds & H. Steiner 1998. *A Debate Over Rights: Philosophical Enquiries*. Oxford: Oxford University Press

Krasner, S. 1999. *Sovereignty: Organized Hypocrisy*. Princeton, NJ: Princeton University Press.

Kukathas, C. 2003. *The Liberal Archipelago: A Theory of Diversity and Freedom*. Oxford: Oxford University Press.

Kymlicka, W. 1989. *Liberalism, Culture and Community*. Oxford: Oxford University Press.

Kymlicka, W. 1995. *Multicultural Citizenship: A Liberal Theory of Minority Rights*. Oxford: Oxford University Press.

Kymlicka, W. 2002. *Contemporary Political Philosophy: An Introduction*, 2nd edn. Oxford: Oxford University Press.

Lacey, M. J. & K. Haakonssen (eds) 1991. *A Culture of Rights: The Bill of Rights in Philosophy, Politics and Law 1791 and 1991*. Cambridge: Cambridge University Press.

Langlois, A. 2003. "Human Rights and Modern Liberalism: A Critique". *Political Studies* 51(3): 509–23.

Leiter, B. 2002. *Nietzsche: On Morality*. London, Routledge.

Levy, J. T. 2000. *The Multiculturalism of Fear*. Oxford: Oxford University Press.

Little, D., J. Kelsay & A. Sachedina 1988. *Human Rights and the Conflicts of Culture: Western and Islamic Perspectives on Religious Liberty*. Columbia, SC: University of South Carolina Press.

Locke, J. [1693] 1902. *Some Thoughts Concerning Education*, R. H Quick (ed.). Cambridge: Cambridge University Press.

Locke, J. 1975. *An Essay Concerning Human Understanding*, P. H. Nidditch (ed.). Oxford: Clarendon Press.

Locke, J. [1689] 1983. *A Letter Concerning Toleration*, J. Tully (ed.). Indianapolis, IN: Hackett.

Locke, J. [1689] 1988. *Two Treatises of Government*, student edn, P. Laslett (ed.). Cambridge: Cambridge University Press.

Lomasky, L. 1987. *Persons, Rights and the Moral Community*. Oxford: Oxford University Press.

Louden, R. B. 2000. *Kant's Impure Ethics: From Rational Beings to Human Beings*. Oxford: Oxford University Press.

Luban, D. 2005. "Liberalism, Torture and the Ticking Time Bomb". *Virginia Law Review* 91(6): 1425–61.

Lukes, S. 1999. "Five Fables about Human Rights". In *On Human Rights: The Oxford Amnesty Lectures*, S. Shute & S. Hurley (eds), 19–50. New York: Basic Books.

Lyons, D. 1977. "Human Rights and the General Welfare". *Philosophy and Public Affairs* 6(2): 113–29.

Machiavelli, N. [c.1513] 1988. *The Prince*, Q. Skinner & R. Price (eds). Cambridge: Cambridge University Press.

Machiavelli, N. [c.1518/19] 1989. *Discourses*. In *Machiavelli: The Chief Works and Others*, A. Gilbert (ed.). Chicago, IL: University of Chicago Press.

MacIntyre, A. 1984. *After Virtue: A Study in Moral Theory*. London, Duckworth.

Macpherson, C. B. 1969. *The Political Theory of Possessive Individualism: Hobbes to Locke*. Oxford: Clarendon Press.

Mamdami, M. 2007. "The Politics of Naming: Genocide, Civil War, Insurgency". *London Review of Books* 29(5) (8 March): 5–8.

Mansfield, H. 2006. "The Law and the President: In a National Emergency, Who you Gonna Call?", *Weekly Standard* 11(17): 12–13.

Marshall, J. 2006. *John Locke, Toleration and Early Enlightenment Culture*. Cambridge: Cambridge University Press.

Martin, R. 1993. *A System of Rights*. Oxford, Oxford University Press.

Marx, K. [1843] 1978a. "On the Jewish Question". In *The Marx–Engels Reader*, R. Tucker (ed.), 26–52. New York: Norton.

Marx, K. [1845] 1978b. "Theses on Feuerbach". In *The Marx–Engels Reader*, R. Tucker (ed.), 143–5. New York: Norton.

Marx, K. [1875] 1978c. "Critique of the Gotha Program". In *The Marx–Engels Reader*, R. Tucker (ed.), 525–41. New York: Norton.

Marx, K. 1992. "Critique of Hegel's Doctrine of the State". In his *Early Writings*, R. Livingstone & G. Benton (trans.), 57–198. Harmondsworth: Penguin.

McCarthy, T. A. 1979, *The Critical Theory of Jürgen Habermas*. Cambridge, MA: MIT Press.

McKinnon, C. 2005. *Toleration: An Introduction*. London: Routledge.

Menand, L. 1996. "The Limits of Academic Freedom", in his *The Future of Academic Freedom*, 3–20. Chicago, IL: University of Chicago Press.

Mendus, S. 1987. "Kant: An Honest but Narrow-Minded Bourgeois?". In *Women in Western Political Philosophy: Kant to Nietzsche*, Ellen Kennedy and Susan Mendus (eds), 21–43. Brighton: Harvester.

Michelman, F. 1986. "Justification (and Justifiability) of Law in a Contradictory World". In *Justification: Nomos 18*, J. R. Pennock & J. W. Chapman (eds), 73–82. New York: NYU Press.

Mill, J. S. 1962. "Utilitarianism". In *"Utilitarianism" and "On Liberty": Including "Essay on Bentham" and Selections from the Writings of Jeremy Bentham and John Austin*, M. Warnock (ed.), 251–321. London: Collins.

Miller, F. 1997. *Nature, Justice and Rights in Aristotle's Politics*. Oxford: Oxford University Press.

Miller, D. 1998. *On Nationality*. Oxford: Oxford University Press.

Miller, D. 2000. "National Self-Determination and Global Justice". In his *Citizenship and National Identity*, 161–79. Cambridge: Polity.

Mills, C. 1997. *The Racial Contract*. Ithaca, NY: Cornell University Press.

Minnow, M. 1990. *Making all the Difference*. Ithaca, NY: Cornell University Press.

Montaigne, M. de [1580] 1965. "Apology for Raymond Sebond". In *The Complete Essays of Montaigne*, D. Frame (ed.). Palo Alto, CA: Stanford University Press.

Moravcisk, A. 2000. "The Origins of Human Rights Regimes: Democratic Delegation in Postwar Europe". *International Organization* 54(2): 217–52.

Morriss, P. 2002. *Power: A Philosophical Analysis*, 2nd edn. Manchester: Manchester University Press.

Mulhall, S. & A. Swift 1996. *Liberals and Communitarians*, 2nd edn. Oxford: Blackwell.

Muthu, S. 2004. *Enlightenment Against Empire*. Princeton, NJ: Princeton University Press.

Mydans, S. 2007. "From their Nation-Turned-Bunker, Burmese Generals Peer Out, and In", *New York Times*, 26 September (www.nytimes.com/2007/09/26/world/asia/26myanmar.html).

Nagel, T. 2003. "Rawls and Liberalism". In *The Cambridge Companion to Rawls*, Samuel Freeman (ed.), 63–85. Cambridge: Cambridge University Press.

Nedelsky, J. 1993. "Reconceiving Rights as Relationship". *Review of Constitutional Studies* 1(1): 1–26.

Neuthouser, F. 2000. *Foundations of Hegel's Social Theory*. Cambridge, MA: Harvard University Press.

Nicholson, P. 1990. *The Political Philosophy of the British Idealists*. Cambridge: Cambridge University Press.

Nietzsche, F. 1982. *Daybreak: Thoughts on the Prejudices of Morality*, R. J. Hollingdale (trans.), M. Tanner (ed.). Cambridge: Cambridge University Press.

Nietzsche, F. 1989a. *On The Genealogy of Morality*, W. Kaufmann (ed.). New York: Vintage.

Nietzsche, F. 1989b. *Beyond Good and Evil*, W. Kaugmann (ed.) New York: Vintage.

Nietzsche, F. 1996. *Human, All Too Human*, D. Fuss (ed.). London: Routledge.

Nozick, R. 1974. *Anarchy, State and Utopia*. Oxford: Blackwell.

Nussbaum, M. 1992. "Human Functioning and Social Justice: In Defence of Aristotelian Essentialism. *Political Theory* 20(2): 202–46.

Nussbaum, M. 1995. "Aristotle on Human Nature and the Foundation of Ethics". In *World, Mind and Ethics: Essays on the Philosophy of Bernard Williams*, J. E. Altham & R. Harrison (eds), 86–131. Cambridge: Cambridge University Press.

Nussbaum, M. 2000. *Women and Human Development: The Capabilities Approach to Justice*. Cambridge: Cambridge University Press.

Nussbaum, M. 2006. *Frontiers of Justice: Disability, Nationality, Species Membership*. Cambridge, MA: Harvard University Press.

Ober, J. 2000. "Quasi-Rights: Participatory Citizenship and Negative Liberties in Democratic Athens". *Social Philosophy and Policy* 17(1): 27–61.

Okin, S. M. 1999. *Is Multiculturalism Bad for Women?*, J. Cohen, M. Howard & M. Nussbaum (eds). Princeton, NJ: Princeton University Press.

O'Neill, O. 1994. "Justice and Boundaries". In *Political Restructuring in Europe: Ethical Perspectives*, C. Brown (ed.), 69–88. London: Routledge.

O'Neill, O. 1996. *Toward Justice and Virtue: A Constructive Account of Practical Reasoning*. Cambridge: Cambridge University Press.

O'Neill, O. 1997. "Kant on Reason and Religion". In *The Tanner Lectures on Human Values, 18*, G. Peterson (ed.), 267–308. Salt Lake City, UT: University of Utah Press.

O'Neill, O. 2003. "Constructivism in Rawls and Kant". In *The Cambridge Companion to Rawls*, Samuel Freeman (ed.), 347–67. Cambridge: Cambridge University Press.

Oswald, M. 2004. "Shares and Rights: Citizenship Greek Style and American Style". In *Dêmokratia: A Conversation on Democracies, Ancient and Modern*, J. Ober & F. Hendricks (eds), 49–62. Princeton, NJ: Princeton University Press.

Otsuka, M. 2003. *Libertarianism Without Inequality*. Oxford: Oxford University Press.

Pagden, A. 1982. *The Fall of Natural Man: The American Indian and the Origins of Comparative Ethnology*. Cambridge: Cambridge University Press.

Pagden, A. 1995. *Lords of All the World: Ideologies of Empire in Spain, Britain and France c.1500–c.1800*. New Haven, CT: Yale University Press.

Pagden, A. 2000. "Stoicism, Cosmopolitanism and the Legacy of European Imperialism". *Constellations* 7(1): 3–22.

Pagden, A. 2003. "Human Rights, Natural Rights and Europe's Imperial Legacy". *Political Theory* 31(2): 171–99.

Pagden, A. & J. Lawrence (eds) 1991. *Vitoria: Political Writings*. Cambridge: Cambridge University Press.

Pangle, T. L. 1988. *The Spirit of Modern Republicanism: The Moral Vision of the American Founders and the Philosophy of Locke*. Chicago, IL: University of Chicago Press.

Pateman, C. 1987. *The Sexual Contract*. Cambridge: Polity.

Patten, A. 1999. *Hegel's Idea of Freedom*. Oxford: Oxford University Press.

Patton, P. 1998. "Foucault's Subject of Power". In *The Later Foucault*, J. Moss (ed.), 64–77. London: Sage.

Patton, P. 2001. "Nietzsche and Hobbes". *International Studies in Philosophy* 33(3): 99–116.

Perry, M. 1998. *The Idea of Human Rights: Four Enquiries*. Oxford: Oxford University Press.

Pettit, P. 1988. "The Consequentialist Can Recognize Rights". *Philosophical Quarterly* 38(150): 42–55.

Pettit, P. 1991. "Consequentialism". In *A Companion to Ethics*, P. Singer (ed.), 230–40. Oxford: Blackwell.

Pettit, P. 1996. "Freedom as Anti-power". *Ethics* 106(3): 576–604.

Pettit, P. 1997. *Republicanism: A Theory of Freedom and Government*. Oxford: Oxford University Press.

Pettit, P. 2000. "Minority Claims under Two Conceptions of Democracy". In *Political Theory and the Rights of Indigenous Peoples*, D. Ivison, P. Patton & W. Sanders (eds), 199–215. Cambridge: Cambridge University Press.

Pettit, P. 2005. "Rawls's Political Ontology". *Politics, Philosophy and Economics* 4(2): 157–74.

Pincus, S. 1998. "Neither Machiavellian Moment nor Possessive Individualism: Commercial Society and the Defenders of the English Commonwealth". *American Historical Review* 103(3): 705–36.

Pinkard, T. 1996. *Hegel's Phenomenology: The Sociality of Reason*. Cambridge: Cambridge University Press.

Pippin, R. 2000. "What is the Question for which Hegel's Theory of Recognition is the Answer?" *European Journal of Philosophy* 8(2): 155–72.

Pippin, R. 2006. "Mine and Thine? The Kantian State". In *The Cambridge Companion to Kant and Modern Philosophy*, Paul Guyer (ed.), 414–46. Cambridge: Cambridge University Press.

Pitts, J. 2005. *A Turn to Empire: The Rise of Imperial Liberalism in Britain and France*. Princeton, NJ: Princeton University Press.

Pocock, J. G. A. 1980. "The Myth of John Locke and the Obsession with Liberalism". In *John Locke*, J. G. A. Pocock & R. Ashcraft (eds), 1–24. Los Angeles, CA: Clark Library.

Pocock, J. G. A. 1985. "Authority and Property: The Question of Liberal Origins". In his *Virtue, Commerce, and History*, 103–24. Cambridge: Cambridge University Press.

Pocock, J. G. A. 1987. *The Ancient Constitution and the Feudal Law: A Re-issue*. Cambridge: Cambridge University Press.

Pocock, J. G. A. 1993. "A Discourse on Sovereignty". In *Political Discourse in Early Modern Britain*, N. Phillipson & Q. Skinner (eds), 377–428. Cambridge: Cambridge University Press.

Pogge, T. 1995. "Three Problems with Contractarian-Consequentialist Ways of Assessing Social Institutions". In *The Just Society*, Ellen Frankel Paul, F. D. Miller, Jr, and Jeffrey Paul (eds), 241–66. Cambridge: Cambridge University Press.

Pogge, T. 2000. "The International Significance of Human Rights". *Journal of Ethics* 4(1–2): 45–69.

Pogge, T. 2002. *World Poverty and Human Rights*. Cambridge: Polity.

Popkin, R. 1979. *The History of Scepticism from Erasmus to Spinoza*. Berkeley, CA: University of California Press.

Post, R. 2000. "Democratic Constitutionalism and Cultural Heterogeneity". *Australian Journal of Legal Philosophy* 25(2): 65–84.

Primus, R. 1999. *The American Language of Rights*. Cambridge: Cambridge University Press.

Pufendorf, S. [1672] 1934. *On the Law of Nature and Nations*. Oxford: Clarendon Press.

Pufendorf, S. [1673] 1991. *On the Duty of Man and Citizen According to Natural Law*, J. Tully & M. Silverthorne (eds). Cambridge: Cambridge University Press.

Rawls, J. 1993. *Political Liberalism*. New York: Columbia University Press.

Rawls, J. 1999a. *The Law of Peoples*. Cambridge, MA: Harvard University Press.

Rawls, J. 1999b. *A Theory of Justice*, 2nd rev. edn. Cambridge, MA: Harvard University Press.

Rawls, J. 2000. *Lectures on the History of Moral Philosophy*, B. Herman (ed.). Cambridge, MA: Harvard University Press.

Rawls, J. 2001. *Justice as Fairness: A Restatement*, E. Kelly (ed.). Cambridge, MA: Harvard University Press.

Raz, J. 1986. *The Morality of Freedom*. Oxford: Oxford University Press.

Redding, P. 1997. *Hegel's Hermeneutics*. Ithaca, NY: Cornell University Press.

Regan, T. 2004. *The Case for Animal Rights*. Berkeley, CA: University of California Press.

Rejali, D. 2007. *Torture and Democracy*. Princeton, NJ: Princeton University Press.

Riley, P. 1983. *Kant's Political Philosophy*. Totowa, NJ: Rowman & Littlefield.

Ripstein, A. 2006a. "Beyond the Harm Principle". *Philosophy and Public Affairs* 34(3): 215–45.

Ripstein, A. 2006b. "Private Order and Public Justice: Kant and Rawls". *Virginia Law Review* 92: 1391–438.

Risse, T., S. C. Ropp & K. Sikkink 1999. *The Power of Human Rights: International Norms and Domestic Change*. Cambridge: Cambridge University Press.

Rose, N. 1999. *Powers of Freedom*. Cambridge: Cambridge University Press.

Ross, W. D. 1930. *The Right and the Good*. Oxford: Oxford University Press.

Rousseau, J.-J. [1754] 1997. "A Discourse on the Origin of Inequality". In *The Discourses and Other Early Writings*, V. Gourevitch (ed.), 111–222. Cambridge: Cambridge University Press.

Ruddock, P. 2004. "A New Framework: Counter-terrorism and the Rule of Law", *Sydney Papers* 16(2): 113–22.

Ryan, A. 1984. *Property and Political Theory*. Oxford: Blackwell.

Sandel, M. 1996. *Democracy's Discontent: America in Search of a Public Philosophy*. Cambridge, MA: Harvard University Press.

Scanlon, T. 1998. *What We Owe to Each Other*. Cambridge, MA: Belknap.

Scanlon, T. 2003. *The Difficulty of Tolerance: Essays in Political Philosophy*. Cambridge: Cambridge University Press.

Scheffler, S. 2006. "Is Terrorism Morally Distinctive?". *Journal of Political Philosophy* 14(1): 1–17.

Scheuerman, W. 2006. "Emergency Powers and the Rule of Law after 9/11", *Journal of Political Philosophy* 14(1): 61–84.

Schmitt, C. 1988. *Political Theology: Four Chapters on the Concept of Sovereignty*, G. Schwab (trans.). Cambridge, MA: MIT Press.

Schneewind, J. 1992. "Autonomy, Obligation and Virtue: An Overview of Kant's Ethics". In *The Cambridge Companion to Kant*, P. Guyer (ed.), 309–41. Cambridge: Cambridge University Press.

Schneewind, J. 1998. *The Invention of Autonomy: A History of Modern Moral Philosophy*. Cambridge: Cambridge University Press.

Sen, A. 1982a. "Rights and Agency". *Philosophy and Public Affairs* **11**(1): 3–30.

Sen, A. 1982b. "Equality of What?". In *Tanner Lectures on Human Values*, S. McMurrin (ed.), 197–220. Cambridge: Cambridge University Press.

Sen, A. 1985. "Well-being, Agency and Freedom". *Journal of Philosophy* **82**(4): 169–22.

Sen, A. 1995. *Inequality Reexamined*. Cambridge, MA: Harvard University Press.

Sen, A. 1999. *Development as Freedom*. Oxford: Oxford University Press.

Sen, A. 2004. "Elements of a Theory of Human Rights". *Philosophy and Public Affairs* **32**(4) (2004): 315–56.

Shachar, A. 2001. *Multicultural Jurisdictions: Cultural Differences and Women's Rights*. Cambridge: Cambridge University Press.

Shapiro, I. 1986. *The Evolution of Rights in Liberal Theory*. Cambridge: Cambridge University Press.

Shapiro, I. 2007. *Containment: Rebuilding a Strategy Against Global Terror*. Princeton, NJ: Princeton University Press.

Shue, H. 1978. "Torture". *Philosophy and Public Affairs* **7**(2): 124–43.

Shue, H. 1996. *Basic Rights: Subsistence, Affluence and US Foreign Policy*, 2nd edn. Princeton, NJ: Princeton University Press.

Simmonds, N. E. 1998. "Rights at the Cutting Edge". In *A Debate Over Rights: Philosophical Enquiries*, M. Kramer, N. E. Simmonds & H. Steiner, 113–234. Oxford: Oxford University Press.

Simmons, A. J. 1992. *The Lockean Theory of Rights*. Princeton, NJ: Princeton University Press.

Singer, P. 2002. *Unsanctifying Human Life: Essays on Ethics*, H. Kuhse (ed.). Oxford: Blackwell.

Skinner, Q. 1978a. *The Foundations of Modern Political Thought Volume One: The Renaissance*. Cambridge: Cambridge University Press.

Skinner, Q. 1978b. *The Foundations of Modern Political Thought Volume Two: The Age of Reformation*. Cambridge: Cambridge University Press.

Skinner, Q. 1989. "The State". In *Political Innovation and Conceptual Change*, T. Ball, J. Farr & R. L. Hanson (eds), 90–131. Cambridge: Cambridge University Press.

Skinner, Q. 1996. *Reason and Rhetoric in the Philosophy of Hobbes*. Cambridge: Cambridge University Press.

Skinner, Q. 1997. *Liberty Before Liberalism*. Cambridge: Cambridge University Press.

Skinner, Q. 2001a. *Visions of Politics Volume II: Renaissance Virtues*. Cambridge: Cambridge University Press.

Skinner, Q. 2001b. *Visions of Politics Volume III: Hobbes and Civil Science*. Cambridge: Cambridge University Press.

Skinner, Q. 2001c. "Hobbes's Changing Conception of Civil Science". In his *Visions of Politics Volume III: Hobbes and Civil Science*, 66–86. Cambridge: Cambridge University Press.

Skinner, Q. 2001d. "Hobbes and the Purely Artificial Person of the State". In his *Visions of Politics Volume III: Hobbes and Civil Science*, 177–208. Cambridge: Cambridge University Press.

Skinner, Q. 2002. "Classical Liberty and the Coming of the English Civil War". In *Republicanism: a Shared European Heritage, vol II: The Values of Republicanism in Early Modern Europe*, M. Van Gelderen & Q. Skinner (eds), 9–28. Cambridge: Cambridge University Press.

Skinner, Q. 2006. "Surveying the Foundations: A Retrospect and Reassessment". In *Rethinking the Foundations of Modern Political Thought*, A. Brett & J. Tully (eds), 236–61. Cambridge: Cambridge University Press.

Skinner, Q. & B. Stråth (eds) 2003. *States & Citizens: History, Theory, Prospects.* Cambridge: Cambridge University Press.

Slattery, B. 1991. "Aboriginal Sovereignty and Imperial Claims". *Osgoode Hall Law Journal* 29(4): 681–703.

Smith, S. B. 1989. *Hegel's Critique of Liberalism: Rights in Context.* Chicago, IL: University of Chicago Press.

Smith, R. M. 2004. "Arraigning Terror". *Dissent* (Spring): 39–44.

Sreenivasan, G. 1995. *The Limits of Lockean Rights in Property.* Oxford: Oxford University Press.

Sreenivasan, G. 2005. "A Hybrid Theory of Claim-Rights". *Oxford Journal of Legal Studies* 25(2): 257–74.

Stainton, T. 1994. *Autonomy and Social Policy: Rights, Mental Handicap and Community Care.* Aldershot: Avebury.

Steiner, H. 1994. *An Essay on Rights.* Oxford: Oxford University Press.

Steiner, H. 1998. "Working Rights". In *A Debate Over Rights: Philosophical Enquiries*, M. Kramer, N. E. Simmonds & H. Steiner, 235–302. Oxford: Oxford University Press.

Steiner, H. 2006. "Moral Rights". In *The Oxford Handbook to Ethical Theory*, D. Copp (ed.), 439–79. Oxford: Oxford University Press.

Steyn, J. 2004. "Guantanamo Bay: The Legal Black Hole". *International and Comparative Law Quarterly* 15 (2004): 1–15.

Sumner, W. 1987. *The Moral Foundation of Rights.* Oxford: Clarendon Press.

Sumner, W. 2000. "Rights". In *The Blackwell Guide to Ethical Theory*, H. Lafollette (ed.), 288–305. Oxford: Blackwell.

Sumner, L. W. 2004. *The Hateful and the Obscene: Studies in the Limits of Free Expression.* Toronto: University of Toronto Press.

Supreme Court of Canada 1998. *Reference re Secession of Quebec*, 2 SCR 217. Ottawa: Supreme Court of Canada.

Taylor, C. 1977. *Hegel.* Cambridge: Cambridge University Press.

Taylor, C. 1979. *Hegel and Modern Society.* Cambridge: Cambridge University Press.

Taylor, C. 1985a. *Human Agency and Language: Philosophical Papers 1.* Cambridge: Cambridge University Press.

Taylor, C. 1985b. *Philosophy and the Human Sciences: Philosophical Papers 2.* Cambridge: Cambridge University Press.

Taylor, C. 1985c. "What is Human Agency?". See Taylor (1985a): 15–44.

Taylor, C. 1985d. "Self-interpreting Animals". See Taylor (1985b): 45–76.

Taylor, C. 1985e. "Atomism". In his *Philosophy and the Human Sciences: Philosophical Papers 2*, 187–210. Cambridge: Cambridge University Press.

Taylor, C. 1985f. "Interpretations and the Sciences of Man". In his *Philosophy and the Human Sciences: Philosophical Papers 2*, 15–57. Cambridge: Cambridge University Press.

Taylor, C. 1989. *Sources of the Self: The Making of the Modern Identity.* Cambridge, MA: Harvard University Press.

Taylor, C. 1991. "The Politics of Recognition". In his *Multiculturalism and the Politics of Recognition*, A. Gutman (ed.), 44–51. Princeton, NJ: Princeton University Press.

Taylor, C. 1994. "Reply and Re-articulation". In *Philosophy in an Age of Pluralism: The Philosophy of Charles Taylor in Question*, J. Tully (ed.), 213–57. Cambridge: Cambridge University Press.

Taylor, C. 1995a. "Liberal Politics and the Public Sphere". In his *Philosophical Arguments*, 257–88. Cambridge, MA: Harvard University Press.

Taylor, C. 1995b. "Cross-purposes: The Liberal–Communitarian Debate" In his *Philosophical Arguments*, 181–203. Cambridge, MA: Harvard University Press.

Taylor, C. 1999. "Conditions of an Unforced Consensus on Human Rights", in *The East Asian Challenge for Human Rights*, J. R. Bauer & D. A. Bell (eds), 234–44. Cambridge: Cambridge University Press.

Taylor, C. 2004. *Modern Social Imaginaries*. Durham, NC: Duke University Press.

Thomson, J. 1986. *Rights, Restitution and Risk*. Cambridge, MA: Harvard University Press.

Tierney, B. 1997. *The Idea of Natural Rights: Studies on Natural Rights, Natural Law and Church Law 1150–1625*. Atlanta, GA: Scholars Press.

Tuck, R. 1981. *Natural Rights Theories: Their Origin and Development*. Cambridge: Cambridge University Press.

Tuck, R. 1987. "The Modern Theory of Natural Law". In *The Languages of Political Theory in Early Modern Europe*, A. Pagden (ed.), 99–122. Cambridge: Cambridge University Press.

Tuck, R. 1993. *Philosophy and Government 1572–1651*. Cambridge: Cambridge University Press.

Tuck, R. 1994. "Rights and Pluralism". In *Philosophy in an Age of Pluralism: The Philosophy of Charles Taylor in Question*, J. Tully (ed.), 159–70. Cambridge: Cambridge University Press.

Tuck R. 1999. *Rights of War and Peace: Political Thought and the International Order from Grotius to Kant*. Oxford: Oxford University Press.

Tuck, R. 2005. "Introduction". In *On the Rights of War and Peace*, vol. 1 [3 vols], H. Grotius. Indianapolis, IN: Liberty Fund.

Tully, J. 1980. *A Discourse on Property: John Locke and his Adversaries*. Cambridge: Cambridge University Press.

Tully, J. 1991. "Introduction". In S. Pudendorf, *On the Duty of Man and Citizen According to Natural Law*, J. Tully & M. Silverthorne (eds), xiv–xxxvii. Cambridge: Cambridge University Press.

Tully 1993a. *An Approach to Political Philosophy: Locke in Context*, Q. Skinner (ed.). Cambridge: Cambridge University Press.

Tully, J. 1993b. "Governing Conduct". See Tully (1993a), 179–241.

Tully, J. 1993c. "Placing the Two Treatises". In *Political Discourse in Early Modern Britain*, N. Phillipson & Q. Skinner (eds), 253–80. Cambridge: Cambridge University Press.

Tully, J. 1995. *Strange Multiplicity: Constitutionalism in an Age of Diversity*. Cambridge: Cambridge University Press.

Tully, J. 1999. "To Think and Act Differently: Foucault's Four Reciprocal Objections to Habermas's Theory". In *Foucault Contra Habermas: Recasting the Dialogue between Genealogy and Critical Theory*, S. Ashenden & D. Owen (eds), 91–142. London: Sage.

Tully, J. 2000a. "The Struggle of Indigenous Peoples For and Of Freedom". In *Political Theory and the Rights of Indigenous Peoples*, D. Ivison, P. Patton & W. Sanders (eds), 36–59. Cambridge: Cambridge University Press.

Tully, J. 2000b. "Democracy and Globalization: A Defeasible Sketch". In *Canadian Political Philosophy: Contemporary Reflections*, R. Beiner & W. Norman (eds), 36–62. Oxford: Oxford University Press.

Tully, J. 2002. "The Kantian Idea of Europe: Critical and Cosmopolitan Perspectives". In *The Idea of Europe: From Antiquity to European Union*, Anthony Pagden (ed.), 331–58. Cambridge: Cambridge University Press.

Tully, J. 2003. "Diverse Enlightenments". *Economy and Society* **32**(1): 485–505.

Tully, J. 2005. "On Law, Democracy and Imperialism", Twenty-First Annual Public Lecture, Centre for Law and Society, University of Edinburgh.

Turner, B. 2006. "The Enclave Society: Towards a Sociology of Immobility". *European Journal of Social Theory* **10**(2): 287–303.

Turpel, M. E. 1992. "Indigenous Peoples' Rights of Political Participation and Self-Determination: Recent International Legal Developments and the Continuing Struggle for Recognition". *Cornell International Law Journal* **25**(3): 579–602.

Venne, S. 1998. *Our Elders Understand Our Rights: Evolving International Law Regarding Indigenous Rights*. Penticton: Theytus Books.

Waldron, J. 1984a. *Theories of Rights*. Oxford: Oxford University Press.

Waldron, J. 1984b. "Introduction". See Waldron (1984a), 1–20.

Waldron, J. 1987. *Nonsense Upon Stilts: Bentham, Burke and Marx on the Rights of Man*. London: Methuen.

Waldron, J. 1989. "Rights in Conflict". *Ethics* **99**(3): 503–19.

Waldron, J. 1991. *The Right to Private Property*. Oxford: Oxford University Press.

Waldron, J. 1992. "Superseding Historic Injustice". *Ethics* **103**(1): 4–28.

Waldron, J. 1993. *Liberal Rights: Collected Papers 1981–91*. Cambridge: Cambridge University Press.

Waldron, J. 1998. *Law and Disagreement*. Oxford: Oxford University Press.

Waldron, J. 2002. *God, Locke and Equality: Christian Foundations in Locke's Political Thought*. Cambridge: Cambridge University Press.

Waldron, J. 2003a. "Indigeneity? First Peoples and Last Occupancy". *New Zealand Journal of Public Law* **1**(1): 55–82.

Waldron, J. 2003b. "Security and Liberty: The Image of Balance". *Journal of Political Philosophy* **11**(2): 191–210.

Waldron, J. 2004. "Terrorism and the Uses of Terror". *Journal of Ethics* **8**(1): 5–35.

Waldron, J. 2005. "Torture and Positive Law: Jurisprudence for the White House". *Columbia Law Review* **105**(6): 1681–750.

Wall, S. 1998. *Liberalism, Perfectionism and Restraint*. Cambridge: Cambridge University Press.

Walzer, M. 1977. *Just and Unjust Wars*. New York: Basic Books.

Walzer, M. 1994. *Thick and Thin: Moral Argument at Home and Abroad*. Notre Dame, IN: University of Notre Dame Press.

Webber, J. 1994. *Reimagining Canada: Language, Culture and the Canadian Constitutio*. Montreal: McGill-Queen's University Press.

Wenar, L. 2007. "Rights", *Stanford Encyclopaedia of Philosophy*, http://plato.stanford.edu/ (accessed October 2007).

White, M. 1978. *The Philosophy of the American Revolution*. Oxford: Oxford University Press.

White, S. 1988. *The Recent Work of Jurgen Habermas: Reason, Justice and Modernity*. Cambridge: Cambridge University Press.

Williams, B. 1973a. *Problems of the Self: Philosophical Papers 1956–1972*. Cambridge: Cambridge University Press.

Williams, B. 1973b. "The Idea of Equality". See Williams (1973a), 230–49.

Williams, B. 1981. "Internal and External Reasons". In his *Moral Luck: Philosophical Papers 1973–80*, 101–13. Cambridge: Cambridge University Press.

Williams, B. 1995a. *Making Sense of Humanity and Other Philosophical Papers*. Cambridge: Cambridge University Press.

Williams, B. 1995b. "Saint Just's Illusion". See Williams (1995a), 135–60.

Williams, B. 2005a. *In the Beginning Was the Deed: Realism and Moralism in Political Argument*. Princeton, NJ: Princeton University Press.

Williams, B. 2005b. "Realism and Moralism in Political Theory". See Williams (2005a), 1–17.

Williams, B. 2005c. "Human Rights and Relativism". See Williams (2005a), 62–74.

Williams, B. 2006. "The Human Prejudice". In his *Philosophy as a Humanistic Discipline*, A. W. Moore (ed.), 135–52. Princeton, NJ: Princeton University Press.

Williams, M. 2007. "Nonterritorial Boundaries of Citizenship". In *Identities, Affiliations, and Allegiances*, S. Benhabib, I. Shapiro & D. Petranovich (eds), 226–54. Cambridge: Cambridge University Press.

Williams, R. 1992a. *Linking Arms Together: American Indian Treaty Visions of Law and Peace 1600–1800*. Oxford: Oxford University Press.

Williams, R. 1992b. *Recognition: Fichte and Hegel on the Other*. Albany, NY: SUNY Press.

Williams, R. 1997. *Hegel's Ethic of Recognition*. Berkeley, CA: University of California Press.

Wolff, J. 2002. *Why Read Marx Today?* Oxford: Oxford University Press.

Wood, A. 1990. *Hegel's Ethical Thought*. Cambridge: Cambridge University Press.

Wood, A. W. 2005. *Kant*. Oxford: Blackwell.

Yack, B. 1993. "The Problem with Kantian Liberalism". In *Kant and Political Philosophy: The Contemporary Legacy*, R. Beiner & W. J. Booth (eds), 224–44. New Haven, CT: Yale University Press.

Yack, B. 1999. "The Myth of the Civic Nation". In *Theorizing Nationalism*, R. Beiner (ed.), 103–18. New York: SUNY Press.

Young, I. M. 1990. *Justice and the Politics of Difference*. Princeton, NJ: Princeton University Press.

Young, I. M. 1997. "Difference as a Resource for Democratic Communication". In *Deliberative Democracy: Essays on Reason and Politics*, J. Bohman & W. Rehg (eds), 383–406. Cambridge, MA: MIT Press.

Young, I. M. 2002. *Inclusion and Democracy*. Oxford: Oxford University Press.

Zernik, K. 2006. "Senate Approves Broad New Rules to Try Detainees". New York Times, 28 September (www.nytimes.com/2006/09/29/washington/29detain.html).

Index

sexual 127
ethics
  communicative 119
  discourse 121, 125
  as distinct from morality 131,
    134, 135, 140–43, 247, 251
  Kantian 97, 101, 105, 142, 242
  naturalistic 22–3, 39, 41, 204
  and rights 71, 91, 156
exception
  from the rule of law 47, 162,
    242
  state of 170–71, 175, 252

Feinberg, J., on claiming rights 2,
  29, 174
feminist critics of discourse ethics
  125
feminist political philosophers 78
Finnis, J. 239
Foucault, M.
  on the conduct of conduct 190
  on contract 187
  on discipline 189
  on domination 192, 193–4
  on freedom 192–3
  and government 188–92, 194,
    196
  on human rights 195–7, 200
  "juridicial power" 187, 194
  on legitimacy on the exercise of
    power 187–8
  on liberalism 191
  and liberty 192–3
  on natural law 195
  "negative and positive?" liberty
    192
  on neo-liberalism 191
  political thought 16, 194
  and power 181, 186–9, 192–4,
    196, 253
  on rights 16, 28, 186–7, 189,
    191–3, 194–7
  on social contract theory 16,
    187, 192
  on sovereignty 190, 194, 196
freedom
  in Constant 3
  in Foucault 192, 194, 196
  in Grotius 50, 52–4
  in Habermas 13
  in Hegel 128, 129–41, 143–5

in Hobbes 53, 58
in Islam 214
in Kant 95–7, 100–109
in Locke 64, 65, 71, 72
movements for 5
as non-domination 229, 243; see
  also Pettit
neo-Roman conception of 128
in Nozick 80
in Pagden 205
in Rawls 110, 112–15, 120
and rights 1, 93, 146–50, 152, 157,
  162, 164, 166, 168, 172, 175,
  178, 180, 182, 183, 192, 210,
  213, 215, 229, 237, 240, 243,
  244, 245, 248, 249, 250, 252,
  254, 256
in Skinner 84, 85
in Steiner 81
Frost, R. 262

Gatens, M. 213, 236
geist 248; see also spirit; Hegel
genocide 61, 176, 185
Geuss, R. 262
  and critique of human rights 29,
    89–91, 92
Gewirth, A., and human rights 4, 30,
  31, 255
government
  broad conception of 5, 20, 46, 52,
    53, 56, 57, 59, 60, 63, 84, 87, 89,
    106, 140, 153, 154, 155, 162–4,
    165, 172, 173, 187, 188, 194, 243
  human rights 195–6, 97, 200, 203,
    221–2, 228, 254
  natural rights 88
  and power 74–7
  rationalities of 189–90, 91, 92
  rights and 53, 59, 60, 63, 84, 85,
    87, 89, 106, 140, 153, 154, 155,
    162–4, 165, 172, 173, 178, 187,
    188, 194
  see also Foucault
Greece, ancient 4, 133
Greek political thought
  and ancient liberty 4
  and ethics 141–2
  and rights 3, 4
Green, T. H. 16
  and recognition of theory of rights
    150–51